BANDUNG REVISITED

BANDUNG REVISITED

The Legacy of the
1955 Asian-African Conference
for International Order

Edited by

See Seng Tan and Amitav Acharya

NUS PRESS
SINGAPORE

© NUS Press
National University of Singapore
AS3-01-02, 3 Arts Link
Singapore 117569

Fax: (65) 6774-0652
E-mail: nusbooks@nus.edu.sg
Website: http://nuspress.nus.edu.sg

ISBN 978-9971-69-393-0 (Paper)

First edition 2008
Reprint 2020, 2023

National Library Board Singapore Cataloguing in Publication Data

Bandung revisited: the legacy of the 1955 Asian-African Conference for international
  order/edited by See Seng Tan and Amitav Acharya. – Singapore: NUS Press,
  c2008.
  p. cm.
  Includes index.
  ISBN-13: 978-9971-69-393-0 (pbk.)

  1. Asian-African Conference (1st: 1955: Bandung, Indonesia). 2. Asia –
Foreign relations. 3. Regionalism – Asia. I. Tan, See Seng, 1965– II. Acharya,
Amitav.

DS33.3
327.5 – dc22   OCN191658776

Cover: President Sukarno of Indonesia giving the opening address at the Bandung
  Conference, 18 April 1955 (private collection of Amitav Acharya)

Typeset by: Scientifik Graphics Pte Ltd
Printed by: Markono Print Media Pte Ltd

CONTENTS

CONTRIBUTORS

Amitav Acharya is Professor of Global Governance and Director of the Centre for Governance and International Affairs at the Department of Politics, University of Bristol, United Kingdom. He received his Ph.D. from Murdoch University, Perth, WA, Australia. His research interests include Asia-Pacific regionalism, Southeast Asian affairs, regional institutions and world order, and Third World security.

Adekeye Adebajo is Executive Director of the Centre for Conflict Resolution, Cape Town, South Africa. He received his Ph.D. from St. Antony's College, University of Oxford, United Kingdom. His research interests are UN reform, regional security, peacekeeping, peacebuilding and conflict management.

Ang Cheng Guan is Head of Humanities and Social Studies Education at the National Institute of Education, Nanyang Technological University, Singapore. He received his Ph.D. from the School of Oriental and African Studies, University of London, United Kingdom. His research interests include international history of post-World War II Southeast Asia, Sino-Vietnamese relations, international history of the Vietnam War and Asian strategic thought.

Dewi Fortuna Anwar is Research Professor and the Deputy Chairman for Social Sciences and Humanities, the Indonesian Institute of Sciences (IPSK-LIPI) and Director for Program and Research at the Habibie Center, Jakarta, Indonesia. She received her Ph.D. from Monash University, Clayton, Vic., Australia. Her primary research interests are Indonesian foreign and defence policies and ASEAN political and security cooperation.

Itty Abraham is Director of the South Asia Institute and Marlene and Morton Meyerson Centennial Chair at the University of Texas at Austin, United States. He received his Ph.D. from the University of Illinois at Urbana-Champaign, Illinois, United States. His research interests include international relations, science and technology studies, and post-colonial theory.

Chen Jian is Michael J. Zak Chair of History for US-China Relations at Cornell University, N.Y., United States. He received his Ph.D. from Southern Illinois University, Ill., United States. His research interests are Sino-American relations, modern Chinese history, Chinese foreign policy and security strategies. In 2008–9, he will hold the Philippe Roman Chair in History and International Affairs at the London School of Economics and Political Science.

Michael J. Montesano is Assistant Professor at the Southeast Asian Studies Programme, National University of Singapore. He received his Ph.D. from Cornell University. His research interests include modern Thai history, the development of commercial banking in provincial Thailand, firms and networks in Southeast Asian business history, and the role of the United States in Southeast Asia.

Rahul Mukherji is Associate Professor at the Centre for Political Studies, Jawaharlal Nehru University, New Delhi, India. He received his Ph.D. from Columbia University, New York, United States. His research interests are comparative political economy, international relations and South Asia.

Helen E.S. Nesadurai is Senior Lecturer at the School of Arts and Sciences, Monash University, Malaysia, and External Associate of the Centre for the Study of Globalisation and Regionalisation, University of Warwick, United Kingdom. She received her Ph.D. from the University of Warwick. Her research interests include globalisation and its governance, regionalism in the Asia-Pacific, theories of international political economy, and international relations.

Anthony Reid is Professor at the Asia Research Institute, National University of Singapore. He received his Ph.D. from the University of Cambridge, United Kingdom. His research interests include social and economic history of Southeast Asia; nationalism, ethnicity and identity in Southeast Asia; modern history of Sumatra, South Sulawesi and Sabah; and religious change in Asia.

See Seng Tan is Associate Professor, Programme Coordinator for Multilateralism and Regionalism research, and Coordinator for Executive Education at the S. Rajaratnam School of International Studies, Nanyang Technological University, Singapore. He received his Ph.D. from Arizona State University, Arizona, United States. His primary research interests include critical social thought, international relations theory, and Asia-Pacific and Southeast Asian security affairs.

PREFACE

The 50th anniversary of the Bandung Conference, in April 2005, provided a timely occasion to consider the legacy of Bandung and to critically assess its contemporary relevance in shaping a new regional order in Asia and Asia's partnership with other parts of the world. At the behest of the Institute of Defence and Strategic Studies (now the S. Rajaratnam School of International Studies) at Singapore's Nanyang Technological University, a distinguished international panel of leading area studies specialists, diplomatic historians and international relations scholars congregated in Singapore shortly before the Asian-African Summit (Bandung II) to take up that challenge. As their contributions to this anthology amply reflect, the dispute over the Conference's legacy and relevance to the contemporary international order continues to linger after five decades, perhaps more trenchantly now than before with the benefit of hindsight. The contestedness over its meaning notwithstanding, what is abundantly clear about Bandung is its unremitting significance as a point of reference, whether intended or otherwise, for a variety of directions—from non-alignment to engagement to regionalism—taken by countries that participated in the 1955 meeting. In this respect, the "beauty" of Bandung clearly rests in the eyes of its beholders. Nevertheless, as the essays in this volume demonstrate, few, if any, today would dismiss the Conference's disputed legacy as irrelevant to international diplomacy.

This book would not have been possible but for the charity, inspiration and encouragement of many to whom we are indebted. The late Roeslan Abdulgani, the Secretary-General of the Bandung Conference, generously gave his time to Amitav Acharya (then Deputy Director and Head of Research of the Institute of Defence and Strategic Studies) to recollect and reminisce on the Bandung Conference and inspired the latter's interest and research on the legacy of the Conference. Despite his heavy commitments, Ali Alatas, the former Indonesian foreign minister and current presidential adviser, delivered the keynote address at our project's workshop—the meeting where the original drafts of the chapters were first deliberated—conducted back in April 2005. We thank Paul Kratoska of NUS Press, as well as the two anonymous reviewers assigned by the press, for their helpful comments on our manuscript. We also gratefully acknowledge the support of colleagues, both past and present, at the Rajaratnam School. Our intrepid research assistants, Karyn Wang, Morten Hansen and Jack Tan, did an outstanding job with data collection. As always, colleagues from the school's corporate support department ably ensured the smooth running of the workshop; in this respect, we especially thank Adeline Lim for her excellent contribution. Last, but not least, Ambassador Barry Desker, dean of the Rajaratnam School, has unstintingly supported this project since its inception.

We dedicate this book to the memory of Roeslan Abdulgani—fighter, diplomat, statesman.

INTRODUCTION

The Normative Relevance of the Bandung Conference for Contemporary Asian and International Order

Amitav Acharya and See Seng Tan[1]

Held in April 1955, the inaugural Asian-African Conference, more popularly known as the Bandung Conference, celebrated its 50th anniversary in April 2005 with a second gathering in Bandung and Jakarta, Indonesia. Described by President Sukarno of Indonesia as "the first intercontinental Conference of colored peoples in the history of mankind,"[2] the original Conference has been variously praised, panned and pilloried, with analysts and pundits rarely in agreement over its long-term legacy as well as the ramifications of that legacy in present-day international affairs. Nevertheless, few would dispute the notion that the inaugural meeting in 1955 constituted, not least for Asia, a watershed in international history—"an unprecedented and unrepeated moment of unity of purpose," as Jamie Mackie has called it.[3] But determining the what, why and how of this ostensibly monumental event would be the crucial challenge for students specifically of the Conference and, more generally, of Third World international politics.

The essays in this volume amply reflect the Conference's contested legacy and relevance to the contemporary international order. But as Ang Cheng Guan reminds us in the second chapter of this study, the contrasting views of George Kahin's mostly sanguine view of the Conference and Michael Leifer's decidedly less generous opinion of the same capture, more or less, the ambivalent disposition that surrounded Bandung.[4] And as the one regional (African) and four country perspectives to this study illustrate, that sense is further complicated by the different and at times divergent views held of the Conference by various nations, including even its foremost constituents, not least China, India and

1

Indonesia, among others. Is the original Bandung Conference best understood as merely a post-colonial ideological reaction to the passing age of empire and its excesses, or an ambitious effort to promote a regional idea and an agenda for regionalism? Are its principles of peaceful coexistence mere rhetoric, or have these facilitated, if only indirectly, attempts by Asian countries to establish goodwill and improve relations with one another? What political, economic, social and/or cultural impacts, if any, has the Conference had on Asian societies other than at the state-to-state level? Has the Conference affected the way in which North-South relations have been conceptualised and conducted? Has the Conference influenced the foreign policy behaviour of individual countries? Conversely, how have these nations appropriated the Conference for their own purposes? These are some of the questions our contributors try to answer. That their arguments evince as many disagreements as concurrences only goes to show how contested and contestable the Conference's legacy has been and continues to be.[5]

Instead of reconciling or synthesising those differences, one of the tasks this volume's authors set for themselves was to highlight the miscellany of views on the Conference, not least those presented below. Yet in a crucial way, this vagueness is in effect reflective of the "nature" of international realities. "Ambiguity in 'international relations'," as Raymond Aron has reminded us, "is not to be imputed to the inadequacy of our concepts, but is an integral part of reality itself."[6] Regarding its legacy and relevance, the Conference, contested as it was, can arguably be seen as having exercised a lasting normative influence, chiefly through its contribution of particular principles and a loosely defined normative framework, which have since, if only in an inadvertent and unexpected fashion, provided important foundations for Asian regional order. Our varied remembrance of Bandung, as Itty Abraham notes in this volume, "particularly seems to invoke symbolic and ideological effects." In this respect, at least three noteworthy normative effects, at best unintended and accidental, emerged out of the Bandung Conference.[7] The first involves the articulation and advancement of basic principles of conduct in international relations. The second effect has to do with the alignment with rival power blocs. The third entails the importance of the consensus principle for the Conference and its legacy *vis-à-vis* contemporary diplomatic practice in Asia.

Notably, in highlighting these three points (discussed at length below), we do not argue that the Conference's architects anticipated these outcomes and actively sought to achieve them. If anything, insofar as it might have encouraged Asian leaders to think more regionally, it might be said that these were, in Anthony Reid's words in this volume, "due more to its [the Conference's] failures than to its successes." To be sure, the Conference produced no standing regional organisation, prompting some to see it as a major failure. However, this view is flawed. As Reid persuasively argues, the Conference was, if anything, a rival to the regional idea, rather than a crucial step towards it. Hence, the conclusion that Bandung "failed" to evolve into a regional institution would be to insist, unfairly and likely incorrectly, on a collective intention towards formal institutionalism on the part of the Conference's conveners. Put differently, if, as Fouad Ajami once noted, "the men who met in Bandung were dreamers,"[8] did their aspirations include a regional idea, a regionalist agenda? Unlikely, the essays in this anthology suggest, even if the regionalism that subsequently took root, for instance, in Southeast Asia—as embodied in the Association of Southeast Asian Nations (ASEAN)—clearly benefited from the normative legacy of Bandung. But the setting up of a permanent organisation was not the objective of the Conference's five sponsors, Indonesia, India, Ceylon, Burma and Pakistan.

In that respect, without provisions for ensuring institutional continuity, Michael Leifer is absolutely right that the notion of Afro-Asian harmony, to which the more enthusiastic supporters of Bandung unfailingly refer, was at best mythic.[9] Instead of setting up an organisation that would have proven unwieldy, what the Conference's sponsors arguably sought was an avenue for dialogue and socialisation among countries that until recently had been appendages of Western colonial powers, in terms of equality and mutual respect. From this vantage point, the nascent post-colonial nation-states represented at Bandung, confronted with the complications brought about by the Cold War (as several contributors to this volume have noted), would likely have held most visions of regionalism suspect, not least because these could potentially serve as fronts for imperialist projects, whether colonialist or communist in orientation. Indeed, it bears reminding that the Japanese vision of a "Greater East Asian Co-prosperity Sphere" was, in 1955, a considerably less-than-distant memory for most Asians, who, a mere decade ago, had endured the Japanese occupation.

A Code of Conduct

Arguably, the most important normative contribution of the Bandung Conference was to articulate and advance the basic principles of conduct in international relations. As Roeslan Abdulgani, the Secretary-General of the Conference in 1955, put it, the purpose of the Conference, if only implicit, was "to determine … the standards and procedures of present-day international relations" and to contribute to "the formulation and establishment of certain norms for the conduct of present-day international relations and the instruments for the practical application of these norms."[10] Comprising the largest ever grouping of new entrants into the international system, 29 states in total, the Conference membership exceeded the number of new states represented at the San Francisco Conference, which founded the United Nations. The dire necessity for the articulation and advancement of a code of conduct for Conference participants rested on at least three key considerations: first, the diffusion and entrenchment of universal norms among newly independent countries for whom the relevance of the former remained to be established; second, the "localisation" of universal norms within a regional context in ways sufficiently innovative and accommodating so as to facilitate cooperation among countries with rival political systems and ideologies; and, third, the establishment of a normative basis upon which peaceful coexistence between the great powers and the new post-colonial states could be fostered.

Not surprisingly, a fundamental concern shared among these mostly nascent nations would be to ensure their own survival through establishing their contestable sovereignty. In other words, Bandung was arguably a venue for norm-setting, not least the principles of state sovereignty and non-interference, which, for Itty Abraham, following Stephen Krasner,[11] comprise the "organised hypocrisy" of the Weberian ideal-type of identity as consisting in one territory, one people, one authority—prerequisites that many newly minted post-colonial Asian nations lacked. Most of the principles articulated at Bandung, such as the ten principles contained in the Final Communiqué, may be regarded as universal "motherhood" ideas that could be found in the UN charter or in European international law. In reality, however, some of these so-called universal norms had not been fully upheld or were yet to demonstrate their relevance for the newly independent countries. Bandung helped to contextualise, uphold and, in some cases, extend these principles. For example, non-intervention in the European states system permitted intervention by the great powers to restore the balance of power. The idea of non-intervention that gained ground at Bandung permitted no such exception, however. Moreover, several participants at Bandung, such as Ceylon and China, were not yet members of the UN, hence the experience of regional norm-setting granted them a sense of belonging to the club of nations and offered an alternative framework for their socialisation into the system of states.

Nevertheless, it was not just a matter of passively transplanting, wholesale, universal principles from the international to a regional context. As has been demonstrated, the norm localisation invariably involves a process of active negotiation between the principles in question, on the one hand, and the local context, customs and players, on the other.[12] Besides seeking to make the principles of sovereignty relevant to the nascent nations amongst its ranks, the Bandung Conference also strengthened, reinterpreted and extended those very principles in a broad, inclusive fashion in order to accommodate diversity and difference. In this regard, a key accomplishment of the Conference, all the more stark in view of the looming backdrop of the Cold War and the growing ideological divide between members of the anti-communist and communist blocs, was the consensus that differing political systems and ideologies should not be the basis for exclusion from international cooperation. Thus understood, a major contribution of the Bandung Conference was the introduction of the People's Republic of China to the Asian and African community—a "getting to know you" encounter, as it were, which highlighted the pragmatism in the foreign policies of the Conference participants, particularly those of the key architects.

For example, India's Jawaharlal Nehru clearly pursued a strategy of engagement of China, arguing that China's communist political system should not be reason enough to exclude it from the club of nations. And as Reid points out in his chapter, although both Nehru and Burma's U Nu "had been cool on the practicality of the [regionalism] idea," it nevertheless "became a feasible reality … when Nehru began to see it, in subsequent meetings following Zhou Enlai's performance at the Geneva peace talks, as a way to draw China out of its isolation." That said, it should be noted that Nehru was no fan of communism. He was not without some serious misgivings about Chinese intentions and power But he believed that China's turn to communism could not be wished away. The best way to cope with China was through a policy of engagement, not isolation or containment. China needed to be made aware of the feelings of distrust and misgiving harbored by its neighbours and their expectation that there should be no interference under any pretext in their internal affairs by the Chinese Communist Party. Similarly, China's neighbours needed to know more about China's policies and attitudes, rather than being simply led to believe what Western intelligence sources had been saying. Nehru secured an invitation for China to Bandung. He also played an important role in introducing Zhou at Bandung, even to the extent of creating a perception of himself being eclipsed by the latter, as Zhou proved adept at socialising with the delegates and projecting a tone of moderation and compromise that succeeded in convincing most delegates that China's political system was by itself not an obstacle to coexistence.

All this is not to imply that the Conference was free of regional circumspection about the People's Republic. Prior to the Conference, there was much apprehension about China, both in the West and among the participants. Some Asian governments that were facing domestic communist rebellions were especially fearful of Chinese subversion of their own polities and societies. They and the Western governments, especially the United States, feared that Zhou would use the Conference to score a propaganda victory for the Chinese. Bandung did not, however, turn out to be a victory for China as the West had feared. As long as Chinese support for communist parties in Southeast Asia continued, thereby constituting a violation of its commitment not to interfere in the internal affairs of neighbours, China had to pay a heavy diplomatic price. Many Southeast Asian countries, including Indonesia and Singapore, delayed having diplomatic relations with Beijing until this interference stopped. At the least, the Bandung injunction to China not to support internally disruptive forces in Southeast Asia created a marker for judging acceptable Chinese behaviour.

Today, Asia is going through another era of engagement with China. While the circumstances are different, the principles and expectations remain similar. Nehru was criticised for putting too much trust on China, while neglecting Indian defense preparedness. But whatever the circumstances and causes of Sino-Indian conflict, few today would deny the fundamental idea that engaging China is likely to yield more benefits in the long term than isolating and containing it. China, too, has learnt a political lesson: violating principles it professes would be counterproductive. China's recent diplomatic successes in Asia are due in part to its adherence to norms associated with Bandung and ASEAN. Any show of hegemony by China will likely backfire, despite allusions, correct or otherwise, to other Asian countries jumping on the China bandwagon.[13] Had it not been for the Bandung Conference, tensions over Chinese intentions would have remained serious. This remains an important reminder of the need for socialisation among nations irrespective of political and ideological differences. In this sense, the Bandung Conference was a precursor of the contemporary "engaging China" policy adopted by ASEAN.

Related to the preceding two observations was the necessity of securing the commitment of the great powers to the non-interference prerogative. A code of diplomatic conduct that could ensure the Conference participants' peaceful coexistence with the great powers through the latters' adherence, even if only tacit, to that code was particularly crucial in the light of the perceived imperialism of the West that the Cold War amplified—a point embodied by Beijing's view during this period, as highlighted in Chen Jian's chapter on China *vis-à-vis* Bandung. Indeed, if the nascent states of Asia were at all worried about possible threats to their sovereignty, the power and influence of the great powers would surely have been of utmost concern. As Wang Gungwu (cited by Ang Cheng Guan in his contribution to this volume) has colorfully described, the Southeast Asian governments harbored a "deep and immediate fear … of the Soviet bear's embrace and the longer-term threat of the Chinese dragon's reach, and the emergence during the 1950s of the American eagle next to the tired Imperial

British lion." If so, could the Bandung Conference be conceivably understood as an effort at constructing regional order, if by this we mean the establishing of common assumptions among states regarding how they were to relate with one another in pacific ways, not least between the strong and mighty, on the one hand, and the weak on the other? Consider, for example, Michael Leifer's opinion on what regional order in East Asia consists of:

> It is possible to argue that the general pattern of the regional balance in East Asia in terms of distribution of power embodies a measure of stability from a sense of prudence. But it is not the same as a viable regional order, which requires more than just a rudimentary code of interstate conduct. It requires also the existence of a set of shared assumptions about the interrelationships among resident and external states.[14]

The current debate in Asian international relations among scholars holding competing theoretical commitments principally revolves around the different conditions under which each analyst thinks regionalism matters most.[15] In view of this, Leifer's rumination on the *normative* prerequisites of regional order—"shared assumptions about the interrelationships among resident and external states"—implies little disagreement among realists (at least of the English School variety) and constructivists alike on the significance of a normative framework to regional order.[16] More importantly, it implies the elusiveness of regional order in Asia so long as external powers, regional key powers and weaker resident states fail to achieve shared normative assumptions about how they ought to relate with one another, despite the existence of an implicit code of diplomatic conduct. Against this backdrop, the years since the original Bandung Conference have shown just how elusive, if not illusory, a viable regional order in Asia has been. In this respect, the monumental achievement of the formation of the ASEAN Regional Forum (ARF) in 1994 was, without doubt, the institutionalisation of a multilateral security dialogue between the great powers (China, Japan, Russia and the United States) and other Asian countries, including the ASEAN ten. Arguably, the ARF, despite its not insignificant problems, could rightly be regarded as a significant step towards the eventual establishment of a region-wide normative framework crucial for moving the Asian region beyond its current instrumentally defined regionalism to an expressly rule-based one.[17]

Alignment with Rival Power Blocs

The second normative outcome of Bandung concerns the question of alignment with rival power blocs. On the one hand, a group of countries comprising India, Indonesia, Ceylon, Burma and Egypt favoured abstention from great power military alliances, such as the Southeast Asia Treaty Organisation (SEATO) and the Central Treaty Organization (CENTO; also known as the Baghdad Pact). India's Nehru criticised such pacts as instruments of domination by great powers that threatened the sovereignty, equality and dignity of the newly independent countries. He considered such pacts as unrepresentative of Asian nations. They exacerbated, rather than lessened, intra-regional tensions. Understandably, this interpretation proved quite controversial, on the other hand, with countries such as Thailand, the Philippines, Iran, Iraq, Turkey and Pakistan defending their membership in such pacts. This latter cluster of states used a formula—"right of individual or collective self-defense"—in justification of such alliances and their participation in them.

How the Conference's participants sought to resolve this tension would have far-reaching implications for Asia's post-war security order. In an exercise in compromise and consensus-building that became its hallmark, the Bandung Conference accepted that countries have the right of individual and collective self-defense, while at the same time calling for their "abstention from the use of arrangements of collective defense to serve the particular interests of any of the big powers."[18] The paradoxical quality of this resolution would prefigure the sorts of settlements that came to define the experience of ASEAN. To be sure, the principle of collective defense was accepted, but not great power pacts of the type that legitimised great power dominance. The Bandung Conference exposed the weak legitimacy of SEATO, in terms of its lack of regional participation and representation. It was not long before SEATO's members became disillusioned with the alliance, and at least two of them—Thailand and the Philippines—later came to accept the view that while SEATO might have provided a temporary relief to their insecurity about communism, it was not a long-term solution. They found a more indigenous form of regionalism, represented by ASEAN, as a more realistic approach to regional security and well-being. But it would be a form of regionalism that not only differed markedly from European regionalism, but one that was defined and would continue to be defined by the divergent perspectives of Asian governments on regionalism—views that arguably have their origins, if at all, in the Bandung Conference. As Anthony Reid observes in this book: "The fact that it moved in the direction of the eventual Non-Aligned Movement, rather than in the direction of regionalism, is therefore of great importance to Indonesia's stance in the following years"; on the other hand, Reid also contrasts Sukarno's disdain for regional cooperation with Tunku Abdul Rahman's evident enthusiasm for it.

The real lesson of Bandung was that direct and overt participation in a great power bloc could provoke the opposing camp and aggravate regional tensions. Importantly, this did not mean that Bandung was specifically aimed against Western interests. Quoting Ali Sastroamidjojo, Ang Cheng Guan notes in his chapter that the Conference's architects harbored no intention of creating "an anti-Western and even an anti-white bloc." Hence, while ASEAN was founded as a grouping of pro-Western governments, it steadfastly refused to be a military bloc. When proposals were made for ASEAN to develop joint military cooperation against communist Vietnam following the US withdrawal from Vietnam in 1975 and the Vietnamese military intervention in Cambodia in 1979, ASEAN wisely avoided them, because it did not want to provoke its adversaries. The norm against "the use of arrangements for collective defence to serve the particular interests of any of the big powers,"[19] originally advanced at Bandung, has more or less endured.

The Bandung Conference was a forerunner of the Non-Aligned Movement (NAM). NAM provided the smaller and weaker states of the Third World a foreign policy framework to assert their autonomy and express their solidarity. NAM's credibility subsequently suffered due to its close association with the Soviet bloc and the anti-Western rhetoric of some of its leading members. With the end of the Cold War, the relevance of NAM as a political platform may be questioned. But the challenge of dealing with a bipolar international or regional order has reappeared, and in this regard, some of the principles of Bandung—especially the need to avoid entanglement with alliances serving the narrow particularistic interests of great powers, and the need for coexistence, dialogue and compromise—remain relevant.

These norms—non-alignment, coexistence, dialogue, compromise and the like—are of considerable relevance for Asia in coping with the Sino-American rivalry. In an important sense, the regional order of post-Cold War East Asia has more or less been bipolar, with the United States and China occupying the two central poles (although the rise of India and the apparent resurgence of Japan offer preliminary grounds to argue the case for multipolarity). Some sections of the US policy-making community advocate a policy of containing China through an intensification of military alliances around the United States. But as ASEAN leaders such as Lee Kuan Yew have argued, such a policy will induce greater insecurity and xenophobia in China and aggravate intra-regional tensions. Such a policy would serve the "particular interests" of the United States and undermine the common security goals of Asia. The common security objectives of Asia—consistent with the Bandung norm—remain the mutual engagement of both China and the United States, and the avoidance of exclusionary security relationships.

Importantly, it was not only entanglement in relations with extraregional powers that concerned the Bandung Conference. A related lesson of no less significance was the perception that neither India nor China, the two big Asian powers, could or should dominate an Asian regional organisation. An Asian regional grouping created under the dominance of regional powers would be as unacceptable as those created under superpower auspices. This reinforced lessons learned from Japan's earlier effort to organise an East Asian regional grouping under its own sphere of influence (the "Greater East Asian Co-prosperity Sphere"). The aversion to regional groupings under the hegemonic influence of either extraregional powers or major Asian powers paved the way for ASEAN, which offered a successful model for relatively less powerful states getting together for mutual benefit. Since the end of the Cold War, both India and China have accepted ASEAN's leadership of regional institutions. This lesson of Bandung remains relevant today, when there is talk in the air of a Sino-centric regional order based on a return to the "benign" tributary system of the past.

Flexibility and Consensus

A third important normative outcome of the Bandung Conference concerned the procedures adopted by the Conference: the recognition of non-intrusive, informal and consensus-based diplomacy over legalistic and formal organisations that might constrain state sovereignty, an important consideration for countries that had just gained sovereign statehood. Nehru was particularly keen that the agenda of the Bandung Conference should be kept as flexible as possible, that no contentious issues that would divide the Conference should be discussed, and that decisions should be reached not by majority voting, but by consensus. As Roeslan Abdulgani would recollect, these procedures, "including the principle of deliberation and consensus, were one of the keys to the success of the [Afro-Asian] Conference."[20]

What is also noteworthy about these principles is that they were not uniquely Asian but were the product of a creative synthesis between the universal and local principles that Bandung best symbolised. One key source of these procedures was the Commonwealth Heads of Government meetings (which were familiar to Nehru). At the same time, the principles of informality, mutual respect, consultation and consensus were also deep-rooted in Indonesian and Asian culture and civilisation. In particular, they called to mind Javanese village principles of *musyawarah* (consultation) and *mufakat* (consensus). Hence, they were easily accepted by Indonesia and other Bandung participants. In an important sense, these procedures adopted at the Bandung Conference marked the birth of consensus diplomacy among Asian nations. Later, this would be called the "ASEAN Way." A common misconception is that the ASEAN Way was itself a post-1967 creation and that it had nothing to do with Bandung. Yet, many core elements of the ASEAN Way had their origins in the Bandung process. These include a preference for informality, avoidance of legalistic approaches and mechanisms found in Western multilateral groups, avoidance of contentious bilateral disputes from the multilateral agenda in the spirit of compromise, the need for saving face, and above all, the emphasis on consultation and consensus.

In an era rife with loose and self-fulfilling talk about a "clash of civilisations," the fit between outside approaches and Asian approaches to negotiations and diplomacy shows that civilisational differences between nations do not preclude dialogue and mutual learning. They also show that supposedly Western concepts can be fitted within Asian local settings—via a process of "localisation," as it were—if they are perceived to be relevant and congruent with existing local beliefs and practices.[21] The Bandung Conference showed that nationalism and regionalism are not necessarily irreconcilable goals but could, under the right circumstances, be mutually supportive. In his opening address at Bandung, President Sukarno described the New Delhi Conference on Indonesia in 1949, which condemned the Dutch Police Action and supported Indonesia's independence as the forerunner of Bandung.[22] Then, as in Bandung, regionalism was seen as a powerful instrument of national independence and sovereignty. In an important sense, this foreshadowed the link between regional resilience and national resilience articulated by Indonesia after the founding of ASEAN in 1967. Bandung also led to the redefinition of the relationship between the West and the rest, or the post-colonial nations of Asia and Africa. The old framework, marked by hierarchy and dependence, gave way to expectations of equality and interdependence in multilateral diplomacy.

Bandung and the Middle East

In lieu of a chapter on Middle Eastern participation at the Bandung Conference, a brief comment particularly on the role of Egypt, under President Gamal Abdel Nasser, is in order. The Middle Eastern participants at Bandung went there ideologically polarised, just like their counterparts from Asia. And unlike the few African participants, who adopted a low profile throughout the Conference—especially since Ghana's Nkrumah, who would later use Bandung as a model for his own pan-African initiatives, was prevented from attending by the British (who still had responsibility for Ghana's foreign and security affairs)—the Middle Eastern delegates were forceful and articulate. Turkey and Lebanon were the most vocal critics of communist powers; many observers thought the Turks were acting on behalf of the Americans. Charles Habib Malik, the Lebanese ambassador to the United States and the United Nations, also savaged the neutralist (especially Nehru's) position on military pacts such as SEATO and CENTO.

The most important Middle Eastern personality at Bandung, however, was Egypt's Nasser. It was Nasser's first major international conference since he seized power from King Farouk in 1952. Before Bandung, Nasser was viewed by the United States as a pro-Western moderate who might be expected not to attack Western interests. If so, either this assessment was dead wrong or Nasser must have left Bandung a profoundly changed man. There is little question that Nasser was one of the most popular leaders at Bandung, both inside and outside of the Conference halls. He could be seen waving to the crowd, holding centre stage at receptions, signing autographs for children. Pictures of the Conference show him radiant, self-assured and charming. He also played a major role in the search for compromises when the pro-Western and the neutral camps at Bandung got into an impasse over the major issues, especially over the wording of the Final Communiqué. It was at Bandung that Nasser first met Chinese leaders, although what exactly transpired between him and Zhou Enlai remains a mystery. Did Nasser speak to Zhou about buying Soviet weapons at Bandung? Did Zhou pass the request to the Kremlin, which agreed and arranged a deal through Prague? This is a matter of speculation only.[23] But what is certain is that after Nasser returned from Bandung, his policies were anything but "pro-Western." Just over four months after his return from Bandung, in September 1955, Egypt signed a historic arms deals with Czechoslovakia. Less than a year thereafter, in July 1956, it nationalised the Suez Canal Company, thereby prompting the Anglo-French-Israeli invasion that would change the history of the Middle East forever. And Nasser would join Nehru and Tito (somewhat eclipsing Sukarno) as a leader of the Non-Aligned Movement, which emerged in the 1960s.

Whither Bandung?

Today, the Bandung Conference serves as a benchmark for judging the progress of multilateral diplomacy in Asia and the developing world. Briefly put, at least three concluding observations can be made in this respect. First, the Conference provided the nascent states of Asia crucial, if somewhat perplexing, lessons in diplomacy and international relations. Recently declassified documents in Western archives reveal that prior to the Conference, Western powers such as Britain and the United States made a concerted effort to counter the influence of neutral countries such as India and Indonesia and offered "coaching" and "guidance" to their allies—Pakistan, Turkey and the Philippines, as well as Ceylon. The British provided a wide range of background and position papers on issues such as the nature of communist colonialism, which turned out, not surprisingly, to be a major bone of contention at Bandung.[24] The United States had an advance copy of the speech that Carlos Romulo gave at Bandung. These exercises, which ironically showed how seriously the West viewed the Conference despite outwardly feigning a lack of concern, reflected the relative unfamiliarity of the newly independent countries with foreign affairs. Now, such propaganda and manipulation by Western powers of Asian conferences would be unthinkable and unacceptable, even to the most pro-Western countries in the region. Thanks mainly to subsequent regional multilateral settings like that provided by ASEAN, the knowledge gap today between Asia and the West on international affairs has narrowed (although not completely been bridged, thus necessitating the creation of a diplomatic academy of Asian or ASEAN nations, perhaps to be located in Bandung as a fitting memorial to the legacy of the Conference).

Second, Asia also faces the need to adapt some of the Bandung principles to new and changing circumstances. Growing economic interdependence dictates that Asia view regional cooperation not merely as a matter of simple "coexistence," but also as "integration" and collective action. The non-interference principle, which served Asia so well at the time of Bandung and subsequently through ASEAN in maintaining regional peace and discouraging great power interventionism, is now facing new challenges. While, in keeping with the Bandung Spirit, differing political systems need not be an obstacle to engagement and cooperation, the doctrine of non-interference should not prevent collective action against common threats and may be used to develop economic cooperation. Moreover, with the end of the Cold War, there is less need today for regional groupings that exclude Western powers. Today, regionalism that includes Western powers, albeit in accordance with principles of equality and mutual benefit, are desirable.

Third, the Bandung Conference would also go down in history as a remarkable feat of organisational success of a young independent nation: Indonesia. Participants and observers (including Westerners), whether speaking privately or publicly, commented favourably on the logistical and residential facilities provided by the Indonesian hosts, not to mention the beautiful physical surroundings of Bandung. Nehru, upon his return from Bandung, wrote an impression of the Conference to Lady Edwina Mountbatten (this has been recently declassified):

> Although there were five sponsors of this Conference—Burma, Ceylon, Indonesia, Pakistan and India—and we shared expenses and had a Joint Secretariat, still a great burden of organising it fell on the Indonesian Government. They discharged this remarkably well. I doubt if we could have provided the same amenities in Delhi. Altogether, therefore, the Conference

was a remarkable success. I think all of us who were there came back a little wiser and certainly with a better understanding of the other.[25]

In sum, the Bandung Conference did not end the Cold War polarisation of Asia, nor did it create a standing regional organisation for the management of intra-regional conflict. But it articulated the normative basis of a regional and international order marked by tolerance of diversity, mutual accommodation, and the softening of ideological conflicts and rivalries. This approach to international order subsequently influenced the outlook and approach of ASEAN and could well be the basis for an emerging Asian security community. The main legacy of Bandung was not so much strategic or organisational, but educational and normative. Bandung was an intercontinental conference, bringing together the newly independent nations of Africa, Asia and the Middle East. Since then, the continents have drifted apart. While there are now inter-regional frameworks for Asian-European and Asian-Latin American cooperation, similar frameworks for Asian-African or Asian-Middle Eastern (West Asian) cooperation have lagged. Yet, Asia's growing demand for oil from the Middle East and the challenge posed by terrorism require the creation of a framework for dialogue and understanding between the western, southern and southeastern parts of Asia. The December 2004 tsunamis underscored the interdependence between Asia and Africa, of the countries bordering the Indian Ocean, in an effort to promote human security. Developing an Asian-African framework for dialogue and cooperation could be a fitting memorial to the historic Bandung Conference more than 50 years ago.

Notes

[1]	This introduction is partly drawn from a paper prepared by Amitav Acharya for President Susilo Bambang Yudhoyono of Indonesia.

[2]	Cited in Fouad Ajami, "The Third World Challenge: The Fate of Nonalignment," *Foreign Affairs* 59, no. 2 (1980/81), available at <http://www.foreignaffairs.org/19801201faessay8162/fouad-ajami/the-third-world-challenge-the-fate-of-nonalignment.html> [25 September 2007].

[3]	Jamie Mackie, *Bandung 1955: Non-Alignment and Afro-Asian Solidarity* (Singapore: Editions Didier Millet, 2005).

[4]	George McTurnan Kahin, *The Asian-African Conference, Bandung, Indonesia, April 1955* (Ithaca: Cornell University Press, 1956), p. 1; Michael Leifer, *Dilemmas of Statehood in Southeast Asia* (Vancouver: University of British Columbia Press, 1972), pp. 136–7.

[5]	That said, the diversity in opinion could be a function of the disparate assemblage of analysts, representing (at least) three distinct disciplinary-cum-methodological traditions, who contributed to this project.

6   Raymond Aron, *Peace and War: A Theory of International Relations*, translated by E. Howard and A.B. Fox (London: Weidenfeld and Nicolson, 1966), p. 7.

7   The following draws heavily from Amitav Acharya, "The Contemporary Relevance of the Bandung Conference for Asian and International Order: Some Reflections" (unpublished paper, 8 March 2005).

8   Ajami, "The Third World Challenge."

9   Leifer, *Dilemmas of Statehood in Southeast Asia*, pp. 136–7.

10 Roeslan Abdulgani, *Bandung Spirit* (Jakarta: Prapantja, 1964), pp. 72, 103.

11 Stephen D. Krasner, *Sovereignty: Organized Hypocrisy* (Princeton: Princeton University Press, 1999).

12 Amitav Acharya, "How Ideas Spread: Whose Norms Matter? Norm Localization and Institutional Change in Asian Regionalism," *International Organization* 58 (2004): 239–75.

13 See the debate between David Kang and Amitav Acharya: David C. Kang, "Getting Asia Wrong: The Need for New Analytical Frameworks," *International Security* 27, no. 4 (2003): 57–85; Amitav Acharya, "Will Asia's Past Be Its Future?" *International Security* 28, no. 3 (2003/04): 149–64. Arguably, the debate has been joined by Evelyn Goh, who posits "enmeshment" rather than balancing or bandwagoning as a plausible explanation for behaviour towards China. Goh, "The U.S.-China Relationship and Asia-Pacific Security: Negotiating Change," *Asian Security* 1, no. 3 (2005): 216–44.

14 Michael Leifer, "The Balance of Power and Regional Order," in Michael Leifer (ed.), *The Balance of Power in East Asia* (London: Macmillan, 1986), pp. 151–2.

15 Amitav Acharya, "Do Norms and Identity Matter? Community and Power in Southeast Asia's Regional Order," in Joseph Chinyong Liow and Ralf Emmers (eds.), *Order and Security in Southeast Asia: Essays in Memory of Michael Leifer* (London and New York: Routledge, 2006), p. 78.

16 Muthiah Alagappa, "Managing Asian Security: Competition, Cooperation, and Evolutionary Change," in Muthiah Alagappa (ed.), *Asian Security Order: Instrumental and Normative Features* (Stanford: Stanford University Press, 2003), p. 14.

17 Ibid.

18 The "Final Communique of the Afro-Asian Conference," in *Asia-Africa Speaks from Bandung* (Jakarta: Ministry of Foreign Affairs, Republic of Indonesia, 1955).

19 Ibid.

20 Roeslan Abdulgani, *The Bandung Connection: The Asia-Africa Conference in Bandung in 1955* (Jakarta: Gunung Agung (S) Pte. Ltd., 1981), pp. 76–7.

21 Acharya, "How Ideas Spread: Whose Norms Matter?" pp. 239–75.

22 "Opening Address by President Sukarno at the Asia Africa Conference," in *Asia-Africa Speaks from Bandung* (Jakarta: Ministry of Foreign Affairs, Republic of Indonesia, 1955).

23 See Mohamed Sid-Ahmed, "The Bandung Way," in *Al-Ahram Weekly*, available at <http://weekly.ahram.org.eg/print/2005/740/op5.htm> [11 July 2007]. The article

claims that Nasser did ask (at Bandung itself?) Zhou about arms and Zhou passed the request to the Soviet leadership, who then arranged for Czech weapons.

24   Amitav Acharya, "Lessons of Bandung, Then and Now," *Financial Times*, 21 April 2005.

25   Ravindar Kumar and H.Y. Sharada Prasad (eds.), *Selected Works of Jawaharlal Nehru*, Second Series, vol. 28 (New Delhi: Jawaharlal Nehru Memorial Fund, 2001).

PART I

PART I

CHAPTER 1

The Bandung Conference and Southeast Asian Regionalism

Anthony Reid

Bandung was undoubtedly a crucial moment in the development of thinking about regional identities, as about many other issues. However, the argument of this chapter is that the Bandung Conference was not so much a step towards the solidarity of the Southeast Asian region, as the emergence of a powerful rival to it. In a sense it was a distraction into the heady world of global politics and global conflicts. Insofar as Bandung played a role in encouraging Southeast Asian leaders to think of themselves as Southeast Asians, this was due more to its failures than to its successes.

Division of Southeast Asia

Colonialism had divided Southeast Asia in profoundly new ways, imposing on it a kind of European nationalism in which artificially exact boundaries separated sovereign domains (potential nation-states). Within these boundaries the languages of education and government, as well as the laws, currencies and economies, were oriented in different ways.

European nationalisms naturally spawned Asian nationalisms, insisting on the same boundaries and the same monopoly of language, legal system, education, etc., within them. While colonial institutions and languages often brought the nationalist elites together in practice, the rhetorical common factor within these boundaries could not be the symbols of colonialism but could be their mirror, the symbols of anti-colonialism. Whatever their differences, societies within these colonially defined boundaries could share an opposition to that colonial presence and the humiliation it represented.

The everyday interactions of a region such as Southeast Asia were significantly impeded by the imposition of different elite languages with their education systems within these boundaries, and the orientation of trade and government to the metropolis. Particularly problematic were the areas that had been crossroads and meeting places in pre-colonial times but were turned into embittered backwaters by the centring of the new national life in colonial capitals. They also became sources of conflict between the new nation-states. What we today call Southern Thailand, southern Philippines, northern and eastern Burma, and Aceh had all been major crossroads in the past, but the imposition of the new boundaries made them problematic peripheries.

In a sense the Peninsula, and particularly the part of it that made up British Malaya, was the archetypal crossroad: difficult to squeeze into nation-state-dom and something of a challenge to it. As the junction of Southeast Asia, the Peninsula had to be central to any practical regional networking. But as a problem for nation-state-dom it was excluded from Bandung and eventually seen as an affront to Sukarno's development of the Bandung idea.

Commercial interaction had been extensive within Southeast Asia and beyond it (especially with southern China in the mid-16th to mid-19th centuries) before European colonial domination and the establishment of fixed boundaries in the second half of the 19th century. But it had been carried on notably by minority traders operating from and through the crossroads—Chinese, Bugis, Malays (in the Dutch sense), Tausug, Mon and Cham. Political interaction among the major state actors had been marked primarily by conflict over status, trade, people and territory. In the mid-19th century this changed. Rama III presciently told his son Mongkut on his deathbed in 1851, "There will be no more wars with Vietnam and Burma. We will have them only with the West."[1] The intense interaction of war and cultural raiding (of artists, builders, poets and Buddhist palladia) gave way by 1890 to conflicts within the lines the Europeans drew on the maps. On the ground there was some truth in what Henry Burney told the Siamese as early as 1826, that only fixed boundaries between territories would "prevent all chance of mistake or dispute" and enable British and Siamese to have more stable and harmonious relations than Burmese and Siamese had had.[2]

In the high colonial era (1870–1930), therefore, most fighting occurred not between states, but around their edges, to force those crossroad areas that had now become problematic peripheries to re-orient to the new colonial capital. Symptomatic were the US war to subdue the Islamic southern Philippines, the Dutch to subdue Aceh, and, to a lesser extent, the British to subdue the Wa and other borderland people of Burma's north and east. The high colonial era was overall an era of unprecedented peace in Southeast Asia, as long as the unsatisfied rising powers, Russia and Germany, were too far away to make Southeast Asia a major issue. Only with the third rising power, Japan, did major conflict return to the region, in 1941.

Searching for New Relationships: Regional or Ideological?

In the era of decolonisation, how would the cards fall? Would the new states pursue regionalism either of a Southeast Asian or a pan-Asian kind, or divide into ideological or religious camps according to their different elite faiths? During the high colonial era there were a number of ventures in all these directions, which developed into competing visions in the 1950s.

Southeast Asian regionalism did begin to find ways to express itself in the colonial 20th century, both in the elite circles of scholars tracing a common heritage and among revolutionaries looking for potential allies. The former manifested itself in the increasing interaction of scholars working on the classic civilisations of Cambodia, Champa, Java, Siam and Burma, culminating in George Coedes' synthetic work (1944) making sense for the first time of the early history of the whole region.[3] It was also manifest in the Pan-Pacific Science Conferences and the work of the Institute of Pacific Relations. Although these growing interactions were dominated by Europeans resident in Asia, we should not overlook the important contribution of Asian scholars such as Prince Damrong, Nguyen Van Huyen and Hoessein Djajadiningrat.

On the revolutionary front, the Comintern (Communist International) was particularly involved in imagining communities of common oppression. On a Southeast Asian level, the great prophet was Tan Malaka, especially during his years as Comintern agent for roughly this region, based in Manila for much of the 1920s. He dreamed first of a "Malay" federation of the Philippines, Malaya and Indonesia, and later of "Aslia" (Asia-Australia), a future socialist federation roughly coinciding with Southeast Asia plus Australia.[4]

Most of the Comintern's activities, however, encouraged commonalities at a global level. The League Against Imperialism notably put together a "Congress of Oppressed Peoples" in Brussels in 1927, encouraged by the Comintern but funded by China and Mexico. It was attended by India's Nehru, Indonesia's Hatta and Vietnam's Ho Chi Minh, among other leaders. Sukarno's welcome speech at Bandung in 1955 specifically mentioned this antecedent for the Bandung idea—"At that Conference many distinguished delegates who are present here today met each other and found new strength in their fight for independence."[5]

The geographically defined Southeast Asian idea certainly made a comeback at the end of the Pacific War, the shared experience of Japanese occupation giving some elites of both right and left an unprecedented sense of commonality. Those on the left perceived a common moment of opportunity for revolution following the sudden Japanese surrender in August 1945. Ho Chi Minh was particularly interested in relations with "fellow Southeast Asian revolutions," and in November 1945 he made an appeal for solidarity to the almost equally embattled Republic of Indonesia. Although there was no response from Indonesia, the leaders of communist-led independence movements in Vietnam, Laos and Cambodia proceeded to call for a Southeast Asian "federation" to comprise all the independence movements of the future ASEAN except the Philippines. In Burma, nationalists wary of their bigger neighbours were early enthusiasts of such a bloc, the nationalist hero Aung San also aspiring for something like a federation of Southeast Asian states in the period 1946–47.[6]

Nehru made a bid for Indian leadership of whatever new solidarities might be emerging, by hosting the Asian Relations Conference in March–April 1947. Southeast Asian delegates were there in force, with both sides of the Indonesian and Indo-Chinese conflicts hoping for support. In turn the Thais hoped for a leadership role in Southeast Asia as an honest broker without claims to domination.

The meeting was a disappointment for the embattled delegations from Vietnam and Indonesia; and the Asiatic Relations Organisation, which was intended to be its outcome, never materialised. This conference probably marked the beginning of the Southeast Asian disenchantment with India as the anti-colonial champion of Asia.

In consequence, there was another surge of the Southeast Asian regional idea in the months that followed, with the Democratic Republic of Vietnam and Thai governments taking the lead in trying to establish a Southeast Asian League. Independence leaders in Burma, the Philippines and Indonesia, however, were careful not to become involved lest their credibility in international negotiations be tainted with communist associations. When the left-liberal Thai Prime Minister Pridi Panumyong was ousted by Phibun Songkram in a military coup in November 1947, the league was quickly buried in Cold War rivalry.[7]

Once the independence of Indonesia and Burma was fully recognised, these countries joined the Afro-Asian group at the United Nations, mainly designed to press France towards decolonisation in Indo-China and Algeria, and to support the Palestinians against Israel. Indonesia had never shown much interest in the Southeast Asian idea, and this grouping at the UN also led Burma away from it towards more global anti-colonial concerns. It was at a meeting in Colombo of the South and Southeast Asian members of this group, designed to generate pressure on the Indo-China conflict, that the idea of a very broad Asian-African conference was born. Indonesia's Ali Sastroamidjojo was very much the inspiration for the meeting, and his government's need for a success that would be anti-colonial without being clear or programmatic enough to exacerbate domestic conflicts was much of the reason why the Conference was so diverse in its makeup.

A Diversion from Regionalism

The Bandung Conference of 1955 has to be considered the major Southeast Asian initiative towards broader solidarities in the post-colonial 1950s. There had been more modest gatherings in post-war Bangkok, such as those described above, and in Rangoon of the early 1950s, such as the Asian Socialist Conference of 1953. The Southeast Asia Treaty Organisation (SEATO) was established in Manila in September 1954, but it clearly resulted from US initiatives to contain China and the spread of communism in Vietnam, and contained only three Asian partners—Pakistan, Thailand and the Philippines. Bandung was far more successful than any of these. Its success was extremely important to Sukarno, even though it had not been his initiative but Ali Sastroamidjojo's. The fact that it moved in the direction of the eventual Non-Aligned Movement, rather than in the direction of regionalism, is therefore of great importance to Indonesia's stance in the following years.

The idea had in fact begun, rather, as regionalism, with the Colombo meeting of April 1954. Ceylonese Premier John Kotelawela had invited four other newly independent Asian states to his capital (but not Thailand or Japan) with the thought that "it was time the united voice of Asia was heard in the councils of the world." Indonesia's Prime Minister had been the one with a wider vision of an Afro-Asian meeting of anti-colonial solidarity. Nehru and Burmese Prime Minister U Nu had been cool on the practicality of the idea, and it became a feasible reality only when Nehru began to see it, in subsequent meetings following Zhou Enlai's performance at the Geneva peace talks, as a way to draw China out of its isolation.

The Conference was widely declared a success, represented particularly by the very wide attendance; by Zhou Enlai's diplomatic opening to Indonesia, India and other states; and by a sense that the Bandung Spirit had managed to frame an agreed Final Communiqué despite the wide ideological differences displayed at the Conference. This success was particularly felt in Indonesia, where the nationalist political elite saw themselves playing, for the first time, a distinguished part in a global drama. Until the military took over in 1966, there was little further interest from the Indonesian leadership in any kind of Southeast Asian regional grouping. Gradually, in the early 1960s, Sukarno was drawn by a variety of factors, not least his memory of Bandung, into increasingly ideological alignments with Beijing and its allies (Pyongyang and Hanoi), directed against neighbours in Southeast Asia.

Finally, Bandung excluded Malaya, save for the Indonesian invitation of hardly-representative Malay nationalist Burhanuddin al-Helmy. Despite their emerging elected leaderships and much internal self-government, Malaya and Singapore were deemed less appropriate invitees than Ghana and Sudan, the soon-to-be-independent countries that had been invited. No doubt this had something to do with China's support for the embattled Malayan Communist Party, and the disdain of some of the Indonesian nationalist elite for the parties participating in the electoral process. Bandung consolidated, thereby, a cleavage at the heart of anything that could be Southeast Asia. The support of Tunku Abdul Rahman for the regional Southeast Asian idea, exhibited in his call for an Association of South-East Asia (ASA) as early as 1959, was met with cold indifference in Jakarta. Jamie Mackie later contrasted Tunku's "enthusiasm for regional cooperation ... and Soekarno's disdain for it."[8]

Separation from South Asia

On the other hand, the Bandung Conference had great importance also in its failures. One of the most striking of these was the way in which India fell out with the group that might have been seen as its natural allies and supporters in post-colonial Southeast Asia. Since much of the debate in Bandung and the lead-up to it was over Nehru's undiplomatic denunciation of any kind of military alliance, and the insistence of smaller countries such as the Philippines, Thailand and Pakistan that they needed such alliances in a way India did not, one might have foreseen a falling out with the SEATO group. Yet Indonesia shared with India its opposition to pacts, its hope for better relations with China, and a firm anti-colonial stance. As Kahin put it, "both the Indonesian and Ceylonese delegations were antagonized by what they regarded as overbearing and patronizing attitudes on the parts of Nehru and Menon."[9] The point was made much more sharply by Philippine Foreign Minister Carlos Romulo:

> Prime Minister Nehru has without doubt a highly cultivated intellect. But while his fellow delegates were impressed by his culture and erudition, many of them were also jolted by his pedantry. His pronounced propensity to be dogmatic, impatient, irascible, and unyielding, especially in the face of opposition, alienated the goodwill of many delegates. Here was a conference which everybody thought would be dominated by him ... [but] he typified the affectation of cultural superiority induced by a conscious identification

with an ancient civilization.... He also showed an anti-American complex
... [although] he has a secret admiration for everything British.[10]

Nehru came to the Bandung Conference as the leader of Asia but left it
as an outsider. His great achievement in bringing China into the Asian dialogue
did not in the long run serve India's purposes. Sino-Indian relations deteriorated
steadily from 1958 to the war of 1962. On the other hand, the quieter aliena-
tion of Southeast Asian leaders from any form of Indian leadership was truly
long-term. Since the China of Mao Zedong was even less acceptable a partner,
Southeast Asia was ultimately obliged to seek some kind of regionalism of its
own. But this could not happen until some of the leading actors in the Bandung
Conference had passed from the scene.

There were multiple reasons why the high expectations for regionalism after 1945
were not realised until the late 1960s. Cold War conflict was certainly high on
the list. But it seems likely that the enthusiasms of the Bandung Conference
led Indonesia, in particular, towards a quest for global roles that did not help
relationships with its immediate neighbours, Malaysia and the Philippines. In
this sense it marked a step backwards.

Notes

1   Cited in David Wyatt, *The Politics of Reform in Thailand: Education in the Reign
     of King Chulalongkorn* (New Haven: Yale University Press, 1969), p. 30.
2   Journal of Burney, 15 February 1826, in *The Burney Papers* (reprint Farnborough:
     Gregg International, 1971), pp. 85–6.
3   George Çoedès, *Histoire ancienne des états hindouisés d'Extrême-Orient* (Hanoi,
     1944). A translation of the third edition is better known as *The Indianized States
     of Southeast Asia* (Honolulu: East-West Center Press, 1968).
4   Helen Jarvis (ed.), *Tan Malaka: From Jail to Jail* (Athens: Ohio University Press,
     1991), pp. xcvi–vii.
5   President Sukarno's speech at the opening of the Asian-African Conference, 18
     April 1955, in George McTurnan Kahin, *The Asian-African Conference, Bandung,
     Indonesia, April 1955* (Ithaca: Cornell University Press, 1956), p. 40.
6   Christopher Goscha, *Thailand and Southeast Asian Networks of the Vietnamese
     Revolution, 1885–1954* (Richmond: Curzon Press, 1991), pp. 135–7, 144n.
7   Ibid., pp. 139–44.
8   Jamie Mackie, *Konfrontasi* (Kuala Lumpur: Oxford University Press, 1974), p. 33.
9   Kahin, *The Asian-African Conference*, p. 36. I well remember the stronger reaction
     of another participant in the Bandung Conference, the Australian volunteer Herb

Feith, when I tried to interest him in the 1980s in some kind of joint Indonesia-India conference. He was quite sure that Bandung had been the turning point in souring Indian-Indonesian relations for decades.

[10]   Carlos P. Romulo, *The Meaning of Bandung* (Chapel Hill: University of North Carolina Press, 1956), pp. 11–2.

CHAPTER 2

The Bandung Conference and the Cold War International History of Southeast Asia

Ang Cheng Guan

Scholars have been divided on the significance of the Bandung Conference, which has often been described as a major milestone in the international relations of the newly independent countries of Asia and Africa. There are essentially two views: One is that the Conference achieved a surprising degree of success, albeit modest;[1] the opposing view is that the success of Bandung was more apparent than real and is based largely on myth.[2] The Conference has, however, not attracted much attention from diplomatic historians, and this occasion—the 50th anniversary of the Conference—provides an opportunity to affirm, augment or correct some commonly held views and understandings of that event as well as highlight certain aspects that have not been described in earlier publications.[3]

From the vantage point of Southeast Asia, the Bandung Conference, held on 18–24 April 1955, must be located in the context of three overlapping developments that took place in Asia—in the context of this essay, more specifically Southeast Asia—from the end of World War II, in 1945. The year 1945 marked the end of the Japanese occupation of Southeast Asia. The end of World War II destroyed the pre-war relationship between the colonial powers (the British, French, Dutch and Portuguese) and their Southeast Asian colonies.[4] By April 1955, when the Bandung Conference was held, with the exceptions of Thailand, which was never colonised, and the Federation of Malaya (including Singapore) and Brunei, which were still part of the British Empire, the other Southeast Asian countries had more or less obtained their independence. The second development was that while the states shared a common goal for independence, the transformation paths of each of the new nation-states and their histories were different and complex. One of the major challenges, if not the most critical, was the achievement and maintenance of national unity. The details of decolonisation and transformation are too convoluted and need not delay us here, although we need to constantly keep them in mind.[5] The third overlapping development was the advent of the Cold War in Asia in 1949, which further complicated the already complex situation in the region.[6] Wang Gungwu memorably described the deep and immediate fear (of the Southeast Asian governments) of the Soviet bear's embrace and the longer-term threat of the Chinese dragon's reach, and the emergence during the 1950s of the American eagle next to the tired Imperial British lion.[7]

Aims of the Conference

The aims and objectives of the Bandung Conference, of which there are four, were clearly spelt out by the Prime Ministers of Burma, Ceylon (now Sri Lanka), India, Indonesia and Pakistan in the joint communiqué issued at the end of their planning meeting in Bogor (28–29 December 1954) and reiterated by Indonesian Prime Minister Ali Sastroamidjojo in his opening speech as President of the Bandung Conference.[8] They are worth reiterating here:

(a)   To promote goodwill and cooperation among the nations of Asia and Africa, to explore and advance their mutual as well as common interests, and to establish and further friendliness and neighbourly relations;

(b)   To consider social, economic and cultural problems and relations of the countries represented;

(c)   To consider problems of special interest to Asian and African peoples, e.g., problems affecting national sovereignty and of racialism and colonialism;

(d)   To view the position of Asia and Africa and their peoples in the world of today and the contribution they can make to the promotion of world peace and cooperation.

The Bandung Conference attempted to persuade Asian and African nations that the above four very broad but undoubtedly desirable objectives could best, if not only, be achieved through "neutralism" and through "peaceful coexistence" amongst themselves and with the major powers. With regards to the latter, the Conference provided the occasion to introduce China, an emerging and to many a dangerous/threatening Asian power, into the community of newly independent countries. Roeslan Abdulgani recalled that for the five Prime Ministers who met at Bogor, especially Nehru and U Nu, good relations with China were vital to their national interests. China was considered a "key factor" that would be decisive in stabilising Southeast Asia. Of particular concern was how to reduce the mounting tensions between Beijing and Washington, which the Bogor meeting acknowledged would not be an easy task.[9]

The organisers of the Bandung Conference were well aware of US concern about the Conference, particularly with the presence of China at the gathering.[10] Unlike Moscow, Washington did not send a message of greetings to the Conference. In his opening address on 18 April 1955, Ali Sastroamidjojo noted that from the time the intention to convene the Conference had been publicised there had been much speculation about its agenda. In his speech, he spoke of the "utterances as well as doubts and even suspicions, as if it were our aim to create another source of tension by constituting an anti-Western and even an anti-white bloc." He emphasised that nothing was farther from the truth, and he proceeded to allay those concerns by reiterating the objectives of the Conference as spelt out in Bogor.[11]

Washington indeed had grave reservations about the Bandung Conference and monitored its development very closely. A week after the Bogor joint communiqué was published, on 7 January 1955, US Secretary of State John Foster Dulles met with his staff to discuss the implications of the impending Conference for the United States and to formulate a US position.[12] Washington was concerned for the following reasons: (a) the communists could introduce anti-colonial resolution(s) that no Asian leaders would dare to oppose and, in the process, "ensnare the relatively inexperienced Asian diplomats into supporting resolutions seemingly in favour of goodness, beauty and truth"; (b) present at the conference would be Zhou Enlai, whose "skilful diplomatic machinations" the Americans had experienced at the Geneva Conference (1954). The Bandung Conference would be an "excellent forum (for Zhou) to broadcast communist ideology to a naïve audience of anti-colonialism," especially when the Conference agenda would be determined only during the Conference itself; (c) the Bandung meeting would put the recent Manila Pact (September 1954) meeting in an unfavourable light, as the latter had had only three Asian participants; and (d) The Bandung meeting had the potential to develop into an effective forum that excluded the United States. The fear was that if the communists succeeded in establishing such groupings in Europe, Asia and Africa, "the communist engulfment of these nations will be comparatively easy." One possible outcome could be the establishment of a very solid anti-Western bloc led by India and China in the United Nations.

Apparently some of the countries that were invited and were closely associated with the United States were seeking "guidance" from Washington. For example, General Carlos Romulo (Philippine ambassador to the United States) had requested papers, ideas and source materials on issues that would arise at Bandung and that he believed only the Department of State was in a position to assist him with.[13] At this point, it was still unclear how many of the invited countries would attend the Bandung Conference. Dulles was of the view that if the Arab bloc decided to attend (and that hinged on the decision of Egypt), many Southeast Asian states, such as Thailand and Japan, would feel obliged to attend. Tokyo was apparently confused, as the Japanese did not know what was to be on the agenda but felt that they needed to attend (if the other Asian countries accepted the invitation) in order to overcome their diplomatic isolation.

The British Foreign Office, too, was greatly interested in this forthcoming Conference. London was very worried about the outcome of the Conference, fearing that it would establish a bloc to outflank and undermine the Southeast Asian Treaty Organisation (SEATO) and the Colombo Plan. There was, therefore, considerable relief when the Soviet Union was excluded from the Conference. The British were, however, far less concerned about China, as Foreign Secretary Anthony Eden had been rather impressed by Zhou Enlai's reasonable attitude at the 1954 Geneva Conference.[14] London's position was that it would be a mistake to either oppose the holding of the Conference or to prevent any country from attending. Instead, they should avoid displaying any signs of anxiety and should encourage "good" or "competent" people/representatives from the friendly countries to attend,[15] a view that coincided with the idea raised at the US Department of State meeting that Washington establish as many contacts with the "friendly" countries as possible to work out courses of action to counter any communist agenda.

Two groups were subsequently established to monitor the evolution of the Bandung Conference and to coordinate efforts in coming out with an agreed US position: the Afro-Asian Working Group led by William Lacy (who would soon assume the position of ambassador to Korea, in March 1955) and the Bangkok Conference Group led by Douglas MacArthur (counsellor with the US Department of State).[16] The 8 February 1955 report stated that two of the 30 invited were communist countries while ten could be counted as pro-Western, so the Conference was likely to avoid contentious issues. As on 8 February, Beijing, Hanoi, Bangkok and Manila had accepted the invitation; Tokyo was likely to accept; and Phnom Penh, Vientiane and Saigon remained undecided. The report further stated that the United States should be concerned about the impact of the Conference on the neutralist and pro-Western countries. Washington should work towards rebutting all communist charges and encouraging endorsement of the "Free World and US achievements and goals." This could be achieved by keeping in close touch through normal diplomatic channels with the governments that were close to the United States. Washington should also counter all issues raised at Bandung by taking public positions on them without directly referring to the Conference.[17]

During 23–25 February 1955, the Manila Pact countries met in Bangkok to establish SEATO. This meeting was seen to be particularly important in the light of the forthcoming Bandung Conference. Dulles emphasised that "it was of first importance that the Bangkok Conference should present a success to the world and thereby demonstrate that free Asian countries and Western countries could deal together with profit and harmony."[18]

It is, therefore, worth highlighting the following points, which have a bearing on the Bandung Conference. The meeting noted that it was particularly important that Ngo Dinh Diem be able to quickly consolidate South Vietnam, as the talks between North and South Vietnam on the 1956 elections scheduled by the Geneva Accords were expected to start in July 1955. The meeting warned that even if South Vietnam managed to hold off the communist challenge, Cambodia and Laos were not necessarily safe. In Cambodia the underground Vietnamese communists, abetted by like-minded Khmers, continued to be a source of instability in the country, although so far Sihanouk had managed to control them. The Pathet Lao activities in Northeast Laos continued to be a serious threat to the government. In Thailand there were 46,000 Vietnamese refugees, many of them inspired by and in constant contact with the Vietnamese communists. This was complicated by Pridi Phanomyong's "Free Thailand" movement. Bangkok was concerned that Pridi might be used by the Chinese communists to launch his movement from the Thai Autonomous Area of Hunan. The meeting judged that the Malayan communists could not achieve their goal as they lacked sufficient external support. But having failed in their military struggle, they had now turned to infiltrating schools, trade unions and other organisations. Last but not least, Indonesia was particularly worrisome and "could be lost (to the communists) without the prior loss of Malaya." Attendees of the Bangkok meeting anticipated that the communists would use the Bandung Conference to attack SEATO but felt comforted that the Asian members of the Manila Pact at Bandung would be there to defend both the objectives and the aspirations of the Manila and Bangkok meetings.[19]

The China Question

We now shift our attention to China, which was the "focus of attention of the international world at that time."[20] China was represented at the Conference by Prime Minister Zhou Enlai. The role of the Chinese Premier has been the most written-about aspect of the Bandung Conference.[21] Roeslan Abdulgani recalled that the address by Zhou received the most attention. Abdulgani reasoned that that was to be expected as it was the first opportunity for most from the outside or Western world to hear firsthand Beijing's views on various world issues from no less than its Prime Minister.[22] It was more than just his speech. Everything that the Chinese Prime Minister did and said at the Conference was followed very closely. We are perhaps all familiar with Richard Wright's report of Zhou's "suave restraint and deliberate avoidance of issues liable to raise contention at the Conference"; of Kahin's report of how Zhou made "a favourable impression on most of the delegates, supporters of the Western bloc as well as members of the uncommitted group," thereby laying "the foundation for a feeling which continued to grow among the Conference's delegations: that he was reasonable, conciliatory, and sincerely anxious to establish the genuineness of China's peaceful inclinations. Likewise the difference in Zhou's two speeches and his apparent sensitivity to both the general tone of the Conference and the particular concern voiced by Cambodia and Thailand impressed many of the delegates."

Of the Southeast Asian countries at the Bandung Conference, Zhou paid particular attention to Thailand, Cambodia, Indonesia and Laos. And those four countries in turn were particularly impressed by Zhou. As for Burma, Zhou had already visited Rangoon and U Nu had also visited Beijing in 1954.

Roeslan Abdulgani had the impression that Prince Wan (the Thai foreign minister, who represented Thailand at the Conference) and Zhou did not get on well because Thailand was a member of SEATO. In her 1994 memoir Sirin Phathanothai, the daughter of Prime Minister Pibul Songgram's closest adviser, throws some light on Sino-Thai relations and the Bandung Conference. She recalls that her father, Sang Phathanothai, had for a long time advocated establishing some form of relationship with Beijing. Pibul Songgram vacillated for fear of antagonising the United States. But at the same time he was fearful of China's power. The crux of the problem was how to balance the need for some long-term understanding with China against the immediate pressing need for US support. The Bandung Conference offered an opportunity that Phathanothai immediately grasped. The Prime Minister was concerned that sending a Thai delegation would anger the Americans. However, Phathanothai felt that not attending the Conference would isolate Thailand from the very neighbours Washington hoped Bangkok would influence. Also, Bangkok did not need to take an active part in the Conference. The Thais could just observe and take note of the proceedings. Pibul was convinced and decided to send Prince Wan (Warnwai), who was himself concerned about Thailand's increasing commitment to the United States and was keen to get to know Zhou Enlai.

At Bandung, Prince Wan was apparently very impressed with Zhou but discreetly maintained a correct and distant attitude in the early part of the Conference. Zhou had invited Prince Wan to a private dinner. The prince was initially hesitant but was persuaded by Nehru (whom he consulted) to accept. The dinner discussion was frank but friendly. Prince Wan brought up Bangkok's concern about China, the overseas Chinese in Thailand, and Beijing's support for Pridi Phanomyong, and he was assured by Zhou that China had no ill intentions. Zhou had expressed surprise at the intensity of anti-Chinese feelings among many of the Asian countries at the Conference and urged the prince to help bridge the gap between their two countries. The private meeting left the prince with the impression that Zhou was "an extraordinarily charming man, and a natural diplomat: astute, patient, unfailingly courteous" and not anything like a communist bandit.

What followed was a top-secret exercise to establish relations with China. In December 1955 a small Thai delegation led by Aree Pirom secretly arrived in Beijing, where they met senior Chinese officials including Mao Zedong and Zhou Enlai. During that meeting, Aree Pirom asked Mao what Thailand should do regarding its relations with the United States and China. Mao said that he personally felt that the most advantageous policy for a small country like Thailand was to remain neutral, although that would not be an easy road for Thailand to take. Both countries signed a secret agreement, and the Chinese Embassy in Rangoon became the point of liaison between Zhou and Phathanothai. The liaison culminated in Phathanothai's sending his two children, Sirin and Warnwai, to China in 1956 as "an offering of goodwill from Thailand's political elite to serve as a 'living bridge' between the two countries."[23]

The Americans were aware that soon after the Bandung Conference some amongst the Thai leadership were making discreet overtures towards Beijing. Philippine General Romulo told Dulles that he was greatly disturbed over Zhou's effect on Prince Wan during the Bandung Conference; he claimed the latter had been completely beguiled by Zhou.[24] The US Embassy was of the view that Thai actions were a manifestation of the "Thai political tradition of attempting, as a small nation, to maintain its independence by keeping in line with apparent trends in the international pattern of power."[25] Rockwood H. Foster (acting officer in charge of Thai and Malayan Affairs) wrote in a letter (dated 22 June 1955) to the American ambassador to Thailand:

> The Thai are scared of the Chinese and dislike them thoroughly, but as long
> as Burma, Laos, Cambodia, and Vietnam give Thailand as little protection
> as they do now, the Thai, having flyspecked the Manila Pact commitments,

realize that diplomatic realities must prevail over abstract principles. I am afraid the Thai have decided that we cannot now be entirely trusted to defend them as we were at the time of Korea.[26]

The US assessment was that in the event of a direct communist attack on Laos, Cambodia or South Vietnam, Bangkok would participate in any military countermeasures only if assured of the prompt commitment of US forces to the region. If not, the Thai would almost certainly seek an accommodation with the communist bloc. If communist control of the mainland Southeast Asian countries were achieved through subversion, then Thailand would move towards a neutralist position.[27]

The Thai coup d'état masterminded by Sarit Thanarat in September 1957, when Pibul Songgram was forced into exile, provided the opportunity for the United States to persuade the new Thai leadership to reverse Thailand's policy towards China in 1958. Despite having doubts regarding US commitment to fight communism in Southeast Asia, Sarit concluded that aligning with the United States was in the best interest of Thailand.[28] Aree Pirom (and his assistant Karuna Kusarasai), who made the secret trip to Beijing at the end of 1955, were imprisoned for many years. Sang Phathanothai, too, was imprisoned. In Zhou's analysis, Pibul was overthrown because Washington had learnt of the scope and character of Bangkok's ties with Beijing and wanted a more pro-United States government.[29]

In Bandung Zhou also impressed Cambodia's Prince Sihanouk, and they remained on personal and friendly terms until Zhou's death in January 1976. Kahin, who had access to the unpublished verbatim record of the Conference, noted the striking amount of time and effort Zhou devoted to Sihanouk relative to leaders of the other small countries.[30] Zhou hosted a special luncheon solely for Sihanouk. According to Sihanouk, Zhou personally assured him that "China would always faithfully adhere to the Five Principles (of coexistence) in its relations with Cambodia and have a friendly feeling toward my country."[31] There was, however, one slight "hiccup," which concerned the subject of a military mission for Cambodia. In Bandung, Nehru, U Nu, Sihanouk and Zhou had apparently discussed the issue of an Indian training mission for Cambodia. The view was that an Indian training mission would be appropriate for Cambodia's neutrality rather than the proposed US Military Assistance and Advisory Group (MAAG), which had been under discussion since the 1954 Geneva Conference. Sihanouk apparently agreed, or at least did not object. However, on returning from Cambodia after Bandung, Sihanouk endorsed the MAAG agreement, which surprised Nehru and U Nu as well as Zhou, who had apparently put a lot of pressure either bluntly or subtly on Nehru to oppose the MAAG agreement or any form of US assistance to Cambodia. But both the United States and Sihanouk believed that there was no theoretical conflict between the MAAG agreement and Indian assistance for Cambodia.[32]

The Bandung Conference also paved the way for closer Sino-Indonesian relations, which lasted until 1965, when Jakarta abandoned its leftist foreign policy. In contrast, US-Indonesian relations became increasingly strained until the 1965 coup. At Bandung on 22 April 1955, both sides signed a treaty whereby China jettisoned its dual citizenship policy. Chinese in Indonesia would have to choose either Indonesian or Chinese citizenship. Soon after the Bandung Conference Zhou visited Jakarta, and the two Prime Ministers issued a joint statement on 28 April emphasising the new relationship between Jakarta and Beijing based on the Five Principles of Peaceful Coexistence. Sukarno visited the Soviet Union and China in August and October 1956 respectively. The visits enhanced Jakarta's relations with the two communist giants (whereas Sukarno's visit to the United States in May–June 1956 did not help improve relations with the United States at all).[33] By August 1957, while the anti-communist forces remained strong in the outer Indonesian islands, the communists were apparently gaining strength in Java. The Indonesian military, which was supposedly the stalwart against communism, was also reported to be not as cohesive as it had been a year ago. The non-communist and anti-communist groups were unable to cooperate against the communist and pro-communist forces. The PKI—the Communist Party of Indonesia—was seen as the best-organised group in Indonesia, with the best opportunity to take control of Java.[34] Former Indonesian Vice-President Mohammad Hatta, too, felt that the situation would turn critical if the non-communist parties failed to get their act together.[35] The political situation by the end of the year can best be described as having been in a fluid state. This state of affairs continued until the communists were completely decimated in late 1965.

Western Rejoinders

Despite the initial apprehensions about the Bandung Conference, it is notable that US Secretary of State John Foster Dulles, in his post-Conference analysis, rightly or wrongly, judged that the Conference had not caused as much damage to the interests of the United States and the Free World as had been anticipated. The secretary of state believed that it was the group of friendly countries rather than Zhou that had dominated the Conference, and that there was so much pressure put on the Chinese that Beijing was now obliged to refrain from acts of violence. After the Conference, both Nehru and Indian Foreign Minister

Krishna Menon believed that the Bandung Conference had given the Chinese a more realistic view of their international environment and the smaller states of Asia less fear of Chinese expansionism.[36]

Dulles was also rather comfortable with the Final Communiqué, with the exception of the Palestine issue. He listed about eight points in the communiqué that were supposedly consistent with US foreign policy. In his words, it was "a document which we ourselves could subscribe to."[37] It is perhaps worth noting that this view was not shared by other, albeit unofficial, assessments of the impact of the Conference on the United States. One view was that while one significant outcome of the Conference was the "damnation of communism as a new form of colonialism," in the same breath there was a strong indictment of the arrogant patronage of the United States.[38] The British came to more or less the same conclusion. The communiqué was described as "gratifyingly moderate in tone" and "neither particularly helpful to us nor as positively harmful as it might have been." The position of the Foreign Office was, "we should not exaggerate the results of the Conference or, on present evidence, assume that they will necessarily be lasting in their effects." London, not surprisingly, was particularly concerned with the implications of the Conference on the former colonial powers but concluded, "the Conference is likely to make the task of the Colonial Powers in the United Nations more difficult than in the past, though not disastrously so." In sum, the consensus was that Britain came out remarkably well from the Conference.[39]

The anti-communist countries at Bandung warned of the "hidden dangers" of the Five Principles of Peaceful Coexistence. In their view, it was communist propaganda meant to lull the Free World into a false sense of security; and they believed that the communist countries would not sincerely carry out those principles.[40] How valid was the anti-communist view? How correct was Dulles's assessment? To answer this question, we will need to enter into the world of the Asian communist camp during this period to understand their motivations and compare their words and deeds.

The Indochina Issue

Indochina is perhaps the appropriate point of entry. It was the frontline of the Cold War in Asia. It is worth noting that whereas the situation in Indochina was discussed at the Colombo Meeting (1954), the subject was avoided in Bandung to preserve the unity of the Conference. Nehru did consider bringing the Indochinese states together in a meeting with Zhou, but Saigon refused.[41] North Vietnamese Prime Minister Pham Van Dong failed to persuade the other participants to recognise the Democratic Republic of Vietnam. Pham Van Dong and Laotian Prime Minister Katay Don Sasorith signed an agreement in the presence of Nehru and Zhou whereby the Vietnamese communists committed to respecting the territorial sovereignty and integrity of Laos.

Despite their differences with the Chinese in the summer of 1954,[42] after the Geneva Conference had ended, the Vietnamese communists continued to consult Beijing as to which strategy to adopt to ensure the unification of Vietnam.[43] Like the Vietnamese communists, the Chinese thought that it would be impossible to reunite the country by elections in 1956 as stipulated in the Geneva Accords. In their view, it was imperative that the Vietnamese communists prepare for a protracted struggle. They recommended their own experience that had been successful against the Guomindang, which was to lie low for a long time, muster strength, keep in touch with the people and wait for an opportunity.[44] According to Hoang Van Hoan, the Hanoi leadership decided to accept the Chinese recommendation[45] because, based on its own assessment, it too did not see itself as strong enough to step up the military struggle in the South at this point. Second, even if it had wanted to back the plan, it would still need to discuss the matter with China and the Soviet Union. Both Beijing and Moscow had made clear that they were not in favour of any moves that could lead to a new military confrontation. Hanoi, in mid-March 1956, thus rejected the 14-point plan of action that had been drawn up by Le Duan and adopted by the Nam Bo Committee.[46] The plan had recommended that military action be used in support of other activities in the South, that support bases and more battalions be created, and that the military organisations in the inter-zones be consolidated. Cambodia was considered to be strategically important, and it was proposed that budgetary assistance should therefore be increased and senior cadres should be seconded to Cambodia. The plan also included the creation of a support base to aid activities in Cambodia and the consolidation of the leading organisations there. Instead, the Hanoi leadership advised Le Duan and the Southern cadres to exploit the agrarian issues in the South until a longer-range strategy could be worked out,[47] thus shifting the emphasis away from a military struggle to an economic one.[48]

Both North Vietnam and China had independently, and for their own specific reasons, concluded that they needed a period of peaceful coexistence. During this period and for the rest of 1957, the Chinese communists were absorbed in their domestic and economic affairs and were content to leave their foreign policy as it was. The policy of peaceful coexistence would allow them to focus on straightening the mess that they had inadvertently created at home (Mao's "Hundred Flowers" policy) as well as to concentrate on economic development.

Sometime in July 1957, Mao is said to have told the Vietnamese communists that reunification might take a long time and the immediate concern was to defend the existing frontier—the 17th parallel.[49] The North Vietnamese did not disagree. They, too, were preoccupied with domestic problems.

Although at the Bandung Conference Nehru and Zhou were able to persuade the North Vietnamese to respect the sovereignty of Laos, events subsequently developed within Laos that the North Vietnamese could not ignore. They had to do with the political survival of the Pathet Lao,[50] which in turn impacted on Hanoi's reunification goal by the July 1956 deadline. After the 1954 Geneva Conference, the Pathet Lao were temporarily regrouped in the two provinces of Sam Neua and Phong Saly. The Geneva Accords had envisioned an internal Laotian political settlement in the form of a general election in 1955. But the Royal Laotian Government (RLG) and the Pathet Lao were unable to reach any understanding, and on 25 December 1955 the incumbent government proceeded with a general election without the participation of the Pathet Lao.

Soon after the unilateral election (6–14 January 1956), the Pathet Lao held a conference at Sam Neua and established the Neo Lao Hak Xat (NLHX, or the Lao Patriotic Front). A *Nhan Dan* article of 16 January described the formation of the NLHX as an important stage in the history of the Laotian people's struggle for national independence.[51] Given the close links between the Pathet Lao and the Vietnamese communists, and judging from the leading personalities in the NLHX, there is no doubt that the new front had the full blessings of the Vietnamese communists. On 15 January the Chinese also greeted the formation of the new front with enthusiasm and described it as a "great event in the political life of the Laotian people" that "conformed to the aspirations of the Laotian people and reflected the growing democratic forces in Laos." The Chinese further urged the RLG to resume its negotiations with the Pathet Lao fighting units so as to reach a political solution in accordance with the Geneva Accords.[52] The Vietnamese communists, in fact, intimated to the Indians that they had no wish to upset the Geneva Accords on Laos.[53] Pham Van Dong told the Indian Charge d'Affaires in Hanoi that he was willing to exercise his "good offices" to help settle the Pathet Lao problem, and he also renewed his invitation to Katay Don Sasorith (who was the pro-Western Laotian Prime Minister from October 1954 until the recent election) to visit Hanoi.[54]

The fact that the Pathet Lao did not resort to open fighting during and after the December elections, the subsequent formation of the NLHX, as well as the conciliatory attitude of the North Vietnamese showed that the Hanoi leadership had an overall strategy in Indochina that had Chinese approval. Sam Neua and Phong Saly were completely taken over by the RLG by 19 January

1958. The occupation of the two provinces by the Royal Laotian Army, which began on 24 December 1957, proceeded speedily and smoothly without incident, which came as a surprise to many foreign observers.[55] Clearly the Pathet Lao had been instructed to be cooperative and not to create trouble.

Demise of a Conference

As early as 1956, India, Ceylon, Burma and Indonesia all seemed cool to the idea of another Asian-African conference, and it did not appear it would be held in mid-1956 as anticipated, which certainly allayed the concerns of some Western powers who were worried that the Conference would become an annual event.[56] As early as August 1957, Ngo Dinh Diem observed that "neutralism" had lost much of its appeal in Asia since the Bandung Conference.[57] The Bandung commitment began to noticeably unravel towards the end of 1958, because goodwill and cooperation amongst the countries could no longer be sustained and were overtaken by nationalist and ideological considerations. In the early 1950s the Soviet Union perceived the Chinese as ideological partners. But in 1958 the Chinese, having achieved a degree of economic and political stability, were gradually exhibiting their independence *vis-à-vis* the Soviet Union. China began to pursue its own interests in the region. According to Aleksandr Kaznacheev, a new period of Soviet policy began to emerge in 1958–59, when the Soviet Union gradually abandoned the earlier agreement on the division of interests. He cited many examples from his experiences while working in the Russian Embassy in Burma to support his claim. The Russians were, however, not very successful in Burma. Kaznacheev also referred to the Soviet Union's generous military assistance in terms of weaponry to Indonesia. As for the Vietnamese communists, the growing Sino-Soviet rivalry could not have escaped their notice; but they were intent on not being drawn into the growing Sino-Soviet discord. Meanwhile, they were able to benefit from the competition between China and the Soviet Union, who were both ready to help their protégé advance towards socialism.[58]

By mid-1958, Diem's renewed efforts to exterminate the communists, which culminated in the passing of Law 10/59 (6 May 1959), were fatally damaging the communist revolutionary struggle in South Vietnam. According to a Vietnamese communist source, at the end of 1958 and in early 1959, Diem's policy of terror in the South had reached its height. This period has been described as the "blackest, most hopeless years" for the people in South Vietnam. Hanoi understood that it could no longer continue to advocate restraint without losing the control and allegiance of the Southern communists as well as the reunification struggle to Diem, who had the support of the United States. According to

Hoang Van Hoan's account, in 1958 it was suggested inside the Lao Dong Party that armed struggle be launched against Ngo Dinh Diem and this proposal was put forward to the Chinese Communist Party Central Committee. But the Chinese were of the view that the time was not yet ripe and suggested that Hanoi reconsider whether it was opportune then to expose its armed forces in South Vietnam.[59]

In November 1958 the Lao Dong Party held its 14th plenary session. It was reported on 8 December that the meeting had discussed the report by Le Duan on the world situation; the report on the three-year plan (1958–60) for economic transformation and cultural development by Nguyen Duy Trinh; and Truong Chinh's report on land reform. The 14th plenary session decided, "the immediate task is to step up the socialist transformation of the individual economy of the peasants and craftsmen and that of the privately run capitalist economy, and at the same time to strive to develop the state-run economy which is the leading force of the whole national economy."[60] Although it was not reported, it is highly unlikely that there was no discussion on the revolutionary situation in South Vietnam. After the 14th plenary session, Le Duan was believed to have left for the South on an extended inspection tour to study the situation there.[61] Meanwhile, the Southern revolutionaries were told that political struggle remained the basis of the revolution in the South. This is confirmed in a document (captured in July 1959) titled "Situation and Tasks for 1959." This document, issued by the Nam Bo Regional Committee, directed that political struggle should remain the basis of the revolution in the South, despite the committee's acknowledgement that the Diemist forces were getting stronger *vis-à-vis* the Southern revolutionaries.[62] But very soon after, the decision to renew the military struggle in the South was reluctantly taken at the landmark 15th plenary session of the Lao Dong Party held in January 1959. The decision was, however, not publicised until a week after the promulgation of Law 10/59 in May. Soon after the communiqué was issued, work on the Ho Chi Minh Trail (much of which was in Laotian territory) began.

Unlike the North Vietnamese, the Chinese were much more ready to accommodate a neutral Laos (had the Americans and North Vietnamese allowed it). However, the internal situation in Laos bedevilled both the Vietnamese and Chinese communists, and the decision of the Vietnamese communists to resume armed struggle immediately spelt the end of any hope for the neutralisation of Laos.

Over in Cambodia, Sihanouk did not think that Beijing had formulated a forward policy with regard to Indochina. Therefore, he believed that any Chinese subversive threat, in so far as Cambodia was concerned, was a very distant one. However, he did feel a sense of grave anxiety about the activities of the Vietnamese communists. In 1958 Sihanouk perceived the Thais and the South Vietnamese rather than the communists as the imminent threat, because of Cambodia's unresolved territorial/border disputes with both countries. On 29 and 30 May the Cambodian government protested to the South Vietnamese government regarding the intrusion of South Vietnamese soldiers into its territory, near Kas Kong District of Peam Chor in PreyVeng. More protests followed on 15 and 19 June. It was reported that on 15 June South Vietnamese soldiers had crossed into Cambodian territory, occupied a number of villages and clashed with the Cambodian patrols. On 19 June the South Vietnamese were said to have moved a frontier post on Route National 19 by three kilometres and subsequently by four kilometres. The South Vietnamese government denied that any of the incidents had taken place. On 27 June a joint meeting of the Cambodian National Assembly and the Royal Council adopted a declaration appealing to foreign countries to send observers to Cambodia to establish the truth of what it described as a South Vietnamese invasion of Cambodia. The King of Cambodia and Sihanouk also demanded that the United States order South Vietnam to withdraw its army from Cambodian territory immediately and unconditionally. The Cambodians revealed that South Vietnamese regular troops had penetrated seven miles into Stung Treng Province and that since the beginning of 1957, the South Vietnamese had intruded into Cambodian territory on 29 occasions and moved the border-marking post deep into that territory. On 30 June Chinese Vice-Premier and Foreign Minister Chen Yi condemned US-South Vietnam encroachment on Cambodian territory and expressed Chinese support for Cambodia. One Chinese Foreign Ministry source believed that Chen Yi's expression of support helped Sihanouk make up his mind to establish diplomatic relations with Beijing. The Stung Treng incident forced Sihanouk to recognise China in the hope of using Chinese support as leverage against the South Vietnamese, and possibly the Thais as well. On 18 July Sihanouk sent a letter to Zhou Enlai proposing that Cambodia and China establish diplomatic relations. The next day Zhou sent Sihanouk a positive reply and added that China would do its utmost to help Cambodia defend its independence. On 23 July (just one day after the resignation of Souvanna Phouma), it was made known that China and Cambodia had decided to exchange ambassadors and that embassies would be set up in Beijing and Phnom Penh. On 27 July a statement was issued by the Royal Council that declared its support for the government's decision to establish diplomatic relations with China. The statement also revealed that "China with its 600 million people and efficient government was giving Cambodia disinterested aid."

Soon after the announcement of the establishment of diplomatic relations, Sihanouk made his second visit to China, where he met Mao Zedong on 16 August in Zhongnanhai and again on 20 August in Beidaiha. In his conversations with Mao, Sihanouk observed that unlike his more flexible and moderate Prime Minister, Mao showed a "certain distrust for non-communist regimes" and seemed unable to compromise as easily. The Chinese also offered to provide Sihanouk with whatever military armaments and equipment he needed. On 24 August a joint statement was signed that again emphasised both countries' adherence to the policy of Cambodian neutrality.[63] But this commitment was not sustained either.

Spirit Alive

This essay has been an attempt to evaluate the two main views mentioned at the beginning of this chapter regarding the significance of the Bandung Conference, on the basis of declassified archival documents and memoirs. It first highlighted the hopes, concerns and interactions of the Southeast Asian participants of the conference as well as China, Britain and the United States. Although neither London nor Washington was invited to the Conference, both were key players in the international politics of Southeast Asia and they monitored the Conference closely. The essay then attempted to reconstruct the major political developments in Southeast Asia during the immediate post-Bandung years, specifically those events that involved and affected the countries that had participated in the Bandung Conference. The conclusion this author arrived at is that the success of the Bandung Conference was more apparent than real. It has been said that all myths are potentially of value to us and what is most important is to agree on what we can find in them and what we can make of them. As the former Malaysian Deputy Prime Minister Anwar Ibrahim recalled in a recent speech at Cape Town University (South Africa), he grew up in the shade of the Bandung Conference and still regarded that Afro-Asian gathering as a great moment of history. Even though he became critical of the subsequent attitude and performance of the Bandung generation leaders, the moment never ceased to inspire him.[64] Indeed, the Bandung Spirit as contained in the Bandung communiqué—which, as we recall, even Dulles described as "a document which we ourselves could subscribe to"[65]—remains very much alive today.

Notes

[1]   George McTurnan Kahin, *The Asian-African Conference, Bandung, Indonesia, April 1955* (Ithaca: Cornell University Press, 1956), pp. 1, 36–8.

2   Michael Leifer, *Dilemmas of Statehood in Southeast Asia* (Vancouver: University of British Columbia Press, 1972), pp. 136–7.

3   See, for example, Richard Wright, *The Colour Curtain: A Report on the Bandung Conference* (Cleveland and New York: World, 1956); Kahin, *The Asian-African Conference*; G.H. Jansen, *Afro-Asia and Non-Alignment* (London: Faber and Faber, 1966); Roeslan Abdulgani, *The Bandung Connection: The Asia-Africa Conference in Bandung in 1955* (Jakarta: Gunung Agung, 1981).

4   Milton Osborne, *Exploring Southeast Asia* (Sydney: Allen & Unwin, 2002), p. 156. See also Osborne, *Southeast Asia: An Introductory History* (Sydney: Allen & Unwin, 1995).

5   See Marc Frey, Ronald W. Pruessen and Tan Tai Yong (eds.), *The Transformation of Southeast Asia: International Perspectives on Decolonisation* (Armonk: M.E. Sharpe, 2003); Leifer, *Dilemmas of Statehood in Southeast Asia*.

6   See Akira Iriye, *The Cold War in Asia: A Historical Introduction* (New Jersey: Prentice Hall, 1974).

7   Frey, Pruessen and Tan (eds.), *The Transformation of Southeast Asia*, pp. viii, ix, 268–9.

8   Ministry of Foreign Affairs, Republic of Indonesia, *Asia Africa Speaks from Bandung* (Jakarta: Ministry of Foreign Affairs, 1955), pp. 11–3; address by Ali Sastroamidjojo, President of the Conference.

9   Abdulgani, *The Bandung Connection*, chap. 5.

10 Ibid., p. 46.

11 Ministry of Foreign Affairs, Republic of Indonesia, *Asia Africa Speaks from Bandung*; address by Ali Sastroamidjojo.

12 Document 1: Minutes of a Meeting, Secretary's Office, Department of State, Washington, 7 January 1955, *Foreign Relations of the United States (FRUS)* XXI, East Asian Security; Cambodia; Laos (Washington, DC: United States Government Printing Office, 1990). All subsequent references are from this volume unless otherwise stated.

13 Document 13: Memorandum for the Record by the Counsellor of the Department of State (MacArthur), Washington, 10 February 1955.

14 Author's correspondence with July Stowe, who was with the British Foreign Office in the 1950s.

15 Document 2: Memorandum of a Conversation, Department of State, Washington, 10 January 1955.

16 The Manila Pact countries were scheduled to meet in Bangkok on 23–25 February 1955 to form SEATO.

17 Document 11: Memorandum from the Acting Chief of the Reports and Operations Staff (Gilman) to the Secretary of State, Washington, 8 February 1955.

18 Document 12: Editorial note.

19 Document 19: Telegram from the Delegation at the SEATO Council Meeting to the Department of State, Bangkok, 23 February 1955; Document 20: Telegram

from the Secretary of State to the Department of State, Bangkok, 24 February 1955. See also Document 14: Telegram from the Embassy in the United Kingdom to the Department of State, London, 11 February 1955.

[20] Abdulgani, *The Bandung Connection*, p. 32.

[21] See footnote 1 and also Dick Wilson, *The Story of Chou En Lai, 1898–1976* (London: Hutchinson, 1984); Ronald C. Keith, *The Diplomacy of Zhou Enlai* (New York: St. Martin's Press, 1989); Han Suyin, *Eldest Son: Zhou Enlai and the Making of Modern China, 1898–1976* (London: Jonathan Cape, 1994).

[22] Han, *Eldest Son*, p. 103.

[23] See Sirin Phathanothai, *The Dragon's Pearl* (New York: Simon & Schuster, 1994), and Daniel Fineman, *A Special Relationship: The United States and Military Government in Thailand, 1947–1958* (Honolulu: University of Hawai'i Press, 1997); Document 472: Memorandum of a Conversation, Department of State, Washington, 3 May 1955, in *FRUS*, 1955–1957, XXII, Southeast Asia (Washington, DC: United States Government Printing Office, 1989).

[24] Memorandum of a Conversation, Department of State, Washington, 24 May 1955, in *FRUS*, 1955–1957, XXI, East Asian Security; Cambodia; Laos, pp. 103–5.

[25] Dispatch from the Embassy in Thailand to the Department of State, Bangkok, 23 May 1956, in *FRUS*, 1955–1957, XXII, Southeast Asia, pp. 875–81.

[26] Letter from the Acting Officer in Charge of Thai and Malayan Affairs (Foster) to the Ambassador in Thailand (Peurifoy), Washington, 22 June 1955, in *FRUS*, 1955–1957, XXII, pp. 825–7.

[27] National Intelligence Estimate 62–57 (Probable Developments in Thailand), Washington, 18 June 1957, in *FRUS*, 1955–1957, XXII, Southeast Asia, pp. 925–6.

[28] Fineman, *A Special Relationship*, chap. 10.

[29] Sirin Phathanothai, *The Dragon's Pearl*, pp. 139–40.

[30] George McTurnan Kahin, *Southeast Asia: A Testament* (London: RoutledgeCurzon, 2003), p. 260.

[31] Quoted in Kahin, *The Asian-African Conference*, p. 15.

[32] Document 211: Letter from the Director of the Office of Philippine and Southeast Asian Affairs (Young) to the Ambassador in Cambodia (McClintock), Washington, 5 July 1955, in *FRUS*, XXI, East Asian Security; Cambodia; Laos.

[33] For details, see Andrew Roadnight, *United States Policy towards Indonesia in the Truman and Eisenhower Years* (Houndmills: Palgrave Macmillan, 2002), chap. 6.

[34] Message from the Department of State to the Ambassador in Indonesia (Allison), Washington, 8 August 1957, in *FRUS*, 1955–1957, XXII, Southeast Asia, pp. 406–7; National Intelligence Estimate (NIE 65-57), Washington, 27 August 1957, in *FRUS*, 1955–1957, XXII, Southeast Asia, pp. 429–31.

[35] Telegram from the Embassy in Indonesia to the Department of State, Djakarta, 30 August 1957, in *FRUS*, 1955–1957, XXII, Southeast Asia, pp. 432–4.

[36] George McTurnan Kahin, *Southeast Asia: A Testament* (London: RoutledgeCurzon, 2003), p. 146.

37   Document 48: Minutes of a Cabinet Meeting, White House, Washington, 29 April 1955.

38   Andrew Roadnight, *United States Policy towards Indonesia in the Truman and Eisenhower Years* (Houndmills: Palgrave Macmillan, 2002), p. 128.

39   *CO 936/350, IRD* 168/164/03, Effects of the Afro-Asian Conference on the United Nations, 4 May 1955, 24 May 1955, 26 May 1955, 27 May 1955, 7 June 1955.

40   For details, see Roeslan Abdulgani, *The Bandung Connection*, chaps. 14 and 15.

41   G.H. Jansen, *Afro-Asia and Non-Alignment*, p. 219; Circular Document No. B.43/55 Secretary of State for External Affairs to Head of Posts Abroad, Ottawa, 27 July 1955, in *Documents on Canadian External Relations (DCER)*, vol. #21-780, S=DEA/12173-40, chap. VII, Far East, Part 7: Bandung Conference of Non-Aligned Nations.

42   See *Socialist Republic of Vietnam Foreign Ministry White Book on Relations with China, Hanoi Home Service*, 6 and 11 October 1979, *SWB/FE/*6238 and 6242. For the replies of the Chinese government and Hoang Van Hoan, see *Beijing Review*, 23 November 1979, 30 November 1979, 7 December 1979.

43   Hoang Van Hoan, *A Drop in the Ocean: Hoang Van Hoan's Revolutionary Reminiscences* (Beijing: Foreign Languages Press, 1988), p. 324.

44   Ibid.; Guo Ming (ed.), *Zhongyue Guanxi Yanbian Shishi Nian* (Guangxi People's Publisher, 1992), p. 65.

45   See Hoang Van Hoan, *A Drop in the Ocean* (Beijing: Foreign Languages Press, 1988), p. 324.

46   United States Department of State "Working Paper on North Vietnam's Role in the South" (27 May 1968), Appendices, Item 19 (Translation of a document found on the person of a political officer with communist forces in Zone 9 of the Western Interzone on 27 November 1956), Item 31 (An intelligence report from an agent of the GVN who had contact with Vietnamese Communist Party members in Saigon area in 1956) and Item 204 (Document purportedly issued probably in late-spring 1956 by Lao Dong Party Central Committee for guidance of senior cadres in GVN zone).

47   See United States Department of State "Working Paper on North Vietnam's Role in the South" (27 May 1968), Appendices, Items 19, 31 and 204.

48   United States Department of State "Working Paper on North Vietnam's Role in the South" (27 May 1968), Appendices, Item 31.

49   *Socialist Republic of Vietnam Foreign Ministry White Book on Relations with China, Hanoi Home Service*, 4–6 October 1979, *SWB/FE/*6238/A3/11.

50   For details of the relationship between the Vietnamese communists and the Pathet Lao, see Paul F. Langer and Joseph J. Zasloff, *North Vietnam and the Pathet Lao: Partners in the Struggle for Laos* (Cambridge: Harvard University Press, 1970); Geoffrey Charles Gunn, *Road through the Mountains: The Origins of Nationalism and Communism in Laos, 1930–1954* (Ph.D. thesis, Monash University, 1985).

[51]   *VNA*, 16 January 1956, *SWB/FE/527*, p. 39.

[52]   *NCNA*, 15 January 1956, *SWB/FE/527*, p. 5.

[53]   *FO 371/123399*, DF 1017/52, 14 February 1956, from UK High Commission in India to Foreign Office.

[54]   *CUSSDCF.* 751 J. 00/3-156, 1107, 1 March 1956, from Vientiane to State Department (Secret).

[55]   *FO 371/135790*, DF 1015/9, 30 January 1958, from Vientiane to Foreign Office.

[56]   *FO 371/116980-1*, D 2231/203, British Embassy, The Hague, 5 April 1955; Memorandum from the Director of the Office of Philippine and Southeast Asian Affairs (Young) to the Assistant Secretary of State for Far Eastern Affairs (Robertson), Washington, 3 January 1956, in *FRUS* XXII, Southeast Asia 1955–1957.

[57]   Document 163: Despatch from the Embassy in Vietnam to the Department of State, Saigon, 12 August 1957, in *FRUS* XXI, East Asian Security; Cambodia; Laos.

[58]   See Aleksandr Kaznacheev, *Inside a Soviet Embassy: Experience of a Russian Diplomat in Burma* (Philadelphia: Lippincott, 1962).

[59]   Hoang Van Hoan, "Distortion of Facts about the Militant Friendship between Vietnam and China is Impermissible," *Beijing Review* 49, 7 December 1979: 15.

[60]   *An Outline History of the Vietnam Workers' Party (1930–1975)* (Hanoi: Foreign Languages Publishing House, 2nd Edition, 1978), p. 81; *VNA*, 8 December 1958, *SWB/FE/827*, pp. 53–4.

[61]   George Carver, "The Faceless VietCong," *Foreign Affairs* 44, no. 3 (April 1966); United States Department of State "Working Paper on North Vietnam's Role in the South" (27 May 1968), Appendices, Item 36: Interrogation of a Vietcong infiltrator captured on 4 April 1964; Janos Radvanyi, *Delusion and Reality: Gambits, Hoaxes and Diplomatic One-Upmanship in Vietnam* (Indiana: Gateway Editions, 1978), p. 23; Carlyle Thayer's interview with Phan The Ngoc from My Tho province, who was Le Duan's escort officer during part of his trip in late 1958. See Carlyle Thayer, *War by Other Means: National Liberation and Revolution in Vietnam 1954–1960* (Sydney: Allen and Unwin, 1989), p. 222, footnote 85.

[62]   Race Document Number 1025: Tinh Hinh Va Nhiem Vu 59 (no date).

[63]   *Zhou Enlai Waijiao Huodong Da Shiji* (Beijing: Shijie Zhishi Chubanshe, 1993), pp. 240–1; *CUSSDCF:* 751 H. 00(W)/9-2458, 386, 24 September 1958, from Phnom Penh to Department of State; *SWB/FE/795*, pp. 19–22; *SWB/FE/797*, pp. 9–18; for Sihanouk's account of the events leading to as well as his visit to China, see Norodom Sihanouk and Wilfred Burchett, *My War with the CIA: Cambodia's Fight for Survival* (Harmondworth: Penguin, 1973), pp. 102–3; Sihanouk's speech in Paris on 19 November 1960 to an audience of Cambodians living in France, *SWB/FE/523/B/3*; *FO 371/152692*, DU 1015/108, 25 August 1960, from Commonwealth Relation Office (CRO) to Foreign Office: Malcolm MacDonald's Talk with Sihanouk (Secret).

64   Anwar Ibrahim's speech at Cape Town University, 1 December 2004. Anwar was eight years old in 1955.
65   Document 48: Minutes of a Cabinet Meeting, White House, Washington, 29 April 1955.

CHAPTER 3

Bandung and State Formation in Post-colonial Asia

Itty Abraham

The Bandung Conference—a week-long meeting of the heads of 29 newly independent Asian and African governments held in Indonesia in April 1955—remains a vibrant symbol of the potency of anti-colonial and anti-racial sentiment and the popular pride associated with national sovereignty even today, half a century on. Although Bandung is remembered for a variety of reasons, most notably its place in the creation of the Non-Aligned Movement and the international voice it gave to the long-marginalised peoples of former European colonies in Asia and Africa, what actually happened at the Afro-Asian conference is in many respects quite removed from those memories. Bandung as a remembered event particularly seems to invoke symbolic and ideological effects. What this chapter seeks to resurrect are the immediate and important political outcomes of the Conference, whose legacies are not all positive, and which produced and reinforced political cleavages important to this day.

This chapter argues that it is not possible to understand what happened at Bandung without also discussing an earlier, lesser known but very significant event, the Asian Relations Conference, held in New Delhi in 1947.[1] Only by seeing Bandung in relation to the Asian Relations Conference does it become possible to trace discursive continuities in the political dilemmas seen to be facing newly independent post-colonial states, framed under the master trope of the "minorities problem." Minorities, as the term is used here, are not simply numerically smaller demographic or communal entities; rather, they signify the domestic presence of ethnic and religious communities *seen as having non-local origins*. In other words, Bandung highlights the political formation of the permanent minority as a necessary by-product of state formation in post-colonial Asia.

Struggles for independence from colonial rule were never restricted to "national" territories. Indeed, it is among the contradictory defining features of anti-colonial struggles that the fight for national political independence took place on a global scale even as the presumed objects of liberation—people and territory—were indeterminately identified. In the case of the world's two largest colonial empires, India and Indonesia, neither the boundaries of the national space being claimed nor those who would be included in these "new" nations was wholly known in advance; contrary to what we might expect, such prior definitions were not central to the struggle for freedom.[2] A similar argument can be made for China, while acknowledging some important differences since it was never completely colonised.[3] In other words, the three largest Asian countries entered and made a claim to sovereign national independence with indeterminate and fuzzy cartographic limits and popular boundaries.

The global scale and extent of Indians living outside "India" were shaped by colonial policies of indenture and migration—largely, but not entirely, within the British Empire—and by long-distance commerce.[4] At the time of Indian independence, Indians could be found across the world.[5] The largest populations were to be found in plantation enclaves in the Caribbean, South America, South Africa, the Indian Ocean island of Mauritius, Ceylon (now Sri Lanka), Southeast Asia and the Pacific Islands. Smaller but significant pockets of Indians were all over Burma, East Africa and the Persian Gulf. Still other communities could be found in the United States, Canada, Australia, as well as the United Kingdom. The same is true of the overseas Chinese, or *huaqiao*, who in successive waves of migration and indenture over two centuries had taken up residence in Thailand, the Malayan Peninsula, the western United States, and the islands of the Indonesian archipelago, the Caribbean and Hawai'i, as well as establishing ethnic enclaves in various European countries.[6] These well-known facts being duly noted, while for the residents of these offshore locations it was natural to identify these recent arrivals as "Indians" and "Chinese" (or some more colourful and derogatory appellation), these labels may not have been the obvious or preferred means of self-identification. In other words, while the presence of "Indians" and "Chinese" may have been self-evident to others, these women, children, laborers, traders, farmers, small business owners, bankers and soldiers were more often than not Biharis, Tamils, Gujaratis, Punjabis, Oriyas and Bengalis, and not necessarily "Indians." Likewise, Chinese migrants, especially those from the southwest, might have spoken Hakka, Yue (Cantonese), Min (Fujian), Xiang (Hunan), Gan (Jiangxi) or Wu (Shanghai) as well as, sometimes, Mandarin.[7] It is not unreasonable to appreciate that relations among "national" compatriots from India and China might have been as distinct and distant as their interaction with their new neighbours in Africa, the United States and the Middle East.

Following this line of argument, it is perhaps more significant than is usually realised that the leading light of the anti-colonial movement in India, Mohandas Gandhi, was after all a diasporic Indian, an NRI (non-resident Indian) in present-day parlance. Gandhi's time in South Africa may well have helped him forge a new identity—or, better, solidarity—as an "Indian," as opposed to being a Gujarati-speaker from a small coastal princely state, and certainly gave him the experience of seeing British colonial rule in another setting, thereby opening the possibility of acquiring the necessary critical distance to analyse the forms and practices of British imperialism in India.[8]

But even beyond Gandhi and his specific role in mobilising and leading an anti-colonial movement is the importance we should ascribe to the familiarity and concern that was expressed by the Congress Party regarding the treatment and standing of overseas Indians. The two most important political forums in the country of the time, the Viceroy's Imperial Council and the Congress Party, both expressed regularly, and with no small amount of vehemence, the need for British imperial authorities to intervene around the world where the condition of Indians was not meeting expected humanitarian and political standards.[9] This concern led to innovations in Indian foreign policy, prior to formal independence, with agents being appointed in different African countries in particular to look over and monitor the state of overseas Indians, regularly sending reports back to New Delhi for the council and the political elites to follow.[10]

The demand for Indians to travel to the white colonies of Canada, Australia and New Zealand, based on their status as British subjects, raised new problems for the imperial authorities, given the hostility of these dominions to the arrival of what they considered racial and cultural inferiors. As Radhika Mongia has shown most effectively, the meaning of imperial citizenship was recast as a result of these movements, demands and counter-responses, as the British scrambled to find a way of keeping the peace in their largest colony, India, while trying to accommodate the racially unequal social practices endemic to South Africa, Australia and Canada.[11]

What this brief recapitulation points to is the ease with which nascent nationalists in India assumed the condition and status of Indians overseas was directly linked to their own struggle. Not to put too fine a point on it, during this period Indian nationals were found not just within the territorial limits of British India, but also all over the British Empire and in Portuguese Africa (Mozambique), the French West Indies (Guadeloupe) and Dutch South America (Suriname). It did not make a difference. It remains to be seen how much the idea of "India" came from overseas back to the peninsular homeland (*des*), but a plausible case can be made that solidarities forged in foreign lands, struggling against political oppression and economic exploitation, were not a trivial factor. If "Indian-ness"—the implicit foundation of the Indian nation—owed some important part of its formation to the presence and activities of Indians abroad, then what we are describing is an Indian nation that far exceeds the territorial limits of "India," recognisably and with material consequences.

Within Asia, the presence of Indians and Chinese outside their traditional homelands had been a part of the local social, cultural and economic landscape for long enough that their nationality was quite ambiguous. Of course, there is a grave danger in attributing meanings of national identity to a time when the norms and meaning of those terms were quite different from the present, but it seems fair to say that the presence and labour of "Indians" and "Chinese" helped define the ethnoscape[12] of contemporary Southeast Asia in a number of important respects. Southeast Asian states (as also India and China) were, in this sense, quite multi-ethnic in their social makeup, linguistically complex and culturally diverse, with varieties of locally defined religious practices: these were inherently hybrid spaces. Indians and Chinese may have been represented in distinct ways, but their social distance was not yet defined primarily as a political problem. Their simultaneously marginal and mainstream social location was a product of the overall lack of political freedom within colonies as well as, at times, the product of multiple, overlapping political authorities. This is not in any way to assume social harmony between communities at all times, or to disavow the important and perceived linkage between Indians and British imperial hegemony, given the widespread use of Indian military personnel and the Indian Army in counter-insurgency operations, punitive missions and outright military conquest.[13] In spite of the colonial state's strongly held racial beliefs and practices, expressed in a discourse that reduced social meaning to racial and cultural essentialisms and that saw inter-communal violence as endemic, wars, riots and communal conflict were not everyday events. For the rest of the time, an inter-communal state of tolerance could be said to be in place, bounded by Native Lines—a spatially distinct ethno-religious habitus—especially where overseen by a colonial regime that was interested in maintaining an absence of inter-communal conflict. This fragile peace became more so as the possibility of political independence came nearer. What changed with the imminent arrival of political independence were the norms that seemed attached to statehood—an increasingly hegemonic idea of the necessary relation between territory and a distinct community of people, coming together to produce the concepts of "nationals" and "national identity."

Nationalism as we know it today may have been invented in Europe, but its export overseas was a contradictory and uneven process.[14] It is important to note that the making of modern French and English nationalism, including the socialisation of their own peripheries,[15] was simultaneous with imperial expansion overseas, its institutional consolidation and the corresponding flows of people from the homeland to faraway places and from one colony to another.[16] Likewise, for Germany and Italy, latecomers to the imperial adventure, defining the territorial roots of identity was not necessarily the first or most obvious step in the making of the national project.[17] Arguing about and identifying who was a German and who an Italian was simultaneous with and followed the consolidation of numerous smaller kingdoms and principalities—often by force, but also by political negotiation and economic agreement.[18] It was not until the First World War that a wider international (Euro-American) consensus emerged that territorially distinct spaces should be coterminous with a single political authority, and recognition of which political entities had achieved that status began to become consensual and uniform. This was the moment when political identity became uniquely linked to national affiliation. Complicating matters considerably was the fact that these processes were taking place even as the republican ideal sought to establish its legitimacy over other forms of rule.[19]

We do not yet fully understand the complex process by which contradictory historical shifts and geographical confusions became consolidated into a common sense about the nature and relation of people-as-nation, state as a sovereign political authority and national identity as a mutually exclusive solidarity. Yet it was this common sense that Asia had to confront, half a century later, as its component elements made claim to international presence and the right to be recognised as independent national entities. Now, to be a state with full international standing assumed the "organized hypocrisy"[20] of the Weberian ideal type: the identity of one territory, one people, one authority. And to meet these unstated yet powerful conditions, the presence of overseas nationals was among the greatest hurdles to cross as both a political and an intellectual problem.

In China, a Nationalist government still struggling to control the vast expanses of land claimed by its imperial predecessors took the historic step of identifying all Chinese, regardless of location, as citizens of the new republic. Almost from its inception in 1911, the Kuomintang regime was deeply beleaguered. Facing internal conflict with the communists, loss of authority from regional warlords, the fear of invasion and eventual occupation of Manchuria, limited sovereignty, tenuous control over the western provinces of Tibet and Xinjiang, and intense competition among European imperialists over major "treaty ports," including the major city of Shanghai, Republican China sought to identify its nationals, anywhere in the world, as constitutive and unimpeachable proof of their demand for international recognition of the idea of China. This step was ostensibly to protect the status of overseas Chinese, living in alien lands and with uncertain legal protections and rights; in fact, it may have had much more to do with the fragile state of political authority in the Central States/Middle Kingdom. Whatever the reason, this simple measure offering dual nationality reversed centuries of indifference to the condition of Chinese living overseas, traditionally considered to be disenfranchised from the homeland, even exiled, and offered them new visibility and recognition in a rapidly changing international legal regime of citizenship and nationality.

Post-1949 and the end of the Republican government, the PRC (initially) continued this recognition. Zhou Enlai, reporting to the Third Session of the First National Committee of the Central Committee in 1951, noted:

> There are more than 10 million Chinese nationals living overseas. Lawful rights and interests of these people, as a result of unreasonable discrimination and even persecution on the part of certain countries, have been deeply infringed. This cannot but arouse the serious attention and deep concern of the Chinese people and Government.[21]

If the initial change of legal status of overseas Chinese had already made the governments of Southeast Asia nervous and apprehensive, the idea of permanent dual nationals as also a potential fifth column was a Damocles' sword too dangerous to contemplate. Not surprisingly, from the advent of the Nationalist period, state-sponsored violence against the overseas Chinese increased substantially in Indonesia, Malaya and Thailand. For the independent states of Southeast Asia, the presence of "overseas" Chinese in their lands was a foreign and domestic policy problem of the first order.

India faced a similar dilemma over its "national problem." Its scattered people expected protection of a sort from an independent India, as a natural extension of the support and concern for their condition that had marked the colonial period. Although British India had been a recognised part of the international system from at least as early as 1919 and its official participation in the Versailles Peace Conference, its membership of the League of Nations, and its participation in the founding of the United Nations Organization in 1944–45, the country that was entering a sovereign political existence was hardly the same as its predecessor. For those who assumed the successor country would inherit naturally the legacy of the colonial regime, political independence ushered in a series of direct assaults on the legitimacy of that claim. First and most obvious was the territorial division of British India into India, East Pakistan and West

Pakistan, and the movement of millions of displaced persons in all directions, creating a humanitarian and political emergency of the highest order. The loss of land and people was followed by the unwillingness of a number of semi-sovereign "princely" states of British India—Hyderabad, Junagadh and Kashmir being the most notorious, but also including Travancore—to accede to the newly founded independent state of India, leading to the selective use of military force and occupation.[22] Added to this was the presence of other colonial enclaves in (Portuguese) Goa and (French) Pondicherry, which showed no sign of taking the British lead and preparing for departure, and the uncertainty over the long-term status and condition of the North East Frontier Agency. It all added up to an enormous political problem that questioned the legitimacy and viability of the new state in fundamental ways.

The abstract problems of international recognition and full statehood would acquire tangible expression in the first international conferences bringing together the free countries of Asia and Africa. India's and China's identity crises would confront the ethno-political fault lines foremost in the minds of delegates from "host" states of Southeast Asia, making it impossible to postpone indefinitely the problem of overseas residents. India was quicker to respond to its own contradictions of state formation, and the concerns of Southeast Asia, and would assert during the Asian Relations Conference in 1947 that overseas Indians had no "right of return;" they were to stay where they were and to make their peace with the people and governments of the countries they were residing in. China would take until the Bandung Conference of 1955 to come to the same solution.

Asian Relations: Communalism and Inter-Asian Migration

Delegates to the Asian Relations Conference, held in New Delhi in late March and early April 1947, a few months before India became formally independent, were quite preoccupied with these questions. Perhaps not by coincidence, chairing the Group B round-table sessions on Racial Problems (Topic II) and Inter-Asian Migration (Topics III) were delegates from the Republic of China, including Dr. Wen Yuan-ning, and Sardar K.M. Pannikar from India.[23]

A Burmese delegate graphically described the problem he found his country in: "It was terrible to be ruled by a Western power, but it was even more so to be ruled by an Asian power."[24] Burma, caught between the great powers of India and China, was thus in a great quandary, as he saw it. The problem was compounded by the fact that, according to him, the growth rates of Indians and Chinese living in Burma constituted half of the population increase in that country, while the "death rate among Burmese was mounting."[25]

A Malayan delegate noted, "only 40 per cent of the population of Malaya is indigenous,"[26] the rest consisting of Indians and Chinese. Demographic issues soon gave way to a discussion of loyalties and the obligations of citizenship. All the delegates agreed that an independent country had the sovereign right to decide who should reside within its boundaries; however, the more pressing political problem facing them was what to do about the non-national populations already resident at the moment of independence.

As a delegate from Ceylon was quick to point out, undoubtedly thinking of the Tamil-speaking population in that country, no law should be passed by the independent country that would "discriminate" against those non-nationals who were already resident there and who wished to remain. Speaking later, another delegate from Ceylon sought to clarify that as much as "a fifth" of Ceylon's population consisted of emigrant labour. He noted that among the migrant community there were two kinds—those who had lived there "for generations" (referring to Jaffna Tamils) and those who were better described as an "itinerant alien labour population" (referring to the "estate Tamils," indentured labour from southern India). Since this latter group had been brought to Ceylon by the colonial power, he argued, the end of colonial rule would presumably take care of this problem.[27]

As a Burmese delegate saw it, non-national residents had two choices: to take on the nationality of their present country of residence or to remain resident aliens, nationals of the country they had migrated from. Both responses were problematic, according to him. If the residents took local nationality, then "such action might go against the indigenous races;" but if they did not, it would be "unfair" to send them back to their former country of residence.[28]

A Malayan delegate, in response, took a harder line on the matter of choice. According to him, local citizenship should be granted only to those "who regarded Malaya as the [sole] object of their loyalty."[29] Indians and Chinese living in Malaya, British subjects and Chinese citizens respectively, should "make a vital and final choice" about which country they would owe allegiance to.[30] Another added, "Chinese in Malaya ... cannot have their bodies there and their minds in China."[31]

Responses to these concerns by Indian and Chinese delegates ranged from the aggressive to the mediatory. In general, the Chinese responses seemed more defensive, with the Indians seeking to establish more general principles for inter-Asian migration and protection for alien minorities. Explanations by the Chinese delegation made clear that they considered overseas Chinese to be part of the Chinese nation, with the right to reclaim Chinese nationality never foreclosed. Indian delegates, on the other hand, were much more forthright in telling overseas Indians that they should not look to India to solve their problems and explaining away migration as the result of imperial needs.

When a Chinese delegate, for example, raised the issue of state legislation against the Chinese community in Indonesia and noted that there had been many killings of Chinese in the recent past,[32] he received a strong response from the Indonesians. After blaming the current state of affairs on the colonial power, Holland, "which had enrich[ed] the Chinese at the expense of the Indonesians and used them as 'agent provocateurs'," the Indonesian delegate argued that the Chinese were "narrow minded" and unassimilated "despite three centuries of stay."[33] The Chinese chairman agreed to some extent with these comments, noting that part of the problem was the "exclusiveness" of these communities and that the wealth generated by them tended not to be spent for the benefit of the country of residence. An Indian delegate sought to explain that a vicious cycle was in effect, where money was sent back to the mother country by Indians and Chinese in Southeast Asia because of the fear among these emigrant communities that their status in their countries of residence was unstable. The righteous anger of local communities that income generated from them was being repatriated only exacerbated fears among rich Chinese and Indian traders. Adding a geopolitical twist to the discussion was the following observation:

> the problem could not be solved unless the immigrant communities accept loyalty to the country of adoption and not look back to their countries of origin … *the problem was not so much of racial dislike as a suspicion … of India and China …* That [the smaller countries of southeast Asia] might get mixed up with these big countries through the immigrant communities.[34]

Chinese delegates sought to explain at length that their country's citizenship policy was not as it seemed to many Southeast Asian delegates. They pointed out that the Chinese government did not encourage emigration and that overseas Chinese communities were primarily commercial communities who did not get involved in politics. As long as they were engaged in commercial activities, the delegate went on to say, they should be allowed to remain in the region. Once they were "economically functionless" [sic] they could be asked to leave and the Chinese government would "devise ways and means" of absorbing them back.[35] A Chinese delegate pointed out that the Chinese position was that no one could be a dual citizen; an individual could hold only one country's citizenship at a time. He added that their consulate in Malaya was asking all Chinese to decide whether they wanted to take on Malayan citizenship and noting that they would lose Chinese citizenship if they did so. However, "under Chinese law, they could become Chinese nationals again on giving up Malayan nationality" at a later date.[36] Another delegate noted, "citizenship was a personal affair." Overseas Chinese often held onto their nationality "as a matter of sentiment." Adding an ominous note, the delegate said that if migrant people were asked to "naturalise within a short period or get repatriated" there was likely to be conflict.[37]

Indian delegates noted that inter-Asian migration had come about through "no fault" of the sending or receiving countries, but due to imperial policies over which they had no control. As far as Indian migrants in Ceylon, for instance, were concerned, they had "lost all touch with India" and hence "did not seem to be in a position to get help from [India]. ... India did not seem to have space enough to take them back but their case demanded human justice all the same." Another delegate noted, "countries such as China and India should not encourage emigrants to look for help to their home country, but that emigrants permanently settling in a foreign country should be advised to identify themselves with that country."[38]

Although these considerable differences and problems were aired quite openly, it did not prevent agreement on some broad principles governing the intercourse of Asian affairs and people. There was little disagreement that the countries of Asia, as they formulated their post-independence immigration policies, should be very concerned about ensuring equal treatment before the law of nationals and already resident non-nationals, even if the latter chose to retain their prior citizenship, and that no racial group should be socially disqualified or discriminated against. What the delegates did not want to be accused of was racialism and race supremacy. As a delegate from Azerbaijan noted, "the grim memories of a war based on doctrines of race supremacy" were very much alive. "We Asian peoples meeting here," he said, "should make a note in the report that we condemn all theories based on the supremacy of one race over another."[39]

The preceding discussion has tried to show the differences between the positions taken on the one hand by Indians and Chinese, representing the "source" of the problem of inter-Asian migration, and on the other hand by Southeast Asian "host" countries, who saw the presence of these alien, unassimilated migrants as a source of internal conflict and threat. Responses by the Chinese and Indians were not identical. Indian delegates were more forthright about their relative indifference to the condition of overseas Indians. They made it clear that as long as legal protections were in place, the local inhabitants and the migrant populations should begin to learn to live with each other. The best way for that to happen, it was implied, was for the "right of return" to be taken away. Indian-ness, however much it was obvious to the external eye, was not an immutable thing, they suggested. The longer the time spent away from the putative homeland, the less the homeland identified with them— "they had lost all touch." This position was in contrast with the view expressed by Chinese delegates, who saw Chinese-ness (and Chinese nationality) as essentially permanent, always available to the Chinese-identified person as soon as it was desired. They would "find ways and means of absorbing them." Comments by ROC delegates reflected an ambivalence on the part of the Republican government to cut ties definitively with overseas Chinese populations.

The Asian Relations Conference discussions, it must be noted, were not official consultations between independent states and credentialed officials. The Conference's significance lay in the novelty of the event and its location, the absence of Western voices in the discussion, the self-identified community— Asia—that was being drawn together based on a racial logic of identification, the common problems it was assumed these countries faced and would face, and their unanimous agreement that certain practices typical of Western colonial regimes—especially colonialism and racialism—should be permanently ended as features of international and even domestic relations. The Asian Relations Conference was the first occasion for Asian political leaders to express, as they saw it, the primary political dilemmas facing new Asian states. These concerns, once articulated, only heightened the sense of concern. Following independence, the most important multilateral forum for their discussion and resolution would turn out to be the Bandung Conference.

Bandung: Resolving the Dual Nationality Problem

In the eight years between the Asian Relations Conference and the Bandung Conference, more countries in Asia had become independent or had new regimes, but ironically, the question of what defined Asia was less obvious than it could have been. If the former conference was all about inclusion, starting from the recognition of a lack of information and familiarity with newly found neighbours, this was far less true a few years later. Greater knowledge, it would seem, had led to less agreement. This necessary starting point—who should be invited to the Bandung Conference—spoke volumes for the changed international political situation of the time and also points to the different political agendas the organising countries sought to achieve. In a preparatory meeting held in Bogor, Indonesia, the host country and the other Colombo Powers (India, Ceylon, Pakistan and Burma) struggled with a complex set of political considerations affecting inclusion, making clear that purely racial distinctions determining "Asian" identity were no longer meaningful. For instance, and unlike in 1947—when a Palestinian Jewish delegation was quite visible in

New Delhi—Israel/Palestine was not invited to Bandung, due to the sensitivities of the Arab states and in spite of strong Burmese protests to the contrary. More contentious among the many disagreements in the process of issuing official invitations to Bandung were the inclusion of countries against which one sponsoring country expressed very strong reservations, almost always due to Cold War wars and alignments that predetermined political stances. Most obviously, these included the Koreas, but also Indochina.

The consensus produced soon after the Conference, in no small respect thanks to an important report written by that eminent observer of Asian politics, Cornell University's George McTurnan Kahin, was that the real story of Bandung was China.[40] This "common sense" was further confirmed by a famous epigram attributed to Burmese Premier U Nu:[41] "There would have been no conference without Nehru and no success without [Zhou] Enlai."[42] China's presence was, from the Indian and Burmese points of view at least, essential for the success of the Conference. This was, of course, another China from the one invited to the Asian Relations Conference in 1947, following the fall of the Nationalist regime and the formation of the People's Republic; but in Nehru's eyes, it was also a far more legitimate representative of the Chinese people, regardless of the political ideology professed by its leaders. Given Nehru's and U Nu's relative doubts about the need for an Asian conference in the first place, one of the factors that won them over was their realisation that China's presence would be an important political statement of Asian difference. In spite of the initial reluctance of the other Colombo Powers to invite Communist China, India and Burma made it clear that without China, their own interest in the Conference would be much diminished.[43] China had to be included first to show the Europeans and Americans that Asia worked to different rules than did the West, that national similarities and differences were more salient and ideological differences less important than in the global Cold War discourse of "friends or others." From a more materialist point of view, China, still lacking recognition by much of the contemporary international community, was nonetheless central to the establishment of peace (or at least the end of military conflict) in the region, given its status as a sponsor of conflict and belligerent in both Asia's global conflicts—Korea and Indochina. Chinese behaviour was, by extension, also the most likely cause of the possible use of nuclear weapons in Asia, given the US fear of losing ground yet needing to hold firm against the spread of communism, and the United States' perceived lack of serious military options other than nuclear weapons. Based on their encounters with John Foster Dulles, who had tried to use India to convey strong deterrent messages to China during the Korean War,[44] and exposure to US diplomacy during the Geneva Peace

Conference,[45] Indian foreign policy mandarins feared that the United States would be quite willing to use nuclear weapons in Asia against Asians, as they had done before. The close ties that had grown between India and China since 1950, and the many meetings between Nehru, Krishna Menon and Zhou Enlai, led Nehru to argue that Chinese communism was a nationalist movement first and a communist movement second, that the Chinese could be reasoned with based on mutual national interests, but also that they were in many respects their own worst enemy. In short, China needed to take certain steps to reduce fears held by their neighbours and negotiate and interact differently in this new international environment, especially within Asia.

Zhou soon proved he was second to none when it came to diplomatic manoeuvring; his performance at the conference showed also why he had the complete faith of Chairman Mao and the Chinese Communist Party high command when it came to external affairs.[46] Two measures in particular must be noted here: first, Zhou's willingness *not* to respond to every charge, real or imagined, brought against China, which defused a number of potentially sensitive situations; and, more important, his forthright assertions backed up by behind-the-scenes negotiations with Indonesia, Thailand and Cambodia, in particular, seeking to resolve the question of overseas Chinese nationals and their ambivalent loyalties. The importance of the dual nationality issue for Thailand, for example, led Prince Wan to raise this issue directly in his opening statement. Given the impassioned and even overblown rhetoric of peace, goodwill and understanding typical of many other opening speeches, the bluntness of Wan's comments was a sign of the seriousness of the matter.[47] Speaking of Thailand's doubts about the meaning of peaceful coexistence[48]—the fifth of the Five Principles (Pancasila) put forward by China and India as expressing the most appropriate norms for international relations—Wan asked:

> What exactly does this mean? Does it mean "live and let live" which is the right principle? Does it imply the practice of tolerance as is explicitly stated in the Charter of the United Nations? For the Charter says: "to practice tolerance and live together in peace with one another as good neighbours." These doubts in my mind must first be cleared up, for its fact (sic) which in all responsibility I have to take into account, that Pridi Banomyong, a Thai politician, is organizing the training of Thai-speaking Chinese and persons of Thai race in Yunan for purposes of infiltration and subversion in Thailand. I have also to know for certain the attitude adopted by the PRC in regard to the so-called person [sic] of dual nationality in Thailand or, in other words, to the Chinese community of 3 [million] in Thailand out of a population of 18 [million].[49]

On hearing this and other speeches that made reference to communism, ongoing conflicts in Asia, and other issues that referred to China implicitly and explicitly, Zhou discarded the original speech he had prepared (and which had already been circulated among the delegates) and spoke directly to these issues. After stating directly, if incorrectly, that the support for dual citizenship for overseas Chinese was a policy associated with the previous Nationalist regime ("old China"), he said:

> Up to date, Chiang Kai-shek is still using some very few overseas Chinese to carry out subversive activities against the country [sic] where the overseas Chinese are residing. The People's government of new China, however, is ready to solve the problem of dual nationality of overseas Chinese with the government of countries concerned.... There is a saying in China: "To hear a hundred times cannot be compared to seeing once." We welcome the delegates of all the participating countries in this Conference to visit China at any time you like. We have no bamboo curtain, but there are people who are spreading smokescreen between us.[50]

This direct statement, coming as it did on the first day of the Conference, would go a long way towards alleviating the fears of the collected delegations and help strengthen the idea that perhaps diplomacy among Asian countries would be different and more likely to lead to peaceful resolution than the patterns of international relations typical of the world thus far. Zhou and Wan would amicably discuss the overseas Chinese in Thailand on the sidelines of the Conference, ending in an agreement that helped allay the fears of the Thai government about the loyalties of their Chinese minority. The same outcome would take place with Prince Norodom Sihanouk of Cambodia.

For Indonesia, apart from the significant boost in international reputation it received by organising the Conference, key issues that received international support and resolution were the ongoing Dutch colonial presence in Western Irian (Irian Jaya) province,[51] and the more sensitive and domestically charged question of loyalties of Indonesian Chinese. The Indonesians received full support for their position in Irian Jaya, consistent with the general agreement among the delegates that the day of European colonialism in Asia was long passed. On the question of the dual nationality of Indonesian Chinese, thanks to Zhou's quick reaction, a separate agreement was reached. Reflecting the importance attributed to this issue, and using it to demonstrate the "spirit of goodwill and tolerance" engendered by this Conference and possible among Asian countries, the head of the Indonesian delegation noted in his closing statement:

I would like to add for your information that two days ago, during this Conference, Indonesia was very fortunate to be able to conclude a treaty with the PRC on the solution of the longstanding double nationality problem, which problem is obviously important also for other countries in southeast Asia.[52]

How differently was the question of overseas migrants and dual nationality perceived in the eight short years between the Asian Relations Conference and Bandung? Not only was the question of Indian overseas populations hardly mentioned at all, suggesting that Indian disavowals made in 1947 were taken to heart by their intended audiences (and that little took place to disturb that new confidence), but the new Chinese government changed its position of just a few years before and made significant efforts to take the issue off the table. As noted above, Zhou took pains to address directly the vocal concerns of Indonesia, Thailand and Cambodia, and given his acknowledged ability to shape the course of Chinese foreign relations, agreements reached on the sidelines of the Conference were given considerable weight by these respective delegations. Inter-Asian migration, it would seem, was no longer an issue of Asian international relations thanks to personal diplomacy, the change of regimes in India and China and corresponding changes in the self-definition of their respective nations, and the increasingly substantive content given to the weakly defined norm of "peaceful coexistence."

Clearly any assessment of the ostensible success of the Bandung Conference must include the issue on which the most political progress was made, and which made possible the reduction of political tensions between the most countries. This issue was the partial resolution of outstanding problems of state formation and national identity in Asia, namely, the presence and significance of non-local communities or ethnic minorities. *What the Asian Relations Conference and Bandung meant was the diaspora no longer had the right to return.* The significance of this shift, beyond the local effects it might have had, lies in what it tells us about the conditions of Asian state formation and the meanings of national sovereignty it produced.

Indians and Chinese, exemplars of inter-Asian migration, were the source of much unease, especially in what we now think of as Southeast Asia, for the positions they occupied in the global "commodity chain" of mercantile exchange and commerce, for their political activism in trade unions and rural plantation economies, for their tendency to segregate themselves from other communities socially and culturally, and for the irredentist claims they might make on their powerful, if erstwhile, homelands for political and economic redress. In short, their political loyalties could not be counted on locally: within dominant representations, they remained "Indians" and "Chinese" regardless of their long sojourns away from "India" and "China" respectively.

Unable to resolve the complex issue of Indian and Chinese nationality—who was an Indian/Chinese—unambiguously, the new states of India and China fell back on their national-territorial limits as a means of forcing the decision. Those living within the stated and claimed borders[53] of the countries were (the only legitimate) Indians and Chinese, respectively. Those outside were not, even if they continued to be seen as overseas Indians and Chinese in their countries of residence. The full import of this decision is only drawn out when seen in historical terms as a complete reversal of long-standing policy in both countries: the close affiliation expressed by Nationalist and Communist China, as well as by the Indian Congress Party, for their overseas compatriots. First India, in 1947, and then China, during the 1955 Bandung Conference, helped assuage the fears of countries such as Burma, Cambodia, Malaya, Indonesia and Thailand by denying their interest in and legally taking away the possibility of divided political loyalties from their overseas populations. By extension, it should be noted that this particular "resolution" of the problem of overseas Indians and Chinese, coming as it did via the closure of the option of the right to return, reminds us of the unstable position of both India and China as independent states seeking full recognition by the international community.

Conclusion

This chapter has argued that among the most under-appreciated yet important outcomes of the 1955 Bandung Conference were its political effects. Among the better known of these political effects were the deliberate efforts by India and Burma, in particular, to force international recognition of the People's Republic of China by including it in the Afro-Asian Conference, and thereby to make visible the coming divergence between ideology and nationalism, between communism as an international revolutionary force and nationalism as a territorially bounded political movement. Less widely acknowledged is the importance of the Bandung Conference, and the Asian Relations Conference eight years earlier, in creating a multilateral forum where international political solutions to core domestic problems—the presence of ethnic and religious minorities—were also discussed, negotiated and even sometimes successfully implemented.

The Bandung Conference was not only a response to the structural exclusion of Asians from what we now call the "international community" of sovereign states nor just the official precursor to the Non-Aligned Movement. It was also a serious effort by new Asian political leaders to address, in a multilateral forum, bilateral issues to do with the perceived problem of persons seen as cultural and political aliens in the land of their residence. Bandung and the Asian Relations Conference were, in other words, the site for the re-inscription of a history of Asian movement and migration into a domestic political idiom, indexed by the master-label of "minorities." Most centrally associated with the presence of Chinese and Indians outside their "homeland," this chapter argues that post-colonial state formation in Asia should be seen as a process where access to citizenship was uneven from the outset, where permanent cleavages were pro-duced between insiders and outsiders on the slippery basis of putative indi-geneity, and where racialised distinctions between various communities were normalised enough to be written into dominant political institutions and practices. In this very different sense, the effects of Bandung—the problems of minorities—are still very visible in Asia today.

Notes

[1]   In this context, another important meeting that preceded Bandung and helped make the latter possible and successful was the 19-country conference on Indo-nesia, held in New Delhi in January 1949 (Conference of Asian, Australasian and Middle Eastern Nations on the Indonesian Question).

[2]   This is not to say that visual or cartographic representations of "India" or "Indo-nesia" were absent from the anti-colonial struggles in either country. Far from it; see Sumathi Ramaswamy (ed.), *Beyond Appearances: Visual Practices and Ideologies in Modern India* (New Delhi: Sage, 2003). For Indonesia, see John Pemberton, *On the Subject of "Java"* (Ithaca: Cornell University Press, 1994). Rather, the limits of "India" and "Indonesia" in terms of the people and lands to be included under those appellations were very much the object of contestation all through the anti-colonial period *and after.* By way of contrast, consider how important were the identification of the geo-location and corresponding ethno-linguistic communities in the original call for the creation of Pakistan as a homeland for South Asian Muslims. Ayesha Jalal, *The Sole Spokesman: Jinnah, the Muslim League and the Struggle for Pakistan* (Cambridge: Cambridge University Press, 1985).

[3]   As Duara reminds us, both Chinese Nationalist (KMT) and communist leaders struggled over the meaning and form of the transition from the universal empire of Qing China to, "in the words of the great reformer Liang Qichao (1873–1929), a 'nation among nations'." Prasenjit Duara, "Sovereignty and Citizenship in a Decentered China," in Susan D. Blum and Lionel M. Jensen (eds.), *China Off Center: Mapping the Margins of the Middle Kingdom* (Honolulu: University of Hawai'i Press, 2002), p. xiv. Among the unresolved issues was the question of what was to be included within the borders of a modern Chinese successor state.

Some degree of this problem is indexed by the Nationalist reference to the "Land of the Five Nationalities," by 50 years of PRC border disputes with neighbouring countries, and the ongoing and unresolved "internal" problems, including Taiwan, Tibet and Xinjiang provinces.

4 For an important rethinking of the historical significance of this scale of movement and "circulation," see Claude Markovits, Jacques Pouchepedass and Sanjay Subrahmanyam (eds.), *Society and Circulation: Mobile People and Itinerant Cultures in South Asia, 1750–1950* (New Delhi: Permanent Black, 2003).

5 High Level Committee on the Indian Diaspora, Dr. L.M. Singhvi, chairman of the committee (New Delhi: Ministry of External Affairs, Government of India, 2001), available at <http://indiandiaspora.nic.in/contents.htm> [14 March 2005].

6 Wang Gungwu, *The Chinese Overseas: From Earthbound China to the Quest for Autonomy* (Cambridge: Harvard University Press, 2000).

7 S. Robert Ramsey, "The Languages of China," in Blum and Jensen (eds.), *China Off Center.*

8 Judith Brown, "The Making of a Critical Outsider," in Judith M. Brown and Martin Prozesky (eds.), *Gandhi and South Africa* (Pietermaritzburg: University of Natal Press, 1996).

9 Hugh Tinker, *Separate and Unequal: India and the Indians in the British Commonwealth, 1920–1950* (London: Christopher Hurst, 1976); Tinker, *A New System of Slavery: The Export of Indian Labour Overseas 1830–1920* (London: Hansib, 1993).

10 Tinker, *A New System of Slavery.*

11 Radhika Mongia, "Race, Nation, Mobility: A History of the Passport," *Public Culture* 11, no. 3 (1999): 527–66.

12 Arjun Appadurai, *Modernity at Large: Cultural Dimensions of Globalization* (Minneapolis: University of Minnesota Press, 1996).

13 As Stargardt reminds us, "the use of Indian troops against Vietnamese [as late as 1946] cast a shadow on Anglo-Indian relations and on the image of Indians in Indochina." A.W. Stargardt, "The Emergence of the Asian System of Powers," *Modern Asian Studies* 23, no. 3 (1989): 561–95, see p. 573.

14 Benedict Anderson, *Imagined Communities: Reflections on the Origin and Spread of Nationalism* (London: Verso, 1983).

15 Peter Sahlins, *Boundaries: The Making of France and Spain in the Pyrenees* (Berkeley: University of California Press, 1989); Eugen Weber, *Peasants Into Frenchmen: The Modernization of Rural France 1870–1914* (Stanford: Stanford University Press, 1976).

16 Edward Said, *Culture and Imperialism* (New York: Knopf, 1993); Gauri Vishwanathan, *Masks of Conquest: Literary Study and British Rule in India* (New York: Columbia University Press, 1989).

17 Rogers Brubaker, *Citizenship and Nationhood in France and Germany* (Cambridge: Harvard University Press, 1992).

[18] Charles Tilly, *Coercion, Capital and European States, 990–1990* (Cambridge: Basil Blackwell, 1990).

[19] The moment of territorial exclusivity is usually identified with the Treaty of Westphalia, which is historically dubious, but also the very scope of and participation in that "inter-state" agreement makes it less effective as a historical marker than is usually assumed. There is much more to be said about the relationship between the process of "normal" state-making and international recognition, but limitations of space prevent us from doing so here.

[20] Stephen Krasner, *Sovereignty: Organized Hypocrisy* (Princeton: Princeton University Press, 1999).

[21] Quoted in David A. Wilson, "China, Thailand and the Spirit of Bandung (Part 1)," *China Quarterly* 30 (April–June 1967): 149–69, see p. 155.

[22] V.P. Menon, *The Story of the Integration of the Indian States* (Calcutta: Orient Longman, 1956).

[23] In the original invitation letter, the topics were identified as "Racial problems with special reference to root-causes of racial conflicts" and "Inter-Asian migration and treatment of immigrants." Round Table Group B, which was to discuss these questions, met on 25 March 1947; the plenary session was held the next day. Asian Relations 1948, *Being Report of the Proceedings and Documentation of the First Asian Relations Conference, New Delhi March–April 1947* (New Delhi: Asian Relations Organization), p. 90.

[24] Ibid., p. 96.

[25] Ibid.

[26] Ibid., p. 92.

[27] Ibid., pp. 94–5.

[28] Ibid., p. 91.

[29] Ibid., p. 92.

[30] Ibid.

[31] Ibid., p. 94.

[32] Ibid., p. 93.

[33] Ibid.

[34] Ibid., p. 94, italics added.

[35] Ibid., p. 97.

[36] Ibid., p. 92.

[37] Ibid., p. 97.

[38] Ibid., p. 100.

[39] Ibid., p. 103.

[40] George McTurnan Kahin, *The Asian-African Conference, Bandung Indonesia, April 1955* (Ithaca: Cornell University Press, 1956).

[41] For a biography and analysis of Nu, see Hugh Tinker, "Nu, the Serene Statesman," *Pacific Affairs* 30, no. 2 (June 1957): 120–37.

[42] M.S. Rajan, *India in World Affairs, 1954–1956* (New Delhi: Indian Council of World Affairs, 1964), p. 212, footnote 1.

[43] A.W. Stargardt, "The Emergence of the Asian System of Powers," *Modern Asian Studies* 23, no. 3 (1989): 561–95, see p. 588.

[44] Rosemary Foot, "Nuclear Coercion and the Ending of the Korean Conflict," *International Security* 13, no. 3 (Winter 1988–89): 92–112, see pp. 98–104.

[45] J.Y. Ra, "The Politics of Conference: The Political Conference on Korea in Geneva, 26 April–15 June 1954," *Journal of Contemporary History* 34, no. 3 (July 1999): 399–416, see pp. 411–5.

[46] Shao Kuo-kang, "Chou Enlai's Diplomatic Approach to Non-aligned States in Asia: 1953–60," *China Quarterly* 78 (June 1979): 324–38.

[47] See Wilson, "China, Thailand and the Spirit of Bandung (Part 1)," for a longer discussion of Thai-Chinese relations.

[48] In the context of Pancasila, this term at a minimum meant the ability of Asian states to choose their own domestic political systems and to acknowledge their willingness to live alongside another country of very different political persuasion without seeing this difference as cause for conflict. Rhetorically, of course, this was seen as a word belonging to the communist lexicon that typically engendered a great deal of suspicion whenever and wherever it was used.

[49] Collected Documents 1983 *Asian-African Conference, Bandung, April 1956* (Jakarta: Ministry of External Affairs), pp. 110–1.

[50] Collected Documents, pp. 46–7.

[51] The Portuguese in East Timor were not mentioned.

[52] Collected Documents, p. 160.

[53] Stating it in this way reminds us that the territories claimed did not always coincide with the formal political authority and presence of the Indian or Chinese state.

CHAPTER 4

Bandung and the Political Economy of North-South Relations: Sowing the Seeds for Re-visioning International Society

Helen E.S. Nesadurai[1]

What has been the impact of the 1955 Bandung Conference on the political economy of North-South relations? Much of the literature on the first Asian-African Conference (popularly referred to as the Bandung Conference) focuses on the international relations of the newly independent countries of Asia and Africa. This is not surprising given that inter-state politics rather than economics was the central focus of high-level deliberations at the Conference.[2] Those works that have addressed the political economy implications of Bandung have done so by interpreting Bandung as the initial stage of an unfolding Third World movement of newly independent countries that sought to transcend their colonial histories by using the state as the means to "freedom, self-determination and modernisation that would unite its inhabitants and carry them towards development."[3] This was argued to be the essence of the Bandung Spirit, and the heyday of this form of "Third Worldism" was the period 1955–75, what Mark Berger terms the Bandung Era.[4] The call for a New International Economic Order (NIEO) by the developing world was, therefore, an integral part of the Bandung Era.

This reading of Bandung allows us to go beyond the narrow perspective of the 1955 Bandung Conference itself to locate Bandung within the wider Third World movement that sought to translate the de jure political sovereignty and rights that previously colonised countries had attained through independence into effective capabilities that would enable them to bring development and progress to their populations and, through that, to renew the bases of legitimacy for post-colonial governments. Conflicting interests among the countries meant that the coalition that emerged was often fragile, while claims that the Third World displayed "extraordinary unity" on the subject of the NIEO[5] needs to be qualified by the reality of radical and reformist camps within the coalition.[6] Nevertheless, both camps subscribed to common interpretations of the causes of Third World underdevelopment, although they differed with respect to their preferred remedies for these problems.[7] Their common perspective came from shared dependency ideas that emphasised external structural causes of Third World underdevelopment.[8] NIEO proponents believed that the unequal position of the developing world in the Cold War hierarchical order helped explain the failure of their states to attain post-independence goals. By framing the development problem in this way, the value of the state as the primary vehicle of development was preserved.[9]

Much has been gained from studies such as Berger's, which have interpreted Bandung as an ideological force centred on Third Worldism and the search for authentic forms of state-mediated development. It is, however, equally important to question the notion that Bandung and the NIEO movement are all of one piece, with the former leading seamlessly into the NIEO and the NIEO having its antecedents in the Bandung Conference, or, more commonly, drawing its inspiration from the Bandung Spirit. This chapter revisits the 1955 Bandung Conference in an effort to identify the connections, continuities *and* differences between the Bandung movement and later developments such as the NIEO. Such an exercise, undertaken in sections 2 and 3, cannot be exhaustive or provide conclusive answers to the question of Bandung's impact on North-South relations, especially when undertaken by a non-historian. Nevertheless, the insights gained can be helpful in identifying and evaluating the legacy of Bandung for the international political economy.

The analysis builds on James Mayall's reading of the Bandung movement as a revisionist alliance that sought to restructure international society,[10] most notably through the principle of non-alignment. Aside from this, the chapter suggests that the 1955 Bandung Conference sowed the seeds for re-visioning international society in two other ways. Bandung's call for equitable representation in international decision-making for the new members of the now expanding international society of states was essentially a call to take seriously international justice principles, particularly that of procedural justice, in the management of world affairs. Bandung participants also articulated an alternative set of principles for inter-state engagement that emphasised dialogue and accommodation, collective and peaceful problem-solving, and the search for consensus or compromise. These principles were regarded as more suited to the expanding and increasingly plural international society of states following decolonisation, and a necessary alternative to the power politics and coercion that had been the basis of colonialism/imperialism and that threatened to become the dominant mode of international relations in a world of superpower bloc politics. These diplomatic principles were identified by those closely associated with the 1955 Conference as the Bandung Spirit. Fifty years on, Bandung's initial articulation of alternative principles for international society remains salient.

The discussion in section 4 reveals that procedural justice remains curtailed for developing states, particularly in the key institutions of global economic governance where power disparities and institutional structures limit the extent to which genuine dialogue and debate over how to organise the "good life" can take place. A range of other justice claims has also emerged, articulated by a wider cast of actors beyond states. The ethical rationale for international economic justice has shifted from one based on the "rights and duties of states" during the 1960s and 1970s to the principle of reciprocity since the 1980s, whereby developing states have to demonstrate a certain standard of "good behaviour" in return for development assistance. While this shift focuses attention on problems internal to developing countries that have undermined development and human rights, there is a downside to the extent that it draws attention away from the essential unfairness of some of the new global rules that impede development. Good governance principles, for instance, have often been conflated with neoliberal economic policies that may not necessarily provide the best way forward for these countries. On the other hand, the shift towards more cosmopolitan notions of justice emphasising individual human rights rather than the rights of states has been progressive on the whole, especially for minority groups and even entire populations that have been subject to abuse by governments. It does, however, bring to the fore tensions with statist notions of international justice, and with the Westphalian norms of sovereignty and non-intervention.

By drawing on insights from the English School of international relations theory and Jurgen Habermas's theory of communicative action, section 5 suggests that in a situation where a range of justice claims are now articulated by a variety of actors, the Bandung principle that endorses dialogue over coercion and confrontation may be the best option to reach consensus on values and agendas, and in problem-solving. Although existing power disparities will continue to intrude into such processes, dialogue or communicative action processes merit greater attention as a means for reaching a reasoned consensus through persuasion and arguing in international relations. In the end, Bandung's lasting legacy for a plural world yet one that is fast integrating could well be its endorsement of deliberative politics. The rest of the chapter elaborates on these arguments.

The 1955 Bandung Conference:
Re-visioning International Society

The Asian-African Conference held in April 1955 in Bandung, Indonesia, was the high point of the Afro-Asian movement, which was itself built on the various Asian and African nationalisms that had emerged since the turn of the 20th century. By the late 1940s, when the first official expressions of African and Asian solidarity were made, the Afro-Asian movement's specific aim had already become clearly defined: to hasten the process of decolonisation and achieve independence for the colonies.[11] Although these objectives constituted the backdrop to the Bandung Conference, the immediate focus at Bandung was the problem of peaceful coexistence in the enlarged society of states, especially between the communist and non-communist worlds.[12] The Conference's five sponsors—Burma, Ceylon, India, Indonesia and Pakistan—also shared a concern that there was dangerous tension building up between the United States and communist China, which they feared would result in a disastrous world war that would unleash frightening atomic consequences on the rest of the world. Moreover, these five governments also wanted to lay the basis for peaceful relations between communist China and their own states.[13]

Underpinning these specific aims for the Bandung Conference was the genuine desire for "association and for brotherhood" amidst an unfolding Cold War in which the two superpowers—the United States and the Soviet Union—sought to broaden their zones of influence through aggressive foreign policies.[14] The Bandung sponsors recognised the importance of solidarity and cooperation amongst newly independent states, all generally weak states having to contend with the "mixture of wooing, bullying, flattery, threats and 'presents'" that marked the attitudes of the two superpowers to these new states.[15] Unsurprisingly, therefore, the Afro-Asian movement devoted considerable attention to international politics at (and after) the 1955 Bandung Conference,[16] notwithstanding the 12 paragraphs on economic cooperation in the Conference's Final Communiqué.[17] Even the preparatory ministerial meetings leading up to the Second African-Asian Conference in 1964 (later cancelled) were concerned primarily with political questions.[18]

Economics: A Neglected Area?

Although the 1955 Bandung Conference had been divided into three committees—political, economic and cultural—observers had from the outset expected that politics would take centre stage, and that meetings of the politics committee would attract the top delegates present.[19] True enough, much of the serious discussion focused on the search for common principles for world peace and cooperation against the backdrop of the unfolding inter-state tensions described above. Debates thus focused on, *inter alia*, the notion of non-alignment, sovereignty and non-interference; the idea of peaceful coexistence; the role of collective defence; principles of inter-state engagement; and even definitions of colonialism. Given the rather contentious debates on these issues, it was not surprising that none of the leaders of the delegations attended the meetings of the economic committee.[20] Perhaps this enabled officials and experts in charge of the economic deliberations to reach an agreed resolution in "record time," as noted by one observer, with the final agenda then approved without amendment by delegation heads.[21]

Despite the overwhelming emphasis on political matters, economics was clearly of some importance even if delegation heads and leaders were engaged with other matters. A 12-point Economic Cooperation agenda was issued as part of the Final Communiqué. This section begins with an acknowledgement that economic development was an urgent priority for the Bandung states. Much of the economic agenda was uncontroversial, however, with Bandung partici-pants calling for increased aid and technical assistance for their countries, while acknowledging that assistance already received from outside the African-Asian region had contributed significantly to their development programmes. Bandung participants also affirmed the importance of economic cooperation with states outside the region, and the value of foreign investment for their countries.[22]

The uncontroversial nature of the economic agenda at Bandung was not surprising. The early 1950s was a time of great optimism in both the Western and post-colonial worlds that development was a technical problem that simply required an injection of the right kind of resources and the creation of the right domestic conditions for economic take-off.[23] Moreover, decolonisation was, at most, a decade old, and leaders had yet to confront the political ramifications of domestic economic problems, especially those associated with rampant poverty.[24] Interestingly, many delegates to the economic committee reportedly chose to avoid issues that they felt had "significant political overtones."[25] Thus, the issue of UN export restrictions to China, which had salience for a number of the delegations present, was studiously avoided in the deliberations. The idea presumably was to ensure that the Conference did not degenerate into a forum for confrontation with the Western world. Western observers, especially the United States, who had expected the Conference to adopt an anti-Western course, had, in fact, been sufficiently reassured by the proceedings, with US Secretary of State John Foster Dulles praising, perhaps grudgingly, the Final Communiqué for its measured tone and non-hostile stance.[26] Bandung participants had taken considerable pains to stress that they were not forming another bloc, which had been the great fear of the United States and Britain.[27] Thus, the Final Communiqué stressed that the call for closer cooperation among Bandung participants did not preclude economic ties with states outside the grouping.[28]

There were, however, two key areas of concern in economics that were debated and mentioned in the Final Communiqué. The communiqué revealed that participants were worried about the sources of instability coming from the world economy. This was clear from the recommendations on commodity trade.[29] The end of the Korean War had led to a rapid decline in the prices of primary products, which had been artificially inflated during the war.[30] Aside from a call to stabilise international prices of commodities and demand for them through bilateral and multilateral arrangements, the Bandung participants also advocated export diversification through raw material processing as a way to reduce countries' economic vulnerability. Participants were also troubled by their lack of participation in the international institutions that had been established to govern world affairs. The Conference thus called on participants to consult with one another prior to international economic forums in order to further their mutual economic interest.[31] This fitted in with the broader theme of the Conference. As Kahin notes, a central motivation of most participants at Bandung, and certainly of its five sponsors, was to protest the failure of the Western states "to consult with them and to share with them sufficiently in decisions affecting the countries of Asia" and Africa, reflecting "their conviction that they have the right to take a greater and more active part in such matters."[32]

As noted above, interpretations of Bandung, for instance Mark Berger's, as an ideological force centred on Third Worldism and the search for authentic forms of state-mediated development help give Bandung its proper place in the story of the Cold War and international development.[33] It does, however, exaggerate the notion that Bandung *endorsed* state-directed approaches to national development. As the Bandung Communiqué reveals, Bandung participants endorsed the rights of governments to freely choose their own political and economic systems. The fact that many states may have opted for state planning or statist approaches to development should not be solely imputed to the Bandung Conference nor to the Bandung Spirit. Moreover, the Bandung Spirit, for those closely associated with that Conference, was "essentially a method of approach" for international diplomacy and the governance of world affairs.[34] In any case, the prevailing understanding of development at that time in policy and academic circles—modernisation theory—did recognise an implicit role for the state in creating the conditions for economic take-off.[35] Likewise, development economics during this period emphasised national planning, aided no doubt by Keynesian ideas on the role of the state in demand management.[36] Thus, Bandung was not the sole inspiration for statist approaches to national development, although Bandung and its successor, the Non-Aligned Movement, celebrated the independent territorial state as the primary medium to achieve freedom, development and modernisation for peoples.

Re-visioning International Society

While interpretations of Bandung such as Berger's are valuable in locating Bandung on the stage of world politics, especially with respect to North-South relations, they tend to miss other facets of Bandung's significance to the international society of states. In this context, James Mayall's suggestion that the "under-lying collective purpose [of Bandung] was to restructure international society" is instructive.[37] In fact, Mayall terms Bandung a "revisionist alliance."[38] This seems to be a rather surprising viewpoint, as Bandung's endorsement of the sovereign, independent state tends to reinforce the prevailing Westphalian international system. Mayall suggests that Bandung's revisionism was based on three objec-tives that Third World leaders at and beyond the 1955 Conference shared: (a) non-alignment in the Cold War; (b) the elimination of all forms of colonialism and racism; and (c) modernisation and economic development.[39]

While these Bandung goals affirmed the existing Westphalian state system, they were revisionist in that they identified alternative approaches to the manage-ment of world order beyond what had been the trend during the colonial period, and what was emerging in the bipolar world of superpower bloc politics. In particular, non-alignment, not to be confused with neutrality, offered a third way in international politics. Non-alignment's chief architect, Indian Prime Minister Jawaharlal Nehru, emphasised that non-alignment did not preclude cooperation or allying with a superpower, provided this was the result of a free choice and not the result of coercion.[40] While detractors point to the numerous breaches of the non-alignment principle in Third World foreign policy practices, the point to emphasise is its emergence as a new international norm that gave states the right to chart an autonomous, freely determined course in the international system without being compelled to follow the dictates of the superpowers and their respective blocs.[41] The United States was, however, initially hostile to the idea of non-alignment.[42]

There was also a preoccupation at Bandung that all states should be re-garded and treated as equal partners sharing in the management of world affairs. Indonesian President Sukarno claimed, in his opening speech at the Bandung Conference, "the affairs of all the world are our affairs."[43] In analysing the Bandung

Conference, Kahin predicted that the determination of participating delegates to "share more fully with the West in decisions affecting the interests of their countries" would endure.[44] Conference participants had also drawn attention to their under-representation on the UN Security Council and called for more equitable participation in bodies such as this.[45] The emphatic call for equitable representation and participation in international decision-making was a second way in which Bandung challenged prevailing approaches to world order. Prior to decolonisation, the question of equitable participation did not really arise. Decolonisation at one stroke increased the number of independent states in the system, with the prospect of more to come, thereby raising questions about how these new states would participate in world affairs.

Decolonisation also led to a qualitatively different system where there were now marked differences in political and economic development between states as well as differences in their cultural contexts. The marked differences in material wealth between the Western world and the newly independent states meant that a novel situation now emerged—one in which sharp inequalities were found in separate political jurisdictions (independent states) but within one international system.[46] This required thinking about questions of international justice, especially international economic justice. The Bandung Conference did not explicitly address issues of fairness and justice in substantive areas. These matters were, however, central to the debates on the NIEO, to be discussed in section 3. In fact, the early 1960s already saw growing acceptance of the social liberal principle that wealth inequality required juridically equal countries to be treated differently. It led to revisions in the General Agreement on Tariffs and Trade (GATT), which added a new chapter to address the special problems of developing countries. These problems included the principle of special and differential treatment for developing states. The Generalised System of Preferences (GSP) adopted by the industrial states from the 1960s directly accorded preferential trade treatment to developing countries on a bilateral basis.[47]

Although the Bandung Conference did not directly address justice and fairness in *substantive* economic matters, Bandung's emphasis on equitable participation and representation in international decision-making implies a concern with matters of *procedural* justice, which is perhaps prior and fundamental to achieving fairness in substantive areas.[48] Equitable representation in the international institutions that govern the world economy, for instance, could provide the developing states with a platform from which to articulate their views, justify their position on substantive matters, and find ways collectively to adjudicate between conflicting claims. With substantive justice claims—distributive justice, for instance—dependent on cultural perspectives, national and regional histories, and economic, political and social circumstances, fair process and genuine dialogue or consultation can facilitate decision-making when parties hold different moral claims.[49] It appears, therefore, that the seeds of international justice concerns, especially the more fundamental procedural justice, were planted at Bandung.[50]

Aside from calling for more voice in international decision-making, the articulation of a set of principles to guide international diplomacy was another instance of Bandung attempting a re-visioning of a now qualitatively different international society. By emphasising diplomacy, and especially the diplomacy of dialogue and accommodation, collective and peaceful problem-solving and rejection of power politics and the use of force, these principles, which some of those involved with the Conference have termed the Bandung Spirit, were offered to the international community as principles of engagement that would contribute to peace and cooperation in a highly diverse world.[51] These principles represented a rejection of the coercion and dominance that had characterised the colonial/imperial mode of interaction between the West and Asia-Africa, and that appeared to be the dominant mode of international relations in the unfolding Cold War.[52] Despite the colonial experience, non-confrontation even with regard to the colonial powers was emphasised, as seen on a number of occasions at the Conference. The decision by the economic committee to avoid issues that were politically sensitive to the Western powers has been discussed above. In another instance, Nehru warned Bandung participants to avoid using "agitational language" in drafting their position on the issue of continued colonialism in French North Africa.[53]

These principles of inter-state engagement were also an acknowledgement that the newly independent states were militarily and economically weak, and that they were therefore unable to use power as a tool of statecraft.[54] By offering these methods of inter-state engagement as a preferable alternative to power politics and wielding "the big stick,"[55] Bandung participants were not only attempting to create a more hospitable international arena for themselves, they were also, in effect, attempting to enhance their ability to meaningfully participate in world affairs. International relations based on dialogue and diplomacy would offer far greater chances for post-colonial states to engage in world affairs than a world based on confrontation, power politics and the use of force. If these principles were to guide dialogue and negotiation processes, the chances for fair process or procedural justice also become enhanced. Theorists working in the English School tradition of international relations point to the importance of dialogue between different states and communities from which basic agreement about order and justice might emerge, and through which process consensual moral principles on international justice could be devised.[56] Amartya Sen similarly endorses the importance of public debate in reaching reasoned consensus in diverse societies, pointing out also that the dialogic tradition of reasoning, debate and argument has a very long history in Asia and Africa pre-dating colonialism, and was a common means by which communities in these settings governed social life.[57]

How much of an impact did these developments at the 1955 Bandung Conference have specifically on North-South relations, and more broadly on the international political economy? The next section addresses this question with respect to Third World demands for a New International Economic Order. Following this, section 4 looks more closely at the issue of international economic justice from the perspective of contemporary global governance.

From Bandung to the NIEO: North-South Conflict or North-South Dialogue?

The history and dynamics of the NIEO have been much studied, and this chapter will try and avoid covering familiar ground.[58] It will, instead, focus on a number of issues salient to the theme of this chapter, namely, the continuities and discontinuities between the Bandung Conference and the NIEO movement as they impinge on re-visioning international society. To be sure, a fundamental difference is that the call for an NIEO was issued by the Non-Aligned Movement (NAM), formally at its 1971 Summit in Algiers but informally from 1964 as a set of demands to reform governance of the world economy.[59] More precisely, negotiations on the NIEO were the purview of the G-77, the largest Third World coalition in the United Nations; it had been established in June 1964 following the first session of the United Nations Conference on Trade and Development (UNCTAD).[60] Although the NAM was itself an offshoot of the 1955 Bandung Conference, the latter was confined to participants from the African-Asian region while the NAM involved Latin American states as well. These latter states, which had gained independence far earlier than the African and Asian colonies, had long been active in the UN on matters pertaining to reforming the international economic system.

More important than the question of membership is the point that the NAM has played a major role in embedding the notion of an international development agenda as a shared international problem that requires collective solutions by the international society of states.[61] It was also at the 1961 NAM Summit and the subsequent economic conference in Cairo in 1962 where it was first proposed that the more dangerous division in the world was the North-South divide between the haves and the have-nots rather than the East-West divide that major Western powers were so preoccupied with.[62] Bandung, too, had devoted a great deal of attention to the East-West divide. Although the Bandung Conference had planted the seeds for the notion of equitable participation and representation in international decision-making and agenda-setting, its participants had not adequately conceptualised *moral* justifications with regard to development as an *international* responsibility. To be sure, the idea of international rights and duties to states had already been articulated at the UN during the 1940s and was the basis of the United Nations Relief and Rehabilitation Administration, which distributed assistance from other states to Europe for the latter's reconstruction.[63] After that, Cold War considerations became more important than the "rights and duties" of states in the provision of development assistance.

Moral claims for international assistance were not formally articulated at Bandung, however. In their communiqué, Bandung participants had simply called for continued Western assistance for development as well as endorsed multilateral approaches to development by calling for the early establishment of the Special UN Fund for Economic Development and the International Finance Corporation as well as the allocation of more resources by the World Bank for Asian and African countries. As already noted, Bandung avoided controversial economic matters, while its primary focus had been on searching for ways to ensure peaceful coexistence in a world characterised by an East-West divide. The economic situation had yet to become pressing in 1955, and optimism prevailed, as pointed out above. However, a number of Bandung's leading lights did not even endorse the idea of an international economic conference of non-aligned countries in the early 1960s, even when the economic situation in many newly independent states had become pressing.[64] It was President Tito of Yugoslavia who provided leadership on this issue during the early 1960s.

Between Belgrade and Cairo: International Development as an International Obligation

By the late 1950s, the economic situation facing many newly independent states had become dire, and the earlier optimism gave way to deep pessimism. The average per capita income of the 112 countries listed as underdeveloped by the UN rose by only 1 per cent from US$90 in 1950 to US$100 in 1959. The end of the economic boom caused by the Korean War revealed the marked volatility of primary product prices. The 20 per cent fall in raw material export prices coupled with a 6 per cent rise in industrial product import prices led to an annual loss of about US$1.6 billion annually to underdeveloped countries.

Moreover, 80 per cent of developing country exports were concentrated in only five products, while three-quarters of their trade was with the industrial world. This structural feature promised to become a serious liability with the decision in Western Europe to form the European Common Market (ECM) and in Eastern Europe to form the Council for Mutual Economic Assistance (COMECON), raising fears of closed regional blocs. In fact, the first three years of the ECM saw the non-aligned countries losing US$1.26 billion in export earnings per annum, which was double the financial aid from the ECM countries to developing states.[65]

President Tito of Yugoslavia publicised these issues at the first NAM Summit in Belgrade in 1961. While criticising the formation of the ECM and COMECON, he emphasised that the response from the non-aligned states should not be a quid-pro-quo regional grouping that would be a "new closed market." This was a realistic position given the dominance of the industrial world in trade relations with developing countries. Instead, Tito suggested convening a world conference at the United Nations to debate these pressing economic matters. Jansen suggests that the idea of a world conference was the primary achievement of the Belgrade NAM Summit, and the starting point of further international dialogues on development issues.[66] Tito also lobbied for an economic conference of NAM countries to be held soon after the Belgrade Summit in order to discuss issues pertaining to economic development.

Tito's economic conference, held in Cairo in July 1962—a year after the Belgrade summit—was largely an Asian-African affair, with only three Latin American states attending and Yugoslavia the sole European participant. Moreover, only nine ministers were in attendance out of the 39 countries represented, a marked contrast to the 1955 Bandung Conference, where leaders and/or foreign ministers of 29 countries had been in attendance. Nevertheless, the 1962 Cairo Conference on the Problems of Economic Development involved a fairly substantial economic agenda. Five areas were emphasised.[67] First, there was a call for industrial countries to put aside 1 per cent of their national income or savings from disarmament for international development.[68] Moreover, preference was expressed for assistance to be disbursed through the UN rather than bilaterally. Interestingly, Cairo participants acknowledged that developing states must also contribute to their own development, but with help from the industrial states. In this regard, the second agenda item proposed at the Cairo Conference reiterated the original Bandung proposal that developing countries focus on primary processing activities and labour-intensive consumer product manufacturing. At Cairo, however, industrial countries were also explicitly called on to leave these areas of activity to the developing countries whilst they moved up the manufacturing ladder into capital goods and other complex manufactures that required resources developing states did not possess. It is difficult to fault this proposal, based as it was on the neoclassical economic principle of comparative advantage. Third, participants emphatically rejected the idea of forming a third economic bloc. Fourth, the ever-present issue of commodity price stabilisation was discussed, including proposals for commodity stabilisation schemes. Finally, the Cairo Conference reiterated Tito's earlier call for the convening of an international conference on trade and development, which dovetailed well with American President John F. Kennedy's idea of the UN Development Decade proposed a year earlier.

Although it reiterated a number of ideas raised at Bandung, the Cairo Declaration was more substantive than the economic component of Bandung's Final Communiqué. Yet, like Bandung, it displayed moderation in terms of its demands. It also attempted to fairly apportion duties amongst all states. Jansen suggests that participants' recognition of the futility of heroic politics and grandstanding, coupled with the reasonableness of their demands, led to greater receptiveness on the part of the industrial world to their agenda, particularly on the need for a UN body to oversee development.[69] The contribution of both the Belgrade NAM Summit and the Cairo Conference must be recognised in UNCTAD's establishment in 1964.

The establishment of a UN agency to address Third World development issues was, in some respects, a significant departure from prevailing "Cold War" thinking that emphasised bilateral assistance, which was often directly or implicitly linked to anti-communist strategies. For instance, the US Marshall Plan of 1948–51 aimed at post-war European reconstruction was motivated by concern within US policy circles that continued economic distress in Europe following World War II could provide a thriving breeding ground for communism. Bilateral development assistance to other countries during the 1950s was likewise linked to political and commercial interests of the donor country. Kennedy's revival of US leadership on development finance in the UN similarly reflected a strong anti-communist commitment.[70] The establishment of the multilateral UNCTAD to address development issues was, therefore, a departure from the prevailing bilateral and anti-communist framework for development assistance, an event rendered even more significant by the potential for the numerically dominant developing world to dominate UNCTAD. At the inaugural UNCTAD session in Geneva in 1964, the G-77 was formally launched. More than a decade later, UNCTAD would become increasingly marginal to global economic governance as industrial powers, notably the United States, rejected any role for the body in trade negotiations.[71]

The NIEO: Radicalism versus Reformism

Where Bandung 1955 had not explicitly articulated *moral* justifications with respect to the international obligation of states to economically assist the developing states, Cairo 1962 tentatively asserted this principle, while Geneva 1964 embraced it wholeheartedly. Furthermore, Latin American economist Raul Prebisch's dependency ideas formed the theoretical basis for the package of demands Third World countries issued at the 1964 UNCTAD Conference in Geneva. Prebisch had by this time been appointed UNCTAD's first Secretary General. These demands included proposals for improved market access to the industrial countries, greater self-reliance amongst the South and, more controversially, the right to nationalise assets and a call to democratise *all* binding international decision-making based on the principle of "one-nation, one-vote." This last proposal had been advanced at the Second NAM Summit in Cairo in 1964.[72] The package of demands was, unsurprisingly, rejected by the industrial states.[73] These proposals also reflected Prebisch's diagnosis of Third World underdevelopment in terms of its structural dependency on a capitalist core that controlled all levers of international decision-making and profitable economic activity, thereby appropriating much of the gains from international economic activity.

Rejection of the UNCTAD proposals, coupled with a growing frustration with the sharply declining economic conditions in many parts of the developing world, led to the emergence of a more sustained radical critique of the international economic system in many of these countries.[74] For a new generation of Asian and African radical nationalists, Latin American-inspired dependency ideas proved appealing. The dependency discourse was further strengthened by the presence in various UN bodies of intellectuals who subscribed to these radical ideas.[75] While the radical critique of the international system helped secure unity within the Third World coalition, radical remedies—de-linking from the capitalist world economy—did not find favour in many developing states. Instead, the preference was for reformist rather than revolutionary remedies that revealed an eclectic mix of theoretical economic perspectives.

In fact, the underlying basis of the reformists' remedies was a social liberal philosophy that sought to treat international society as a domestic social welfare state writ large. At the domestic level, welfare principles endorse income redistribution through taxation and welfare entitlements. The international counterpart to these policies was readily evident in the reformist proposals—resource transfers (aid), preferential trade and pricing arrangements, and technology transfer as a right.[76] Many Western scholars and policy analysts also endorsed the reformist agenda. A few, notably the American economist Fred Bergsten, went so far as to acknowledge that the Third World's assertive actions in the mid-1970s on a number of economic issues, including the formation of the OPEC cartel and the price hike, were "fully understandable and at least partially just."[77]

For Bergsten, Third World demands were not unreasonable, because terms of trade for primary products, including oil, had declined markedly for producers during the 1950s–60s, while Western states had been slow to negotiate the commodity agreements developing states had long requested. In fact, industrial states had often manipulated commodity trade, including through stockpiling policy.[78] Industrial countries had high levels of protection in place against exports from developing countries, especially primary processed goods and simple manufactures. Most important, Third World states had been left out of much of the discussions on the international economic rules and institutions that had taken place during the early 1970s, especially on monetary and exchange rate matters following the unilateral US decision to abandon the post-war fixed exchange rate system. For Bergsten, the United States' opposition to Third World demands and its refusal to negotiate on these pressing matters had contributed significantly to the "radicalisation of Third World policies."[79] To him, the correct response was a revised US strategy based on dialogue and genuine interdependence rather than dominance,[80] incidentally principles that had also been articulated at the 1955 Bandung Conference.

The Brandt Commission Report, which was commissioned by World Bank Director Robert McNamara and placed under the chairmanship of retired West German Chancellor Willy Brandt, likewise acknowledged Third World demands as reformist rather than revolutionary. The report, therefore, advocated negotiation and compromise with the Third World, as did the American Council on Foreign Relations. There was much recognition amongst certain quarters in the industrial world that Third World concerns were justified even if the statist logic of the proposals was not altogether appealing.[81] In fact, the Third World reformist movement depended on such allies to provide the intellectual and political support for its negotiations with the industrial countries.[82] Importantly, these allies acknowledged the fairness of Third World demands, especially for their inclusion in international decision-making.[83]

The OPEC oil price hikes in 1971 and 1973, which shocked the industrial world, also altered the balance of power in favour of the South, albeit temporarily, and led to a greater willingness on the part of the industrial countries to negotiate on the NIEO demands.[84] Mayall, however, points out that following the 1973 price hike, the Third World coalition miscalculated its relative bargaining strength and presented its NIEO proposals as a set of categorical or unconditional demands. The industrial world responded negatively to such a strategy, which prompted the coalition to abandon its confrontational stance. A return to a "dialogue" approach saw some progress being made as negotiations on the NIEO resumed.[85]

The Moral Claim for International Justice: Rights and Obligations but not Restitution

There was clearly much sympathy for the Third World predicament and its reformist agenda, although powerful critics warned against any negotiations with or concessions to the developing world.[86] The NIEO package broadly reflected social liberal principles and was an attempt to institute an international Keynesianism that went farther than the embedded liberalism of the post-war GATT and Bretton Woods economic order. The post-war embedded liberal order endorsed a range of departures from external liberalisation to maintain domestic employment and social stability. Thus, an essentially liberal international economic order accommodated Keynesian economic principles and practices at the domestic level.

The NIEO package was qualitatively distinct from the status quo in that it sought to emplace Keynesian inspired principles of demand management and economic regulation as well as social liberal inspired welfarist principles *at the international level.* Although this went against the liberal economic principles at the heart of the post-war economic regimes, the industrial countries during the mid-1970s acknowledged the essential fairness underlying the NIEO demands even if they would not agree to adopt all the proposals in the package.[87] The adoption of the 1975 Charter of Economic Rights and Duties of States at the United Nations General Assembly reflected, at least at that point in time, a successful addition to the prevailing principles of international society to include the "rights and duties of all states to aid the economic development of other states along the path chosen by its government."[88] To be sure, the notion of international obligation could be based on underlying justice claims or on benevolence and charity.[89] The writings and pronouncements of sympathetic Western academics and officials, however, pointed to justice as the fundamental ethic behind the charter.

Although the ethic of "rights and duties" had prevailed during the 1940s, as already noted, it had become less salient since then given that emerging Cold War interests had intruded into issues of international aid for the developing states. The "rights and duties" principle was tentatively revived in the 1960s. The 1975 charter meant a further assertion of this principle in international society. Unfortunately, the accommodative climate that permitted the adoption of such a reformist charter was undermined by a revival amongst elements in the G-77 of the moral claim of "restitution," which was based on the notion that the North owed something to the South as compensation for colonialism.[90] The principle of restitution had long been held by radical African governments, such as Ghana and Guinea, during the 1960s, and its inclusion as part of the NIEO package by radical elements in the Third World coalition helped split the coalition into two camps by 1970 and contributed to its decline. The coalition was only revived following the OPEC price hikes in 1971 and 1973.[91]

The mid-1970s revival of the restitution principle by some quarters in the Third World coalition as the basis for reforming the post-war economic institutions hardened Western opinion once more against the NIEO. The American economist Martin Bronfenbrenner was scathing in his criticism of the restitution argument that UNCTAD had used to justify the NIEO demand for the GSP system.[92] While Bronfenbrenner was prepared to support specific concessionary policies such as the GSP on the grounds that the industrial world's long history of protectionism had prevented developing states from utilising their comparative advantage to develop, he was nonetheless adamant that the broader NIEO programme for greater influence in international economic decision-making, what he termed a "conspiracy or lunacy," should be resisted.[93] He was especially scathing of the flawed political logic behind the restitution claim.

The Failure of the NIEO: What about International Justice Principles?

One of the reasons suggested for the failure of the NIEO was the depiction of its proposals as irrational and revolutionary, and the Third World as malign and self-serving in proposing them, a position that soon dominated over more sympathetic readings.[94] It was, therefore, not surprising that the NIEO collapsed in the end. Moreover, there were instrumental reasons for the growing inflexibility of the Western position, one being the growing constellation of interests coalescing against the NIEO proposals, especially from industries uneasy with developing country demands for easier access to Northern technology.[95] Aside from hardening Western opinion, internal splits within the coalition resurfaced during the late 1970s as the world headed for another recession. This, coupled with the 1980s debt crisis, provided the political space for the United States to undertake a major reform of the international economic system, but away from international Keynesianism and the search for international economic justice.

President Reagan's ideological belief in the superiority of the market mechanism and his quest to reform the international economic institutions meant that alternative paths to development based on different mixes of market and state were slowly discredited at the ideational or rhetorical level, even if state intervention in markets continued to remain an empirical reality in the industrial world and in the developmental states of Northeast Asia. The ideational ascendance of the neoliberal model of development—the so-called Washington Consensus—and the discrediting of Keynesianism shaped the programmes and advice of these institutions throughout the 1980s and well into the 1990s. In the face of these developments, the more sympathetic Western readings of the NIEO that advocated compromises and negotiations with the Third World became marginal despite these being the views of scholars and development practitioners with deep knowledge of the developing areas in question.[96]

The 1980s thus saw a shift away from collective efforts to relieve world poverty and underdevelopment towards a market-centred approach that saw development as resulting simply from liberalising markets and retrenching the state through privatisation and deregulation.[97] In the international economic institutions, the position of the United States was predominant, and unassailable, with the 1980s debt crisis allowing these institutions unprecedented access to developing countries to reform their economic governance institutions and practices in line with the new thinking. The North-South conflict was effectively over, at least for some time. The North-South *dialogue* was similarly put aside. Whether the failure to make progress on reducing the conflict between the developing and the industrial worlds was primarily due to the oftentimes inflexibility of the opposing camps remains unclear. Clearly, the distribution of power played a key part in how Western states responded to the NIEO and in determining its outcomes. However, it was also clear that some progress had been achieved, and usually when the negotiations had taken place in a conciliatory environment of give-and-take and genuine dialogue on both sides.

The North-South divide resurfaced in the late 1990s with the collapse of the 1999 WTO Ministerial Meeting at Seattle and the ongoing stalemate at the WTO despite five years of negotiations. The growing criticism of the Washington Consensus and neoliberal globalisation during the 1990s, which was heightened after the 1997–98 Asian financial crisis, led to a reconsideration of international justice principles. In particular, the thorny question of fairness and accountability in the international economic institutions and in international decision-making is once again a central issue in global governance. However, there is a difference. There is now a tension between competing notions of international justice, particularly between claims for inter-state justice, as was the case from Bandung to the NIEO, *and* justice claims that privilege not states but individuals as human beings deserving of human rights. The latter emerged in the post-Cold War 1990s as the principal approach to justice in international affairs.

Contemporary Global Governance and International Justice

Contemporary global economic governance is characterised by multiple networks of authority, ranging from intergovernmental bodies such as the World Trade Organization (WTO) to private networks such as the credit-rating agencies and transnational networks of non-governmental organisations (NGOs) and civil society groups as well as regional institutions. Debates about economic governance invariably raise questions with respect to fairness, accountability and distributive justice. The developing world in particular has had long and sometimes conflictual relations with the key multilateral institutions, particularly the International Monetary Fund (IMF) and the WTO, over these issues.

Both the IMF and the WTO have been criticised for, among other reasons, the following: (a) they have ill-judged privatisation and liberalisation programmes that often leave developing countries in a fragile state through exacerbating internal inequalities and worsening poverty; (b) they represent the interests of powerful industrial country groups; and (c) as a result, their programmes are politicised.[98] There is much literature on this subject, which will not be repeated here. Instead, the discussion focuses on a more specific issue related to the broad theme of the chapter—the extent to which justice concerns have become incorporated in the processes through which these institutions make decisions about and engage with the developing world. Do developing countries continue to experience exclusion from these key institutions of global economic governance, or have recent internal reforms improved their representativeness and accountability to the developing world? As John Toye notes, the institutional structures and processes of these organisations, especially how decisions are made and new rules adopted, will determine whether the outcomes of these organisations may be considered "just" to developing countries.[99]

The International Monetary Fund

Representation of the developing states in the International Monetary Fund remains inadequate. The executive board, which is responsible for the day-to-day operations and the major work of the Fund, does not sufficiently represent all its members, especially those countries that are the most affected by the Fund's decision-making and programme design, namely, the recipients of its loans. While the largest members are directly represented by their respective executive directors, other countries are grouped within constituencies and represented by just one director for each grouping. Thus, the United States has the largest voting share at 17.11 per cent, followed by the second largest voting bloc of 6.14 per cent for Japan. Thirteen Arab states are collectively accorded 2.95 per cent of voting shares, while 23 African states hold just 1.16 per cent.[100] China holds 2.94 per cent. Despite the presence of formal voting shares, executive board decisions are usually taken by consensus. Voting power does matter, but in a "behind-the-scenes" fashion.[101] It is usually taken into consideration in determining the extent of agreement reached, which is calculated based on the formal voting share of those taking part in these informal discussions. In addition, IMF staff and management, mindful that board approval will be needed, tend to keep voting shares in mind when designing loan agreements and policies.

This problem of representation is compounded by the fact that much of the IMF's decision-making takes place through informal processes of consultation in which developing states lack influence, a problem that is also evident in the WTO.[102] Many decisions, for instance on loan approvals, are often reached outside of these formal board meetings.[103] For many of these decisions, US approval is a necessity. In fact, without US approval, matters often do not even get placed on the table for discussion by the executive board.[104] The United States also holds an effective veto in the IMF, as other countries rarely act collectively to challenge the United States.[105] Moreover, it is often assumed that the voting structure is fair because it correlates with the capital contributions of the shareholders, which constitute the core asset base of the IMF, with the United States contributing 17.67 per cent (while its voting share is 17.11 per cent). This is misleading, however, for two reasons. First, all creditors to the IMF have been remunerated since 1968, and second, the actual expenses in running the institution come from income that the IMF earns from the charges it levies on borrowers, which are mainly the developing states.[106] These charges have, moreover, increased since the 1970s. Thus, the voting structure of the IMF does not adequately reflect the burden borne by the developing states in financing the institution.

Contrary to claims by the IMF that its decision-making is apolitical, the US government has intervened in the allocation and design of loan agreements. During the Cold War, IMF and World Bank lending was directed towards the key allies of the Western world.[107] In 1987 and 1991, Washington overruled the tough conditionalities in the IMF agreements with Egypt that had been agreed to by IMF staff and the Egyptian authorities following their Article IV Consultations. Nevertheless, Egyptian representation to the US government led to more lenient agreements being adopted following US pressure on the executive board.

In this instance, US power worked to Egypt's advantage.[108] In other instances, the United States insisted on harsher conditionalities, especially following the end of the Cold War, when it had to worry less about strategic alliances.[109] During the Asian financial crisis, the IMF worked closely with the US Treasury to develop strict reform policies that would be part of IMF emergency lending to the East Asian states.[110] These policies have been roundly criticised for going beyond what is needed to regain access to capital markets.[111] The point to note is that the combination of voting shares in the IMF and its preponderant power in the international system has given the United States unprecedented influence in the IMF and over its dealings with member states, although it is not the only major power that has exercised such leverage.[112]

The problems at the IMF with inadequate representation and accountability have been compounded by the considerable expansion in its remit or agenda. Since the debt crisis and the end of the Cold War, the IMF, as well as the World Bank, have embraced areas of policy that extend into virtually all areas of public policy-making, including judicial reform, corporate governance, labour policy, education, and health and social welfare, to name a few. In many instances, health care and education policy have ended up being decided on the narrow criteria of efficiency and cost effectiveness rather than the broader criteria required to evaluate any social sector programme.[113]

To be sure, both the IMF and the World Bank have undertaken reforms to enhance their accountability and transparency.[114] One of their more significant moves has been to open dialogue with civil society groups. Although NGOs have not been accorded a formal participatory role in IMF decision-making, they have exercised significant power and influence, particularly the Northern NGOs. In some instances, these NGOs seem even more influential than the developing country governments, whose formal participation is undermined by the problems of representation identified above.[115] Certainly, engagement with civil society is a good thing. As Woods points out, however, these innovative attempts at reaching out to a broader cast of stakeholders should not deflect attention from the "core lack of accountability to developing country governments."[116]

The World Trade Organization

The WTO's establishment in 1995 was hailed as a positive development for developing states as it would provide a consistent rules-based environment for trade liberalisation, particularly through an enhanced dispute settlement mechanism. Moreover, the continuation of the "one-country one-vote" system from the GATT also suggested developing countries could not be marginalised in this new institution. Finally, the Uruguay Round negotiations (1986–93) had succeeded in bringing agriculture and textiles/clothing under WTO trade disciplines, which represented yet another plus for developing countries, given the importance of these sectors to their development efforts. Their previous exclusion from GATT disciplines had worked to the great disadvantage of developing states.

The reality of the WTO for many developing states has, however, been very different. Industrial country protectionism has continued in sectors such as agriculture, primary product processing and labour-intensive manufactures, which developing states, with their large, especially rural, populations, could have easily specialised in on the basis of comparative advantage.[117] The trade regime as it stands locks poor states into low value-added activities or confines them to commodity production, impeding their development prospects.[118] Moreover, commodity markets such as in cotton and sugar have long been distorted by industrial country subsidies that keep prices artificially low, while tariff escalation, which means higher tariffs on processed commodities, reduces the incentive in commodity producing countries to shift into primary processing export activity. Likewise, simple labour-intensive activities with which most countries begin their industrialisation, notably textiles and clothing, have been long protected in the industrial world, with protection having ended only in 2005.

Power disparities explain much of the bias against developing states in the WTO. Although the WTO was expected to provide a consistent rules-based environment that would benefit developing states, critics claim that its institutional structures and negotiating processes have allowed these power disparities to influence negotiating outcomes.[119] For instance, the process of decision-making in the WTO relies not just on the formal mechanisms but also on informal processes both inside WTO meeting rooms (Green Room meetings) as well as outside, in "corridors, cafes and restaurants."[120] Developing states found themselves excluded from the Green Room consultations at the 1999 Seattle Ministerial.[121] Many developing country negotiators have admitted that they are often subject to pressure from the industrial states to take particular positions on negotiating issues.[122] These tendencies tend to undermine the "one-member one-vote" mechanism that was seen as an instrument that should theoretically have helped overcome power disparities in the international system.

To be fair, there have been many instances where developing states have themselves exercised their power to block, notably at the 2003 Cancun Ministerial Meeting. Furthermore, a mixed coalition of governments, NGOs and the media successfully challenged the pharmaceutical companies and altered intellectual property rules at the WTO to allow generic HIV/AIDS drugs to be produced in developing countries. However, the fact remains that the power to block is far less satisfactory than the ability to influence agendas and engage meaningfully in negotiating processes. Other observers of the WTO reject the idea that the WTO has delivered unfair outcomes for developing states, pointing out instead that the WTO provides avenues for these countries to challenge the unfair trade practices of other states. In 2004 Brazil successfully challenged the subsidies the US government paid to its cotton farmers. Small, poor West African states such as Burkina Faso, Benin and Mali, which are heavily dependent on cotton for the bulk of their export earnings and have been hit hard by the sharp fall in cotton prices as a result of US subsidies, will also gain from the ruling, provided the subsidies are dismantled.[123] In addition, legal assistance is now provided to countries through the WTO Secretariat, thereby assisting those governments lacking sufficient legal resources to assess and file legal challenges at the WTO. While there was little genuine consultation and dialogue amongst the diverse WTO membership between the 1999 Seattle Ministerial and the 2003 Cancun meeting, greater efforts have been made since then to consult more with developing states following the breakdown of the Cancun talks.

Toye, however, cautions against drawing overly optimistic conclusions from such trends. In reality, the WTO is a highly intrusive organisation that has the authority to compel changes in a wide range of domestic policies in support of open markets. While open markets are broadly a good thing, developing states aiming to "catch up" need a wider range of policy instruments than permitted by neoliberal frameworks. To be fair, the WTO has not gone completely down the neoliberal path, since many industrial policies—including subsidies, performance requirements and infant industry protection—are still available to developing countries, though for a limited period of time.[124] Robert Wade, nevertheless, warns of the potential for a "shrinking of the development space" available to developing states, an argument also put forward by Toye.[125] Toye argues that the presence of ambiguities in the different agreements that make up the WTO could result in a situation where legal challenges to the use of industrial policies could result in judicial interpretations that move the organisation closer towards the neoliberal position. In a world where states do not confront one another as economic equals and where agenda-setting and rule-writing in global organisations have been governed less by fair process and more by power distribution, "judicialisation [only] tightens the screws of unjust rules."[126]

Thus, an emerging consensus seems to be to limit the scope and agenda of these bodies. However, the more fundamental shift required is to get these organisations to recognise the presence of alternative models of development rather than the single, neoliberal model that has dominated international economic policy-making for much of the 1990s and that continues to influence global economic governance.[127] In fact, there are a range of market models that combine different mixes of state and market, distinct institutions and rules, and a variety of policy instruments, which emphasise a wider range of legitimate end goals than market efficiency and competitiveness and have successfully aided development in various parts of the world.[128] UNCTAD and its economists and development specialists who articulate alternative approaches to development, albeit still within the capitalist framework, have, unfortunately, been marginalised from the core of global economic governance. Following the failed Cancun WTO talks, the industrial countries stepped up their moves to limit UNCTAD to a capacity building and technical assistance role, and to curtail its renewed interest in providing independent analysis to developing countries on trade matters.[129] UNCTAD analysis had helped developing states put together a coherent argument rejecting the US and EU agenda at Cancun that would have further expanded the remit of the WTO into still more areas of domestic regulation and policy. It is not surprising, then, that the United States and the European Union were unhappy with the draft conference text prepared for the UNCTAD XI Conference in June 2005, which called for greater policy space to be given to developing states to design trade policies that would benefit development.[130]

Global Governance and Contrasting Notions of International Justice

International justice concerns did not simply disappear during the 1980s following the collapse of the NIEO project and the consolidation of the neoliberal globalisation project.[131] Instead, the neoliberal free trade project was based on an implicit utilitarian notion of justice that, irrespective of differences between countries, unrestricted trade would generate a higher level of aggregate welfare *for all parties.*[132] Moreover, the 1980s witnessed a shift in view amongst academic and policy circles that underdevelopment was caused by poor policy choices in the Third World and inefficient and/or corrupt governments rather than structural barriers in the international political economy. These new views helped undermine whatever consensus had been emerging on the validity of the Third World's international justice concerns, especially its moral claims for collective approaches to addressing underdevelopment and poverty and the obligation of rich states to help poor states. The indictment of the Third World state reinforced neoliberal prescriptions to retrench the state, which unfortunately contributed to situations where hollowing out of the state has taken place.[133] Such stark policy positions have been replaced since the late 1990s by approaches that recognise that the state has a crucial role to play, but often, this role tends to be seen in terms of a purely regulatory function to embed market governance in the economy and society.[134]

Alongside this shift in attitude towards the state has been renewed attention to standards of good governance by which states are now judged. Under its Millennium Challenge Account, announced in 2002 to provide increased development assistance to poor states, the US government is explicit that assistance will be available only to countries that demonstrate, *inter alia*, a commitment to good governance defined as rooting out corruption, upholding human rights, and adhering to the rule of law.[135] That such conditionalities may be appropriate and necessary is not the issue here. The point to note is that the move towards conditionalities for development aid, a practice that took off during the structural adjustment programmes of the 1980s, reflects an embrace of notions of justice rooted in *reciprocity*. Previously, moral claims for development assistance during the 1950s–70s had not required states to act in certain ways in order to qualify for development assistance or to be treated fairly (justice as impartiality) in international economic decision-making.[136] Although international development and poverty reduction as international obligations are back on the world's agenda, reflected especially in the adoption of the UN Millennium Development Goals in September 2000,[137] the norm of reciprocity is now embedded in the contemporary thinking and practice of development. In contrast, international justice claims raised by bodies such as the NAM and the G-77 in the past had emphasised impartiality rather than reciprocity.

The 1990s also saw attention shifting towards cosmopolitan notions of justice that emphasise justice and human rights for individuals rather than notions of inter-state justice.[138] In fact, a range of actors aside from states is now articulating justice claims. As already noted, international organisations increasingly open to pressure from NGOs are articulating justice claims on behalf of disadvantaged groups, while marginalised groups and individuals are themselves pressing these issues on international (global and regional) agendas. It appears that international justice considerations are increasingly reflected in the new global norms that are now being created or strengthened, for instance, good governance, fairness and accountability in multilateral institutions, and participatory governance involving civil society. Whether these norms are mutually reinforcing or whether their advocates are pushing along parallel tracks remains unclear.[139] What is clear, however, is that cosmopolitan justice claims often conflict with claims of inter-state justice coming from states (or their governments) that perceive themselves to be disadvantaged and/or unfairly treated in international forums and in the world economy.

Conclusion: The Importance of Deliberation in International Society

This chapter builds on James Mayall's reading of the Bandung movement as a revisionist alliance. Beyond the non-alignment principle, the chapter suggests that the 1955 Bandung Conference sowed the seeds for re-visioning international society in two other ways. The Conference's call for equitable representation in international decision-making for the new members of the now expanding international society of states was essentially a call to take seriously the issue of international justice, particularly that of procedural justice in the management of world affairs. The Conference did not, however, deal explicitly with the more substantive issues of international economic justice, although it endorsed the principle of international development assistance by rich states. Successor groups such as the NAM and the G-77 were more explicit in articulating the moral justification for international economic assistance. Bandung participants also articulated an alternative set of principles for inter-state engagement that emphasised dialogue and accommodation, collective and peaceful problem-solving, and the search for consensus or compromise that they saw as more suited to the expanding and increasingly plural international society of states, therefore rejecting power politics and coercion as the basis for international relations. These diplomatic principles were identified as the Bandung Spirit by those closely associated with the 1955 Conference. These alternative principles for international society remain salient in the 21st century.

Procedural justice remains curtailed for developing states, particularly in the key institutions of global governance, while the moral claims that had underpinned calls for distributive justice during the 1960s and 1970s, especially under the rubric of the NIEO, have shifted from claims based on the "rights and duties of states" to norms of reciprocity whereby developing states have to demonstrate a certain standard of "good behaviour" in return for development assistance. This is not necessarily a bad thing, as it has drawn attention to problems internal to developing countries that have undermined prospects for development in some states and worsened human rights abuses in others. It is a problem to the extent that it draws attention away from the essential unfairness of some of the new global rules that have impeded the development process. Good governance principles, for instance, have often been conflated with neo-liberal economic policies that may not necessarily provide the best way forward for these countries.[140] On the other hand, the shift towards more cosmopolitan notions of justice emphasising individual human rights over the rights of states has been progressive on the whole, especially for minority groups and even entire populations that have been subject to rule by incompetent, corrupt or abusive governments. It does, however, bring to the fore tensions with the norms of sovereignty and non-intervention.

The emergence of a range of justice claims has, however, not been accompanied by the emergence of a genuine "world society based on a consensus of values."[141] Processes of global governance continue to reveal the exercise of power rather than fair process, which can mean that the understandings of justice held by certain groups are privileged over others.[142] English School theorists suggest that the way to reach a consensus on values is through dialogue, a position that echoes Jurgen Habermas's theory of communicative action. In the ideal communicative action situation, each participant should treat the others as equals, not as objects to be manipulated or coerced. In addition, each participant should be willing to accept that the outcome of the dialogue could be open-ended rather than expecting the other parties to change their preferences while keeping their own unchanged.[143] Deliberation or arguing, according to Thomas Risse, is a necessary though not sufficient step in negotiation processes, facilitating the development of common understandings about a situation or problem and a shared normative framework and in devising an optimal solution to that problem.[144]

These principles reflect the approach to inter-state engagement endorsed at Bandung. Unfortunately, much of international affairs involving North-South relations has demonstrated strategic rather than communicative action and the continuation of power politics, exemplified by the WTO stalemate since the Seattle debacle. Contemporary realities suggest that power disparities are likely to intrude into communicative or dialogue processes and hinder prospects for reaching consensus. Even in the absence of power politics, the diversity inherent in the world today means that there are many different conceptions of the good life, making it difficult in practice to reach consensus or even compromise. Yet, the NIEO episode also reveals that when dialogue rather than confrontation was adopted, some degree of accommodation that took account of the interests of both sides did emerge. It is in this regard that a revival of Bandung's emphasis on deliberative politics may have salience for global governance in the 21st century. To many detractors, unfortunately, dialogue is seen simply as a "talk-fest" that allows its participants to avoid making hard decisions. Moreover, continuing power disparities do undermine possibilities for genuine deliberation. There is, however, merit in endorsing approaches that emphasise the search for reasoned consensus and optimal solutions and compromises in a plural though fast integrating world. In this regard, the adoption by the 2005 Bandung Conference of a number of self-help and cooperative projects towards development and growth[145] can help enhance the economic and political standing of Asian and

African developing states in international society and, through that, pave the way for processes of genuine dialogue among equals.

However, there must not be an uncritical revival of the ideas and practices encountered at the 1955 Bandung Conference. Debate on politically sensitive issues should be embraced rather than avoided. Proper rules should be developed to guide the communicative process, to prevent dialogues from degenerating into hostile confrontations. In addition, inter-state approaches to justice must give way to broader notions of justice within a renewed Asian-African movement to emphasise individual human rights and the responsibilities of developing states towards their populations, including minorities. It is in such a plural context of complex notions of justice that the Bandung Spirit of diplomacy and accommodation, dialogue and consensus building, and the search for compromise need to be extended to non-state actors. In the end, the Conference's lasting legacy could well be its emphasis on deliberative politics.

Notes

1   The author thanks Alan Chong for his helpful and constructive comments on an earlier draft.

2   George McTurnan Kahin, *The Asian-African Conference, Bandung, Indonesia, April 1955* (Ithaca: Cornell University Press, 1956), pp. 10–1.

3   Mark T. Berger, *The Battle for Asia: From Decolonisation to Globalisation* (London and New York: Routledge, 2004), pp. 47–55. Other works include James Goodman, "Reforming the United Nations and Global Governance," paper presented to the *Conference on the Golden Jubilee of the 1955 Bandung Conference*, organised by the Asia-Pacific Research Network, Bandung, Indonesia, 14–16 April 2005, available at <www.aprnet.org/activities/2005/bandung_paper01.htm> [3 August 2005].

4   Berger, *The Battle for Asia*.

5   This is Krasner's observation. See Stephen Krasner, "Transforming International Relations: What the Third World Wants and Why," *International Studies Quarterly* 25, no. 2 (1981): 119–48.

6   James Mayall, *Nationalism and International Society* (Cambridge: Cambridge University Press, 1990), p. 126.

7   Ibid., p. 128.

8   Craig N. Murphy, *Global Institutions, Marginalisation and Development* (London and New York: Routledge, 2005).

9   Berger, *The Battle for Asia*, p. 52.

10   "International society," a concept from the English School of international relations theory, refers to the ensemble of states in the international anarchic system plus the norms, rules and institutions that these states adhere to or use to govern the

conduct of their relations with each other. See Hedley Bull, *The Anarchical Society: A Study of Order in World Politics* (London: Macmillan Press, 1977). Also see Iain McLean (ed.), *Oxford Concise Dictionary of Politics* (Oxford: Oxford University Press, 1996), pp. 248–9.

11   David Kimche, *The Afro-Asian Movement: Ideology and Foreign Policy of the Third World* (Jerusalem: Israel Universities Press, 1973), pp. 1–2.

12   Kahin, *The African-Asian Conference*.

13   Ibid., pp. 4–5.

14   Kimche, *The Afro-Asian Movement*, p. 13.

15   Ibid., p. 263.

16   Ibid., p. 268.

17   Final Communiqué of the Asian-African Conference, reproduced in Kahin, *The African-Asian Conference*, pp. 76–85.

18   The Conference Secretariat, *Meeting of Ministers in Preparation for the Second African-Asian Conference, Djakarta, 10–15 April 1964* (Djakarta: The Conference Secretariat, 1964), p. 9.

19   Kahin, *The African-Asian Conference*, pp. 10–1.

20   G.H. Jansen, *Afro-Asia and Non-Alignment* (London: Faber and Faber, 1966), p. 309.

21   Ibid.

22   See paragraph 1 in section A on economic cooperation, as found in the Final Communiqué.

23   Richard Higgott, *Political Development Theory* (London and Sydney: Croom Helm, 1983), p. 18.

24   Jansen, *Afro-Asia and Non-Alignment*, p. 308.

25   Kahin, *The Asian-African Conference*, p. 33.

26   See the chapter by Ang Cheng Guan in this volume.

27   Jansen, *Afro-Asia and Non-Alignment*, p. 309.

28   See the Final Communiqué, paragraph 1, section A.

29   See paragraphs 4, 5 and 6 in section A on economic cooperation, as found in the Final Communiqué.

30   Jansen, *Afro-Asia and Non-Alignment*, p. 209. Artificial price inflation has been attributed to the effect of raw material stockpiling. US stockpile policy developed in the early 1950s. See Fred Bergsten, "The Response to the Third World," *Foreign Policy*, no. 17 (Winter 1974–75): 3–34.

31   See paragraph 12 in Section A on economic cooperation, as found in the Final Communiqué.

32   Kahin, *The Asian-African Conference*, p. 4.

33   See Berger, *The Battle for Asia*.

34   Roeslan Abdulgani, *Bandung Spirit: Moving on the Tide of History* (Jakarta: Prapantja Publishers, 1964), p. 64. Roeslan Abdulgani was the elected Secretary General of the 1955 Bandung Conference and had been the Chairman of the Preparatory Secretariat in Indonesia, the host state.

35 Higgott, *Political Development Theory.*

36 Berger, *The Battle for Asia,* pp. 61–85.

37 Mayall, *Nationalism and International Society,* p. 126.

38 Ibid.

39 Ibid., pp. 126–7.

40 Nehru was one of the five sponsors of the Bandung Conference, and the principal exponent of non-alignment. For a discussion of the Nehruvian conception of non-alignment, and especially its distinction from neutralism, see Kanti Bajpai, "Indian Conceptions of Order and Justice: Nehruvian, Gandhian, Hindutva, and Neoliberal," in Rosemary Foot, John Lewis Gaddis and Andrew Hurrell (eds.), *Order and Justice in International Relations* (Oxford: Oxford University Press, 2003), pp. 236–61.

41 Part of the problem stems from critics equating non-alignment with neutrality. In any case, behaviour that contradicts that prescribed by a norm does not necessarily signal a breakdown in that norm or its absence. See Friedrich Kratochwil, *Rules, Norms and Decisions: On the Conditions and Practice of Legal Reasoning in International Relations and Domestic Affairs* (Cambridge: Cambridge University Press, 1991).

42 Mayall, *Nationalism and International Society,* p. 119.

43 Reproduced in Kahin, *The Asian-African Conference,* p. 47.

44 Ibid., p. 38.

45 Ibid., p. 33.

46 During the colonial era, inequalities were found within different imperial or colonial jurisdictions. See Chris Brown, *International Relations Theory: New Normative Approaches* (New York: Columbia University Press, 1992), p. 158.

47 Mayall, *Nationalism and International Society,* pp. 134–6.

48 On the distinction between the two forms of justice, and for a comprehensive discussion of international justice, see Andrew Hurrell, "Order and Justice in International Relations: What is at Stake?" Foot, Gaddis and Hurrell (eds.), *Order and Justice in International Relations,* pp. 24–48.

49 Ibid., pp. 44–5.

50 I am indebted to Alan Chong for pointing this out to me.

51 Abdulgani, *Bandung Spirit,* p. 64.

52 China's military skirmishes in disputed Indian territory, Indonesia's Confrontation with Malaysia, and other inter-state conflicts within the Asian-African alliance do not negate the value and utility of these principles as the basis for international relations.

53 Kahin, *The Asian-African Conference,* p. 18.

54 President Sukarno's opening speech at the 1955 Bandung Conference. Reproduced in Kahin, *The Asian-African Conference,* p. 45.

55 See Sukarno's speech, reproduced in Kahin, ibid.

56 Andrew Linklater, "Rationalism," in Scott Burchill and Andrew Linklater (eds.), *Theories of International Relations* (London: Macmillan Press, 1996), pp. 93–118.

57   In fact, public discussion has been a characteristic means of managing diversity in India since classical times, with clear rules laid down for the proper conduct of debates and disputation by the Buddhist Emperor Ashoka during the third century BC and by the Mughal Emperor Akbar in the 16th century. Amartya Sen, *The Argumentative Indian* (London: Allen Lane/Penguin Books, 2005).

58   For a comprehensive review of debates and different perspectives on the NIEO, see Robert Cox, "Ideologies and the New International Economic Order: Reflections on Some Recent Literature," *International Organisation* 33, no. 2 (Spring 1979): 257–302. See also Murphy, *Global Institutions, Marginalisation and Development*.

59   Goodman, "Reforming the United Nations and Global Governance."

60   On the Western side was Group B, the negotiating committee of Western industrial countries. See Mayall, *Nationalism and International Society*, p. 143.

61   Ibid., p. 147.

62   Jansen, *Afro-Asia and Non-Alignment*, p. 311.

63   Murphy, *Global Institutions, Marginalisation and Development*, p. 109.

64   Nehru was especially opposed to the idea. See Jansen, *Afro-Asia and Non-Alignment*, p. 313.

65   All statistics obtained from ibid., p. 310.

66   Ibid., p. 312.

67   These are discussed extensively in ibid., pp. 315–8.

68   This figure was later reduced to 0.7 per cent.

69   Jansen, *Afro-Asia and Non-Alignment*, p. 318.

70   John Toye and Richard Toye, "From Multilateralism to Modernisation: US Strategy on Trade, Finance and Development in the United Nations, 1945–63," in Louis Emmerji (ed.), *The History of Ideas: An Introduction to the United Nations Intellectual History Project*. Extracts viewed at <www.unhistory.org> [July 2005].

71   Ian Taylor, "The United Nations Conference on Trade and Development," *New Political Economy* 8, no. 3 (November 2003): 409–18.

72   Branislav Gosovic, *UNCTAD: Conflict and Compromise* (Leiden: A.W. Sifthoff, 1972).

73   Alfred George Moss and Harry N.M. Winton, *A New International Economic Order: Selected Documents, 1945–1975* (New York: UNIPUB, 1976), pp. 43–51.

74   Mayall, *Nationalism and International Society*, p. 129.

75   Ibid.

76   Ibid., p. 131.

77   Bergsten, "The Response to the Third World," p. 5.

78   Carlos F. Diaz-Alejandro, "North-South Relations: The Economic Component," *International Organisation* 29, no. 1 (Winter 1975): 213–41.

79   Bergsten, "The Response to the Third World," p. 6.

80   Ibid., p. 27. See also Diaz-Alejandro, "North-South Relations: The Economic Component," p. 213.

81 Murphy, *Global Institutions, Marginalisation and Development*, p. 115.

82 Mayall, *Nationalism and International Society*, p. 132.

83 Diaz-Alejandro, "North-South Relations: The Economic Component," p. 241.

84 Susan Sell, *Power and Ideas: North-South Politics of Intellectual Property and Antitrust* (New York: State University of New York Press, 1998).

85 Mayall, *Nationalism and International Society*, p. 132.

86 Murphy elaborates further on the powerful NIEO critics, especially from US academic and policy circles. See Murphy, *Global Institutions, Marginalisation and Development*.

87 Bergsten, "The Response to the Third World," outlines the NIEO package of demands.

88 Murphy, *Global Institutions, Marginalisation and Development*, p. 113.

89 Brown, *International Relations Theory*, p. 158.

90 Murphy, *Global Institutions, Marginalisation and Development*, p. 113.

91 Mayall, *Nationalism and International Society*, p. 128.

92 Martin Bronfenbrenner, "Predatory Poverty on the Offensive: The UNCTAD Record," *Economic Development and Cultural Change* 24, no. 4 (1976): 825–31.

93 Ibid., p. 831.

94 Murphy, *Global Institutions, Marginalisation and Development*, pp. 113–7.

95 Sell, *Power and Ideas*, p. 130.

96 Murphy, *Global Institutions, Marginalisation and Development*, pp. 115–6.

97 Brown, *International Relations Theory*, p. 183.

98 Ngaire Woods, "Order, Justice, the IMF and the World Bank," in Foot, Gaddis and Hurrell (eds.), *Order and Justice in International Relations* (Oxford: Oxford University Press, 2003), pp. 80–102.

99 Toye notes that there are different conceptions of justice, with the current free trade ideology justified on utilitarian notions of justice. John Toye, "Order and Justice in the International Trade System," in Foot, Gaddis and Hurrell (eds.), *Order and Justice in International Relations*, pp. 103–24.

100 Bessma Momani, "American Politicisation of the International Monetary Fund," *Review of International Political Economy* 11, no. 5 (December 2004): 880–904.

101 Ngaire Woods, "The IMF and the World Bank," in *Routledge Encyclopaedia of Politics* (London and New York: Routledge, 2002).

102 Woods, "Order, Justice, the IMF and the World Bank," p. 85.

103 IMF, *External Evaluation of IMF Surveillance*, Report by a Group of Independent Experts (Washington, D.C.: International Monetary Fund, 1999), p. 34.

104 Woods, "Order, Justice, the IMF and the World Bank," pp. 87–8.

105 Woods, "The IMF and the World Bank."

106 Ibid.

107 Ibid.

108 Momani, "American Politicisation of the International Monetary Fund," pp. 880–904.

[109]   Kimberley Elliot and Gary Hufbauer, "Ambivalent Multilateralism and the Emerging Backlash: The IMF and the WTO," in Stewart Patrick and Shephard Forman (eds.), *Multilateralism and US Foreign Policy: Ambivalent Engagement* (Boulder: Lynne Rienner, 2002), p. 383.

[110]   Joseph Stiglitz, *Globalisation and its Discontents* (London: Allen Lane, 2002), p. 100.

[111]   Martin Feldstein, "Refocusing the IMF," *Foreign Affairs* 77, no. 2 (March/April 1998): 20–33.

[112]   Currently, the 50-year-old compromise between the United States and the Europeans that an American national heads the World Bank while a European is appointed to head the IMF continues.

[113]   Woods, "The IMF and the World Bank," p. 89.

[114]   These are detailed in Woods, "Order, Justice, the IMF and the World Bank."

[115]   Ibid., p. 97.

[116]   Ibid., p. 98.

[117]   Ronald Mendoza and Chandrika Bahadur, "Toward Free and Fair Trade: A Global Public Goods Perspective," *Challenge* 45, no. 5 (2002): 21–62.

[118]   Oxfam, "Running into the Sand: Why Failure at the Cancun Trade Talks Threatens the World's Poorest People," *Oxfam Briefing Paper*, no. 53 (Oxford: Oxford Famine Relief, 2003).

[119]   Amrita Narlikar, "Developing Countries and the WTO," in Brian Hocking and Steven McGuire (eds.), *Trade Politics*, 2nd Edition (London and New York: Routledge, 2004), pp. 133–45.

[120]   Amrita Narlikar, "The Ministerial Process and Power Dynamics in the World Trade Organisation: Understanding Failure from Seattle to Cancun," *New Political Economy* 9, no. 3 (September 2004): 413–28.

[121]   Ibid., p. 421.

[122]   Ibid.

[123]   "Unpicking cotton subsidies," *The Economist*, 30 April 2004.

[124]   Ha Joon-Chang, *Globalisation, Economic Development and the Role of the State* (London and New York: Zed Books, 2003), pp. 325–8.

[125]   Robert Hunter Wade, "What Strategies are Viable for Developing Countries Today? The World Trade Organisation and the Shrinking of 'Development Space'," *Review of International Political Economy* 10, no. 4 (2003): 621–44. See also Toye, "Order and Justice in the International Trade System."

[126]   Wade, ibid., p. 123.

[127]   See the arguments in Dani Rodrik, "Development Strategies for the Next Century" (Cambridge: Kennedy School of Government, Harvard University, 2000), available at <http://ksghome.Harvard.edu/~drodrik>.

[128]   Ha, *Globalisation, Economic Development and the Role of the State*.

[129]   Alexandra Stricker, *Geneva Update 5th February 2004*, Institute for Agriculture and Trade Policy, Geneva, available at <www.investmentwatch.org/articles/gu5feb2004.html> [4 August 2004].

130   Ibid.

131   On the neoliberal globalisation project, see Philip McMichael, "Globalisation: Myths and Realities," *Rural Sociology* 61, no. 1 (1996): 25–55.

132   This, however, ignored other notions of justice—social liberal versions, for instance—that recognise that differences between countries call for differential treatment, as was the moral basis of international justice claims articulated during the 1960s and 1970s. Toye, "Order and Justice in the International Trade System," pp. 105–6.

133   Francis Fukuyama, *State Building: Governance and World Order in the 21st Century* (London: Profile Books, 2004), pp. 53–4.

134   On the role of the state in a globalising world, see Peter Evans, "The Eclipse of the State? Reflections in an Era of Globalisation," *World Politics* 50, no. 1 (1997): 62–87.

135   United States Agency for International Development, *Millennium Challenge Account Update*, Fact Sheet of 3 June 2002, available at <www.usaid.gov/press/releases/2002/fs_mca.html> [2 August 2005].

136   See Brian Barry, "Justice as Reciprocity," in Brian Barry (ed.), *Democracy, Power and Justice* (Oxford: Clarendon Press, 1989).

137   United Nations, *United Nations Millennium Declaration*, (55/2), a resolution of the 55th session of the UN General Assembly, available at <www.un.org/millennium/declaration/ares552e.htm> [2 August 2005].

138   Rosemary Foot, "Introduction," in Foot, Gaddis and Hurrell (eds.), *Order and Justice in International Relations*, pp. 1–23.

139   Ibid., p. 11.

140   Ian Taylor, "Hegemony, Neoliberal Good Governance and the International Monetary Fund: A Gramscian Perspective," in Morten Boas and Desmond McNeill (eds.), *Global Institutions and Development: Framing the World* (London and New York: Routledge, 2004), pp. 124–36.

141   Foot, "Introduction," p. 23.

142   Hurrell, "Order and Justice in International Relations: What is at Stake?" p. 48.

143   Marc Lynch, "Why Engage? China and the Logic of Communicative Action," *European Journal of International Relations* 8, no. 3 (June 2002): 187–230.

144   Thomas Risse, "Let's Argue: Communicative Action in World Politics," *International Organisation* 54, no. 1 (Winter 2000): 1–39.

145   See Ali Alatas, "Towards a New Strategic Partnership between Asia and Africa," *IDSS Commentaries*, no. 18/2005, 19 April 2005 (Singapore: Institute of Defence and Strategic Studies), available at <www.idss.edu.sg/publications/Perspective/IDSS182005.pdf>.

PART II

PART II

CHAPTER 5

From Bandung to Durban: Whither the Afro-Asian Coalition?

Adekeye Adebajo[1]

The year 2005 marked the 50th anniversary of the famous conference in Indonesia's West Java town of Bandung, where there was a diplomatic banquet at which Egypt's Gamal Abdel Nasser and India's Jawaharlal Nehru made common cause to help spur the creation of the Non-Aligned Movement (NAM) to challenge Western domination of the globe. This was the most symbolic event in the Afro-Asian "revolt against the West," which unleashed the greatest change in the international order during the 20th century, with the eventual decolonisation of two continents. South Africa's port city of Durban hosted a meeting of the NAM foreign ministers in August 2004. This was particularly appropriate since Durban hosts a large Asian community that has lived in South Africa for generations. Mahatma Mohandas Gandhi also lived in South Africa for 21 years, between 1893 and 1914, and honed his "non-violence" method of *satyagraha* (truth force) in the then racist enclave before returning to his native India to lead the independence struggle.[2]

The legacy of Bandung is the independence of Africa and Asia, which culminated in the end of apartheid by 1994. The decolonisation struggles were waged through the NAM, the United Nations, the Organisation of African Unity (OAU)—now the African Union (AU)—and the Arab League. The NAM can, in a sense, be regarded as a political strategy to ward off foreign intervention in Afro-Asia, while the UN was the legal instrument to protect the newly won sovereignty of these states. From the 1970s throughout the 1980s, Bandung's legacy moved from being purely political to being economic. Ghana's Kwame Nkrumah famously urged his fellow leaders to "Seek first the political kingdom and all other things would be added onto it." But Nkrumah's political kingdom

would eventually be replaced by Malaysian leader Mahathir Mohammed's economic kingdom, as battles over unequal terms of trade, redistribution of wealth,
exploitative multinational corporations, and neocolonial dependency took on
a special urgency. The Organization of the Petroleum Exporting Countries
challenged the international trading system in 1973, resulting in the tripling of
global oil prices as Southern states flexed their economic muscle. Many of these
battles were spearheaded by the NAM, but they were also waged through the
UN, as marked particularly by the struggles in the UN Conference on Trade
and Development.

As Gandhi and Nkrumah had been symbols of the Afro-Asian political
struggle, Mahathir Mohammed became a symbol of the South's economic decolonisation. Mahathir was a respected leader of the Association of Southeast
Asian Nations (ASEAN), the Organization of the Islamic Conference and the
NAM (hosting the 2003 summit). Malaysia recovered from its bitter divorce
with Singapore in 1965 and its own communal riots in 1969 to create a prosperous economy and a Malay economic class.[3] Mahathir has also been a leading
proponent of "Asian values," celebrating Asian identity and dignity as a counter
to Western cultural hegemony. He championed an East Asian economic bloc as
a "Caucus without the Caucasians" involving ASEAN, China, Japan and Korea,
but excluding the United States, Australia and New Zealand; he has been a fierce
and fearless critic of US policies in the Middle East; and as host, he gently chided
Britain's Queen Elizabeth II at a Commonwealth summit in Kuala Lumpur in
1989 for presiding over a body in which "the wealth was far from common."
During the Asian financial crisis between 1997 and 1998, Mahathir boldly and
uniquely rejected the International Monetary Fund's dictates, helping Malaysia
to avoid some of the worst effects of the crisis.[4]

By the 1990s, Mahathir's economic kingdom would be replaced by Thabo
Mbeki's security kingdom. South Africa became the leading peacemaker and
Nigeria the leading peacekeeper in a decade of troubles in which the spillover of
the Cold War's destructive support of autocratic regimes and fuelling of proxy
wars led to a new generation of conflicts in countries such as Somalia, Liberia,
Sierra Leone, Burundi and the Democratic Republic of the Congo (DRC).
African regional organisations such as the Economic Community of West African
States (ECOWAS) and the Southern African Development Community (SADC),
originally established to promote economic integration and development, were
forced to adapt new security roles. They sought—under the leadership of local
hegemons such as Nigeria and South Africa—to tackle these conflicts, before
the UN eventually took over many of these peacekeeping missions. In Asia, the
end of the Cold War also enabled the UN to deploy peacekeepers to Cambodia

and East Timor, and troops from ASEAN played a tentative and limited role in assisting these efforts. Asia thus has lessons to learn from African security cooperation efforts undertaken by ECOWAS and SADC, as well as the AU. ASEAN has, however, been much more successful than Africa at promoting economic integration and development, and Africa has lessons to learn from the "Asian tigers"—Singapore, Malaysia and South Korea—who have greatly stressed education and the promotion of "national economic champions" in their industrialisation strategies.

This chapter is divided into five main sections. We start by examining the "revolt against the West:" the decolonisation of Africa and Asia that the Bandung Conference of 1955 was seeking to complete. The second section explores the goals, methods and achievements of the Non-Aligned Movement from Bandung to Durban, while assessing the contributions of three of its leading figures: Nehru, Nasser and Nkrumah. The third section focuses on the UN: the most important stage for promoting the legacy of Bandung. Through the UN, the Afro-Asian coalition waged the decolonisation and anti-apartheid struggles; pursued the establishment of a "New International Economic Order" in the 1970s; and sought multilateral support for peacekeeping efforts in Africa and Asia in the 1990s. The section discusses the failed efforts to expand the UN Security Council from 15 to 25 members, including the proposal to create four permanent seats for Africa and Asia. This section also assesses the role of the four UN Secretaries-General produced by Africa and Asia: Burma's U Thant, Egypt's Boutros Boutros-Ghali, Ghana's Kofi Annan and South Korea's Ban Ki-moon. The fourth section of the chapter offers possible lessons for ASEAN from security cooperation in West and Southern Africa under the auspices of ECOWAS and SADC. We conclude the chapter by suggesting ways in which the Bandung coalition, which played such a critical role in the decolonisation struggle, can work together to promote Southern interests in the more contemporary struggles for fair trade, human security and debt cancellation.

The Afro-Asian Revolt against the West

The father of Pan-Africanism, William E. Du Bois, famously and correctly predicted in 1900: "The problem of the twentieth century is the problem of the colour line—the relation of the darker to the lighter races of men in Asia and Africa, in America and the islands of the sea."[5] By the end of the century, with the independence of apartheid South Africa in 1994, the decolonisation of Asia and Africa had been effectively completed. European imperialism had reached its apogee at the start of the 20th century. Between 1945 and the *annus mirabilis* of 1960, 40 African and Asian countries with populations of 800 million—more than a quarter of the global population at the time—had won their independence. In Asia, Japan had shattered the myth of white invincibility through military victories over British, French and Dutch armies during World War II.[6]

These struggles, however, had earlier antecedents. The first Pan-African Congress, held simultaneously with the Paris Peace Conference in 1919, called for the right of Africans to participate in their own governance. The Indian National Congress's struggles were spurred by Gandhi's return from Africa to the subcontinent in 1915. He organised the successful "civil disobedience" campaigns, which culminated in India's independence in 1947. Gandhi had correctly, and somewhat patronisingly, prophesied in 1924 that if Africans "caught the spirit of the Indian movement their progress must be rapid."[7] He had also opined in 1936 that it was "maybe through the Negroes that the unadulterated message of non-violence will be delivered to the world."[8] The Mahatma's beliefs were to inspire five black Africans and Americans who won the Nobel Peace Prize: Ralph Bunche (1950), Albert Luthuli (1960), Martin Luther King Jr. (1964), Desmond Tutu (1984) and Nelson Mandela (1993).[9]

Africa and Asia had changed the world from a Western-dominated one to a more truly international society. The Afro-Asians had humanised international diplomacy and given birth to the concept of "non-alignment" as a substitute to the destructive power politics that had lost Europe its global primacy and brought untold suffering to millions of people around the world during Europe's two civil wars between 1914 and 1945. A year before the Bandung Conference, Vietnamese freedom fighters had famously defeated France at Dien Bien Phu in 1954 (they would also later defeat the United States), helping to blunt the prejudiced arrogance of Western powers. The resistance of Algerian freedom fighters during France's savage colonial war from 1954 also brought down the French Fourth Republic and laid the foundation for Algerian independence in 1962.[10]

It must, however, be noted that the Afro-Asian bloc is not monolithic. Countries such as Singapore, South Korea and Malaysia are closer to joining the ranks of the international *Brahmins* of the rich world, while South Africa has some world-class manufacturers and multinational companies, though the majority of its population continue to live in stark poverty as a result of the inequities of apartheid. Many countries on both continents also belong to the group of international *dalits* whose impoverishment puts them in the ranks of international "untouchables." But Africa and Asia still have *enough* in common: both were colonised by European powers based on ideologies of racial supremacy; both have suffered civil wars, famines, military strongmen and autocrats; and both have struggled to evolve political and economic models based on the West but adapted to local circumstances.

The Non-Aligned Movement

The "Terrible Triplets"

The Bandung Conference, held in April 1955, expressed what Jawaharlal Nehru described as the "new dynamism" of Asia and Africa. Bandung sought to promote economic and cultural cooperation, to support the decolonisation of Africa and Asia, to promote world peace, and to end racial discrimination and domination. Ending the "politics of pigmentation," in which arrogant white statesmen set themselves up as overlords over "lesser peoples" who were considered to be unable to stand on their own feet in the difficult conditions of Western civilisation, was very much a driving force of this conference. Three titanic figures towered over the southern landscape in this "revolt against the West," and it is worth briefly assessing their legacy. India's Jawaharlal Nehru was the intellectual father of the concept of "non-alignment;" Egypt's Gamal Abdel Nasser was the leader of pan-Arabism, federating for a while with Syria; and Ghana's Kwame Nkrumah (who was prevented by the British colonial government from attending the Bandung Conference) was the leader of Pan-Africanism, creating for a while a union with Mali and Guinea.

India's founding premier, Nehru, genuinely identified with Africa. As he noted in 1963: "We think this awakening of Africa is of historic importance not only for Africa itself, but for the whole world."[11] Nehru pushed strongly for the NAM and the UN to support Africa's decolonisation efforts, and counselled African leaders against the dangers of one-party rule and military governments, though he remained firm friends with the autocratic Nasser. As Nkrumah was developing a personality cult in the 1960s, Nehru famously asked him: "What the hell do you mean by putting your head on a stamp?"[12] This was a rebuke that Ghana's *Osagyefo* (saviour) never forgave nor forgot. Nehru visited Nigeria, Sudan and Egypt in the early 1960s and sought to rally the Afro-Asian coalition at the UN to support the anti-apartheid struggle, to settle the Arab-Israeli dispute, and to establish an Indian Ocean zone of peace. He consistently warned Indian settlers in Africa that the interests of indigenous Africans must always be paramount.

Seven Africans have since won the Jawaharlal Nehru Award for International Understanding, established by the Indian government after the death of its "founding father:" Zambia's Kenneth Kaunda (1970), Tanzania's Julius Nyerere

(1973), South Africa's Nelson Mandela (1979), Senegal's Léopold Senghor (1982), Zimbabwe's Robert Mugabe (1989), Egypt's Hosni Mubarak (1995) and Kenya's Wangari Maathai (2005). Nehru's controversial military annexation of the former Portuguese colony of Goa in 1961 helped to legitimise the use of armed force to liberate colonial territories. During the Suez Crisis of 1956 (described below), Nehru helped to mobilise NAM support for Nasser, and the UN General Assembly rallied almost unanimously to condemn the Anglo-French action. On receiving the Nehru Award, Mandela paid the Indian aristocrat a fitting tribute from Robben Island in August 1980: "Truly, Jawaharlal Nehru was an outstanding man. A combination of many men into one—freedom fighter, politician, statesman, prison graduate, master of the English language, lawyer and historian. As one of the pioneers of the nonaligned movement, he has made a lasting contribution to world peace and the brotherhood of man."[13]

Egypt's Nasser staged Africa's first military coup d'état in 1952 and became the foremost champion of pan-Arabism, as well as a leading figure in the politics of the Third World. He strongly backed the Algerian independence struggle against France. Nasser, like Nkrumah, championed "positive neutrality:" he bought arms and received assistance from both East and West. In his *Philosophy of the Revolution*, Nasser saw Egypt as being at the centre of three circles involving the Arab world, the Muslim world and Africa. As Nasser noted: "we cannot in any way stand aside, even if we wish to, from the sanguinary and dreadful struggle now raging in the heart of the continent between five million whites and two hundred million Africans. We cannot do so for one principal and clear reason—we ourselves are in Africa."[14] Significantly, Egypt is described as being *in* rather than *of* Africa, and Nasser's patronising offer of "diffusing the light of civilization into the furthest parts of the virgin jungle"[15] went down badly with many black Africans. Some, such as Nigeria's nationalist leader Obafemi Awolowo, argued that though Egypt's body was in Africa, its heart and head were really in the Middle East. Nasser, though, stood at the intersection of the Non-Aligned Movement as the gatekeeper of North Africa as well as the political and cultural leader of the Arabian Peninsula, which is classified in NAM terms as being part of Asia.[16] Undoubtedly, the most significant historical event involving Nasser was the Suez Crisis of 1956, when the Egyptian leader—shortly after buying arms from the Soviet bloc—nationalised the Suez Canal in July 1956 in response to Washington, London and the World Bank reneging on an earlier promise to fund the building of the Aswan Dam in retaliation for Nasser's purchase of arms from the communist bloc. The British and French launched an invasion with Israel three months later, seeming to have forgotten that the Old European World of "gunboat diplomacy" had been replaced by the bipolar world of the nuclear age. Economic and political pressure by American President Dwight Eisenhower and his forceful secretary of state, John Foster Dulles, on their Western allies finally forced an end to the Anglo-French-Israeli takeover of the canal.[17] Nasser had scored a famous political victory and added perhaps the sharpest nail to the imperial coffin.

The third of our "terrible triplets," Kwame Nkrumah, noted shortly after his country's liberation in 1957: "The independence of Ghana is meaningless unless it is linked up with the total liberation of the African continent."[18] Nkrumah spent 12 years in the United States and Britain, where he established strong ties with other African liberation leaders and helped to organise the fifth Pan-African Congress in Manchester in 1945. He returned to Ghana to champion a brand of "populist nationalism" and used his great charisma and formidable organisational skills to win power as "Leader of Government Business" in 1951.[19] Nkrumah's "positive action" was clearly inspired by Gandhian methods of "passive resistance," which other African leaders such as Nyerere and Kaunda also adopted. After gaining independence for Ghana in 1957, Nkrumah sought to keep the torch of Pan-Africanism alive by promoting the independence of the entire continent, backing liberation movements with training and other support, and proposing the idea of an African High Command as a common army to ward off external intervention and help support the continent's liberation struggles. Nkrumah was, however, a visionary who was too far ahead of his time. His ideas were rejected by the majority of African leaders, who were too busy guarding their newly won independence and were not prepared to pool their sovereignty in a supranational continental body. Nkrumah was also a fierce champion of non-alignment. He sent Ghanaian troops to the UN mission in the Congo in 1960 in a bid to prevent the country becoming a Cold War theatre; and when China invaded Indian territory in 1962, Nkrumah criticised Britain's provision of arms to Nehru as threatening the principle of non-alignment.[20]

The Birth of the Global South

The Non-Aligned Movement was founded six years after Bandung—in Belgrade, Yugoslavia, in 1961, at a summit under the chairmanship of Marshall Tito. Tito, Nehru and Nasser are usually considered the "founding fathers" of the movement. A total of 25 Arab, Asian and African countries attended the Summit. A highlight of the Summit was the condemnation of "imperialism" in the Middle East and support for the Arabs in Palestine. The NAM held further summits in Cairo (1964) and Lusaka (1970), setting up a 25-member New York-based Coordinating Bureau at the UN to oversee the movement's affairs between summits. Preparatory meetings of NAM foreign ministers were held a year before summits, and Algiers (1973), Colombo (1976), Havana (1979), New Delhi (1983), Harare (1986) and Belgrade (1989) hosted further summits. The NAM, however, suffered from the problems of trying to maintain unity among such a large, diverse group. The Sino-Soviet split and the border war between China and India in 1962 shook the group's cohesion. Questions continued to be raised about the non-alignment of countries that hosted foreign military bases. Former Nigerian Foreign Minister Joe Garba offered a scathing critique of the 1976 NAM Summit in Colombo, which he attended:

> From the very beginning, speaker after speaker dwelt principally on divisive political issues. The usual rhetorical flourishes involving accusations and counter accusations as to which countries were progressive and which were merely neo-colonialist went on seemingly without end … of what relevance is the Non-Aligned Movement to solving the Third World's problems? My answer is none at all. The ideological diversity and the disparity of economic development of member countries has meant that arriving at a common position on crucial international issues has become almost impossible.[21]

Other NAM Summit highlights include the rejection of Cuba's unsuccessful bid to introduce a socialist, leftist tilt to the movement at the Havana summit in 1979, and an angry summit in Harare, Zimbabwe, in 1986 that revived many of the "radical" slogans of the past. China has been a NAM "observer" since 1992, preferring not to jeopardise key bilateral relations through membership in the group but using relations with Southern states to garner NAM support in fora such as the UN Human Rights Commission (now the Human Rights Council).[22]

With the end of the Cold War and the collapse of the Soviet Union, many analysts started questioning the NAM's *raison d'être*. Critics wondered whether the movement had not become a relic of the Cold War and asked what the organisation was aligned against in a unipolar US-dominated age. Like the North Atlantic Treaty Organization, the NAM had to define a new role for itself in a rapidly changing international order. By the time of its 13th summit in Kuala Lumpur, Malaysia, in 2003, the NAM's 116 members were focusing more on issues of peace, security, justice, democracy and development. The organisation was also pushing for strengthening and democratising the UN; for stronger regional organisations; for Palestinian liberation; and for strategies to reverse the marginalisation of developing economies as a result of globalisation. Where foreign *intervention* had been opposed in the past, external *neglect* now seemed to be the greater concern. The NAM adopted a more pragmatic and less confrontational attitude towards the West, as its summits in Jakarta (1992), Cartegena (1995) and Durban (1998) demonstrated. The United States is now invited as a guest to NAM summits.

The 50th anniversary of Bandung was held in the historic Indonesian town in April 2005. The Asian-African Subregional Organisations Conference also took place in Bandung, co-hosted by Indonesia and South Africa, in order to launch a "new strategic partnership" between both continents.

We next turn our attention to the most important forum in NAM's strategic political battles: the United Nations.

The United Nations

The Diplomacy of Liberation

Most, but not all, NAM members are part of the Group of 77 Developing Countries, set up in June 1964 in the context of the first UN Conference on Trade and Development. The G-77 continues to dominate the UN General Assembly's agenda. Asian and Arab states opposed the partition of Palestine at the UN General Assembly in November 1947. The African Group at the UN was created in 1958 and soon made its presence felt on decolonisation and anti-apartheid issues, eventually ostracising South Africa at the UN and maintaining pressure for the liberation of Rhodesia-Zimbabwe and Namibia. NAM states led the expansion of the UN Security Council and the Economic and Social Council by the mid-1970s. During this period, the Convention on the Elimination of Racial Discrimination was agreed; a committee on decolonisation was established; and the special committee against apartheid was created. Members of the Palestinian Liberation Organisation were also invited to address the General Assembly's Special Political Committee from 1965. The unspoken Afro-Arab pact of this era involved the Africans agreeing to support the Palestinian struggle against Israel in exchange for the Arabs backing the black struggle against apartheid South Africa. Due to the pressure of a determined Southern majority, the People's Republic of China took its permanent seat on the UN Security Council in 1971 in the teeth of US opposition. Western disenchantment with the global South's dominance of multilateral diplomacy eventually led to the creation of the Group of Seven industrialised advanced nations in 1975.[23]

Peacekeeping

We next turn from the diplomacy of liberation at the UN to the critical issue of international peacekeeping. The need for UN peacekeeping in Africa is clear:

nearly half of the 50 UN peacekeeping missions in the post-Cold War era have been in Africa; the continent currently hosts the most numerous and largest UN peacekeeping missions in the world; much of the UN's socio-economic and humanitarian efforts are located in Africa; and the world body has established subregional offices in West Africa, the Great Lakes and Central Africa, as well as peacebuilding offices in Liberia, Guinea-Bissau and the Central African Republic.[24] The UN's Brahimi report on peacekeeping of August 2000[25] — named after its chairman, Algeria's Lakhdar Brahimi—increased the size of the UN's Department of Peacekeeping Operations from 400 to 600 but was disappointingly short on details on how to improve relations between the UN and Africa's subregional organisations: the continent's main peacekeeping preoccupation. The report's constant warnings that the UN should not undertake certain missions where it could not guarantee success were seen by many Africans as prejudiced code for avoiding African conflicts after the UN debacles in Somalia (1993) and Rwanda (1994). In 2005 more than 85 per cent of UN peacekeepers were deployed in Africa, and 40 per cent of peacekeepers deployed on the continent were African, while 31 per cent of peacekeepers deployed outside the continent came from Africa. Asian countries, most notably India, Pakistan and Bangladesh, have contributed to UN peacekeeping in Rwanda, Sierra Leone and Somalia. China deployed peacekeepers to Liberia and the DRC under the auspices of the UN. African countries such as Nigeria, Ghana and Senegal have been involved in peacekeeping in Lebanon and Iraq. It is, however, important that peacekeeping in Africa does not become an apartheid system in which Africans and Asians spill most of the blood while the West pays some of the bills.

In the aftermath of the US-led military invasion of Iraq in 2003, which had been launched without the authorisation of the UN Security Council, Kofi Annan—the UN Secretary-General at the time—set up a High-Level Panel on Threats, Challenges and Change.[26] The panel was mandated to examine the main global threats and challenges to peace and security and to make recommendations to the UN Secretary-General for a collective response to these threats. The UN panel—with seven of its 15 members coming from NAM states and China—held one of its meetings in Addis Ababa in April 2004 and met with senior AU officials and African civil society actors to gain their own perspectives on relations with the UN. Four regional consultations were also held, in China (two in April 2004), Singapore (April 2004) and India (July 2004). The panel released its report in December 2004.[27]

In order to influence the Security Council—the UN's most powerful decision-making body—African Union members, at a meeting in Swaziland in February 2005, called for two permanent African seats with veto power and two additional rotating seats (the continent currently has three rotating seats on the council) on a reformed Security Council. This became known as the Ezulwini Consensus.[28] The AU set up a ten-member committee to oversee the process of identifying Africa's representatives, but the continent's divisions were embarrassingly laid bare when its leaders failed to reach consensus on giving up the veto demand in August 2005. This stalled the reform of the UN Security Council at the UN General Assembly summit in New York in September 2005. Regarding Asian representation on an expanded council, there appears to be wider regional consensus that any seats would go to Japan and India, though China and Pakistan remain fierce opponents of Tokyo and New Delhi becoming permanent Security Council members.

In concluding this section, it is worth noting the views of Kishore Mahbubani, Singapore's respected former permanent representative to the UN who earned favourable reviews while serving a two-year stint (2001–2) on the UN Security Council. Mahbubani notes about the council: "There is a pattern of behaviour that is shared by the members of the Council, who, willingly or not, are often tempted to believe that agreement between the five [the United States, Russia, China, France and Britain] is the same as agreement between 15 … the P-5 [Permanent Five] have been given power without responsibility; the E-10 [the 10 members elected to two-year terms] have been given responsibility without power."[29] The scholar-diplomat notes that the council as an institution never took responsibility for the massacres in Rwanda and Srebrenica despite the UN's peacekeeping presence in both countries and the publishing of reports by the UN and other international commissions of inquiry. Mahbubani notes that while the formal use of the veto by the five permanent council members has declined, the veto is still effectively exercised in the closed-door consultations of the council, which is where most of its serious business is conducted. Many of the arcane procedures and policies of the council are well-known to the five permanent members, who also have privileged access to UN documents from secretariat staff. Often, decisions are based on complex and not always visible trade-offs between the P-5 that have been worked out over many years. Since no written records of the closed-door consultations are kept, the five permanent members represent the council's institutional memory, giving them a huge advantage over the ten rotating members, who serve only two-year terms.

Mahbubani likens the selective use of UN peacekeepers to the New York fire brigade responding only to fires on Park Avenue but not to blazes in Harlem or the Bronx. Finally, in a sobering comment, he notes that in May 2001, P-5 ambassadors told a lunch meeting that the UN was unlikely to react any differently if a genocide occurred in Burundi than it had reacted to the massacre of one million people in Rwanda in 1994.[30] As four Asian and African countries continue to seek to become permanent members of the UN Security Council, it is worth bearing this insider's insights in mind in order to devise effective strategies to influence future efforts to reform the Security Council. Countries from Africa and Asia-Pacific occupy 109 of the UN's 192 seats (more than half the membership), and this coalition continues to exert considerable influence on the organisation's work. If the UN Security Council is eventually democratised to include more African and Asian representation, the Afro-Asian peacekeeping coalition at the UN must work together to ensure that the UN does not respond only to what former UN Secretary-General Boutros Boutros-Ghali described as "rich men's wars" in Europe, but also to "poor men's wars" in Africa and Asia.

Three Prophets and a Pharaoh

We will next assess the four UN Secretaries-General produced by Asia and Africa: Burma's U Thant, Egypt's Boutros Boutros-Ghali, Ghana's Kofi Annan and South Korea's Ban Ki-moon. The role of Afro-Asian UN Secretaries-General in promoting the decolonisation, development and security interests of the global South is of particular relevance here. The Burmese diplomat U Thant was the UN Secretary-General between 1961 and 1971. He had big shoes to fill, having succeeded the most popular head of the UN, the Swede Dag Hammarskjold, who had died in a mysterious plane crash in 1961 while trying to resolve the tangled Congo Crisis. Brian Urquhart, the long-serving UN Undersecretary-General for Peacekeeping and a former aide to U Thant, notes in his 1987 memoirs:

> U-Thant has, in the West at any rate, been virtually written out of history. Very few people seem to remember his nobility of character, his integrity, or his courageous efforts over the Cuban missile crisis, the Vietnam war, and other international convulsions. His memoirs ... went virtually unre- viewed and unnoticed. He is, in popular Western memory, responsible for the 1967 war in the Middle East, a disaster which, virtually alone among world statesmen, he tried desperately to prevent.[31]

Urquhart goes on to describe U Thant as "decent, brave and responsible." Through firm but quiet leadership, U Thant managed to steady the rocky UN ship after Hammarskjold's untimely death. The Burmese diplomat was a devout, principled Buddhist who practised meditation every morning based on *metta* (good will) and *karuna* (compassion). U Thant was remarkably stoic and un- flappably calm, and he neither took credit for successes nor blamed others for failures. He was critical of the Vietnam War and appalled by the tremendous loss of civilian life. American President Lyndon Johnson angrily rejected U Thant's efforts to arrange talks in Rangoon, which the North Vietnamese had agreed to. US Secretary of State Dean Rusk even accused U Thant of pursuing a Nobel Peace Price. It was under U Thant's stewardship that the UN's agenda shifted to reflect the priorities of its new General Assembly majority from issues of armed conflict to issues of decolonisation and economic development. U Thant was the first UN Secretary-General to order the use of force during a UN peace-keeping operation to end the secession in the Congo in December 1962 after attacks on UN peacekeepers.[32] He was re-elected to a second term in 1966 and will be remembered as one of the global South's most solid diplomats, a Buddhist prophet who steered the UN through one of the most difficult periods in its history.

The Egyptian scholar-diplomat Boutros Boutros-Ghali was the first post-Cold War UN Secretary-General; he held the post between 1992 and 1996. He was widely known as "the Pharoah" by UN staff, due to his aloof and authoritarian leadership style. Irresponsible American politicians eventually turned Boutros-Ghali into a bogeyman, blaming him for everything from the deaths of American soldiers in Somalia to the failure to protect "safe havens" in Bosnia and the obstruction of the reform of the UN bureaucracy. The Pharoah eventually became a pawn in a cynical US political chess game that resulted in the end of his reign. Boutros-Ghali was particularly scapegoated for the Somali debacle, a fiasco that had been entirely planned and directed from the Pentagon. Bosnia's failures were largely due to European *realpolitik* and US policy vacillations. Anglo-French pressure prevented Boutros-Ghali from ordering air strikes against the Serbs, as they argued that this would have put their own troops in harm's way. But relations between the pugnacious American ambassador at the UN, Madeline Albright, and Boutros-Ghali deteriorated badly, leading to his eventual ouster. Boutros-Ghali's tenure witnessed one of the most far-reaching reforms in the history of the organisation. He cut the UN bureaucracy from 12,000 to 9,000 and froze the UN budget, saving US$100 million a year. Departments were slashed by a third, and increased computerisation cut down on the organisation's notorious paper-load. However, in November 1996 Washington vetoed Boutros-Ghali's re-election: the United States was in a minority of one out of 15 countries voting against the Secretary-General's re-election.

During his tenure in office, Boutros-Ghali displayed a fierce and often courageous independence, chastising his political masters in the Security Council for turning the UN into an instrument of parochial national interest over Iraq and Libya. He bluntly condemned the double standards of the UN's Western powers in selectively sanctioning UN interventions in Europe while ignoring

Africa's "orphan conflicts." His bitter 1999 memoirs, *Unvanquished*,[33] contain a devastating indictment of the United States in blocking UN action to halt the genocide in Rwanda in 1994. Boutros-Ghali's tenure as UN Secretary-General was, however, not without achievements: UN peacekeeping successes in Cambodia, El Salvador and Mozambique occurred under his watch, while his landmark 1992 report, *An Agenda for Peace*, remains an indispensable guide to the tools and techniques employed by the UN. For all his achievements, however, Boutros-Ghali earned himself the unenviable distinction of being the only UN Secretary-General to have been denied a second term in office.[34]

Kofi Annan, the Ghanaian UN Undersecretary-General for Peacekeeping Operations and American favourite, was elected UN Secretary-General in 1996. Annan was widely regarded as a competent administrator who rose within the UN system after a 30-year career spanning the fields of finance, personnel, health, refugees and peacekeeping. He was widely seen as charming, affable, humble and, like U Thant, unflappably calm. Like U Thant, he also appeared better suited to the discreet role of a faceless bureaucrat than the high-profile role of a prophetic statesman. However, critics accused Annan of not standing up to the United States when it used the UN to spy on Iraq and violated the UN Charter by raining down bombs on Kosovo, Sudan, Afghanistan and Iraq without the approval of the Security Council. His supporters argued that the enduring lesson of Boutros-Ghali's departure was to not directly confront the world's sole superpower. Annan never quite shook off the impression of being totally indebted to Washington, which almost single-handedly ensured his ascent to the top UN job.

Another accusation that Annan was never able to shake off totally was that while serving as Undersecretary-General of UN Peacekeeping in 1994, he did not respond appropriately to a cable warning of an impending genocide in Rwanda. A subsequent UN inquiry later criticised Annan and his deputy Iqbal Riza for this incident. Though the failure to act was also due to the powerful members of the Security Council who erroneously viewed Rwanda through a tainted Somali prism, Annan was blamed for not taking the information he had received directly to the Security Council and to the Secretary-General. Instead, he instructed that it be passed on to the US, French and Belgian missions in Kigali. Annan's promotion of humanitarian intervention in cases of grotesque human rights abuses and his publishing of reports on Rwanda and the Balkans critical of the UN cannot be separated from some sense of responsibility that he felt at the lacklustre reaction of the UN secretariat and its diplomats to these tragedies. Though he never publicly admitted it, the time he devoted to championing the issue of "humanitarian intervention" as well as the related doctrine of the "responsibility to protect" (which was agreed during the UN reform process in 2005) and the political risks he incurred to place these issues on the international agenda suggest that the Rwanda experience left some emotional scars.

Annan's relations with Washington were negatively impacted by his refusal to give carte blanche to US policies in Iraq. He somewhat clumsily declared the war in Iraq "illegal" in the middle of the US election campaign of 2004. This led to several US Congressmen calling for Annan's resignation and, coupled with the Oil-for-Food scandal in Iraq (in which Annan's son Kojo was rewarded by Cotecna, a Swiss company hired by the UN, to the tune of possibly US$484,000), turned him into something of a lame duck two years before the end of his term. The UN reform process in September 2005, on which Annan had pinned so much hope for bequeathing a legacy, also produced a disappointingly watered-down text that called for establishing a Peacebuilding Commission and Human Rights Council and committed states to a "responsibility to protect" victims of extreme state violence but fell far short of the expectations of most observers. Kofi Annan was awarded the Nobel Peace Prize in 2003, but the difficult end to his ten-year tenure somewhat besmirched his legacy.[35]

The third Afro-Asian prophet in our trio is Ban Ki-moon, who replaced Annan in January 2007. South Korea's former foreign minister described himself as a "harmoniser" and "bridge-builder" and was determined to adopt a low-key style and restore the credibility of the UN's management processes after the Oil-for-Food scandal. But his first five months in office were widely seen to have been dogged by a series of missteps. As China's permanent representative to the UN, Wang Guangya, noted: "His intentions are good ... But, personally, I feel that he's a newcomer, and he does not understand the culture and the environment in this house."[36] Ban has been seen, like Annan, to be indebted to Washington, as demonstrated by some of his early appointments (including awarding the position of head of UN political affairs to an American national) and his frequent quoting of former US Permanent Representative at the UN John Bolton. The South Korean ran into trouble for seeking to restructure the UN departments of peacekeeping and disarmament—another action viewed as directed by a US hand—without proper prior consultation with his staff and national governments, and he was embarrassingly forced to amend his plans. Ban has, however, been energetic in pursuing security issues of importance to the global South. In January 2007 he attended the African Union Summit in Addis Ababa, where he pushed Sudan's reluctant leader, Omar Al-Bashir, to implement a plan to deploy UN peacekeepers in Darfur to bolster a weak AU force. He also attended the Arab League summit in Saudi Arabia in April 2007 and has been energetic in efforts to promote peace in the Middle East.[37]

Regional Security Mechanisms

ECOWAS and SADC: Lessons for ASEAN

We next turn our attention from UN peacekeeping to regional security mechanisms in Africa and Asia. Africa, during the bipolar era of the Cold War, was the
perfect example of the pernicious effects of Northern actors exporting insecurity
to the South through foreign "proxy" wars in order to preserve their own security
at home. The United States, the Soviet Union and France turned the continent
into a strategic playground to conduct their ideological games, resulting in the
deaths of millions of Africans. Africa was flooded with billions of dollars of
weapons provided to local proxies in countries such as Angola, Ethiopia, Liberia,
Mozambique and Somalia. Since 1960 about 40 African wars have been fought,
resulting in more than seven million deaths and spawning more than nine million refugees. Asia also suffered hundreds of thousands of deaths and destruction
from Cold War conflicts, most notably in Korea and Vietnam.

The post-Cold War neglect of Africa by external actors forced local actors
such as the AU, ECOWAS and SADC, many of them primarily economic
organisations, to adopt security roles. The loss of external support also led African
leaders to seek to protect their regimes from rebels and putschists through these
security mechanisms. However, these organisations remain weak institutions,
lacking financial and logistical means as well as adequate and well-trained staff.
Regional interventions have become embroiled in political difficulties and often
been viewed as partisan and lacking legitimacy. Despite these difficulties, progress
has been made in stemming some of Africa's most intractable conflicts, largely
through the efforts of regional peacekeepers. Nigerian-led ECOMOG (ECOWAS
Ceasefire Monitoring Group) interventions in Liberia and Sierra Leone between
1990 and 1998 cost Nigeria's treasury more than US$3 billion and resulted in
more than 1,000 peacekeeping fatalities. Both interventions managed to halt
some of the worst excesses of these conflicts, protected hundreds of thousands
of civilians, disarmed factions, and helped to organise elections. ECOWAS also
sent peacekeepers to Guinea-Bissau (1999) and Côte d'Ivoire (2003), while West
Africa's aspiring hegemon, Nigeria, led back a peacekeeping force into Liberia
in August 2003 that was subsumed under a UN mission.[38] South Africa, the
continent's other potential hegemon, launched an intervention into Lesotho in
1998 that became embroiled in clashes with the civilian population until the
situation was brought under control. South Africa deployed peacekeepers in
Burundi and the DRC under a UN umbrella, while Thabo Mbeki was the lead
mediator of Côte d'Ivoire's crisis until 2006.[39]

Just as Southern African states had established the Southern African Development Coordination Conference—the precursor of SADC—in 1980 to counter a rampaging apartheid South Africa, ASEAN[40] was formed in part as a bulwark against Chinese expansionism. Though ASEAN was active in peacemaking efforts in Cambodia between 1979 and 1991, the organisation has made less progress than ECOWAS and SADC in developing a security mechanism to resolve regional conflicts. It was notably Australia that led the International Force for East Timor (INTERFET) in September 1999, much to regional embarrassment, as a largely non-Asian state violated the "racial sovereignty" of the region to intervene in a territory claimed at the time by the more natural hegemon: Indonesia. Though Singapore, Malaysia, Thailand and the Philippines contributed troops to INTERFET, most of these countries offered support, medical, engineering and security task forces that provided regional cover for what was effectively an Australian intervention. The UN Transitional Authority in East Timor replaced the force in February 2000 and eventually steered the country to independence.

Considering that ASEAN was seen as the "Balkans of the East" in the 1960s, it is a tribute to the organisation that it has helped to prevent its members from going to war with one another through closer economic integration.[41] There were disputes in 1963 between Malaysia and Indonesia; *konfrontasi* between Malaysia and the Philippines over Sabah in the same year; a dispute between Indonesia and Singapore in 1968; and the more recent Philippines/Singapore crisis of 1997 over the hanging of a Filipino maid. Tensions have also simmered periodically between Singapore and Malaysia, and between Singapore and Indonesia. Farther afield, there are tensions on the Korean Peninsula, the South China Sea and the Taiwan Strait. ASEAN's Treaty of Amity and Cooperation (TAC) came into force in 1978, establishing a code of conduct and six key principles to be observed by member states: mutual respect for one another's independence, equality, sovereignty, territorial integrity and national identity; the right of each state to live free from external interference, subversion and coercion; non-interference in the internal affairs of one another; peaceful settlement of disputes; renunciation of the threat or use of force; and effective cooperation among members. Most of these principles are contained in the UN Charter, which all ASEAN states have signed. TAC's High Council is empowered to use "good offices," mediation and conciliation to resolve disputes. But the council has never been used, though ASEAN has made progress in completing its Rules of Procedure.[42]

In 1999 ASEAN created a troika of past, present and future foreign ministers who chair the ASEAN Standing Committee. This troika was established to allow the organisation to respond more effectively to important political and security issues and is similar to SADC's troika in Southern Africa. ASEAN members have enunciated norms and principles such as dialogue, consultation (*musyawarah*), consensus (*mufakat*) and non-confrontation. But for all these high-sounding principles, ASEAN has never in its history directly resolved a regional dispute. States have been left to settle their bilateral discords through commissions such as those on Malaysia-Thailand and Malaysia-Indonesia. ASEAN is also the only major regional organisation without observer status at the UN, and its members continue to argue that only the UN has the legitimacy and capability to undertake peacekeeping missions. However, at the ASEAN/UN summit in Bangkok in February 2000, then UN Secretary-General Kofi Annan bemoaned the fact that both bodies "have found little to say to each other on peace and security at the time when new forms of security challenges are presenting themselves."[43]

In 1997 Malaysia's former deputy prime minister, Anwar Ibrahim, called for ASEAN to adopt a policy of "constructive involvement" over Cambodia; the Thai foreign minister at the time, Surin Pitsuwan, similarly called for "flexible engagement" in implementing ASEAN's non-intervention principles. These sound very similar to South Africa's "quiet diplomacy" policy in engaging Zimbabwe's Robert Mugabe. But both African and Asian leaders are still, in most cases, very much committed to principles of "non-intervention," as seen by African reactions to Mugabe and Asian reactions to the military junta in Myanmar. African states, however, pressured Liberia's Charles Taylor into exile in August 2003 and have sanctioned military regimes in Côte d'Ivoire and Comoros (barring them from an OAU summit in 2000), as well as opposing military-installed regimes in Guinea-Bissau (2003) and Togo (2005). Twenty-seven African countries have signed up for the African Peer Review Mechanism, a voluntary system for monitoring governance performance on the continent. This is an initiative that could perhaps profitably be adopted by Asian governments.

The Evolving Security Architecture in West and Southern Africa

ECOWAS and SADC have struggled to achieve their *raison d'être* of economic development and integration. Both are, however, regarded as being in the avant garde of subregional organisations in the security field: ECOWAS and SADC have established security mechanisms with political and military institutions and signed mutual defence pacts; both conducted regional peace support operations; and both have established subregional parliaments and legal tribunals for arbitrating disputes. The ECOWAS security protocol of 1999 established the following organs: a Mediation and Security Council, a Defence and Security Commission, and a Council of Elders. The protocol called for improved cooperation in early warning, conflict prevention, peacekeeping operations, cross-border crime, and the trafficking of small arms and narcotics. SADC's Organ on Politics, Defence and Security was created in 1996, and a protocol on politics, defence and security cooperation was signed in 2001. The protocol called on SADC states to coordinate their security policy through a troika of members under a one-year rotating chair supported administratively by the SADC secretariat in Botswana. The SADC protocol further seeks to harmonise its members' foreign policy and calls for initiatives ranging from conflict prevention to peace enforcement. By 2004 the organisation unveiled a Strategic Indicative Plan for the Organ (SIPO) as a five-year programme to implement its security protocol. SIPO outlined plans for work in the four broad sectors of politics, defence, state security and public security. The plan seeks to work with civil society actors and think tanks in the subregion, and even attempts to coordinate the participation of its members in UN peacekeeping missions.

ECOWAS' Defence and Security Commission advises its Mediation and Security Council on mandates, terms of reference, and the appointment of force commanders for future military missions. The ECOWAS Council of Elders consists of 15 eminent personalities who have been sent by ECOWAS to observe elections in Gambia, Sierra Leone, Nigeria, Togo and Zimbabwe. The ECOWAS security mechanism of 1999 further broadened the powers of the organisation's executive secretary to give him the authority to take initiatives for the prevention and management of conflicts, including fact-finding, mediation, facilitation, negotiation and reconciliation of parties. These powers are more extensive than those of the SADC Executive Secretary—and ASEAN chief—who are clearly more secretary than general. ECOWAS' protocol also calls for a peace and security observation mechanism as well as an early warning system, both of which SADC is also developing. The issue of financing remains a major challenge to the building of the proposed ECOWAS and SADC peacekeeping forces, which are two of the five subregional pillars of an AU-led African Standby Force to be established by 2010. But despite these constraints, ASEAN could learn some lessons from Africa's more advanced security mechanisms.

Conclusion: Rekindling "The Spirit of Bandung"

In concluding this chapter, it is important to identify ways of rekindling the "spirit of Bandung" to foster greater Afro-Asian cooperation. Generally, Asia has done better economically than Africa in the first five post-independence decades, and several Asian states have joined the ranks of the *nouveaux riches*. The Asian financial crisis between 1997 and 1998, however, highlighted the region's continuing vulnerability to Western financial actors and demonstrated the fragility of the "Asian miracle." Both Africa and Asia have adopted the Westphalian system of nation-states and largely accepted colonially imposed national boundaries. The few exceptions in which these borders have been changed include the creation of Singapore from Malaya in 1965, the creation of Bangladesh from East Pakistan in 1971, the creation of Eritrea from Ethiopia in 1993, and the creation of East Timor from Indonesia in 2001. With the exception of Singapore, military intervention was required in all of these cases, underlining the durability of colonial borders. Secessionist tendencies, though, remain strong in parts of Indonesia, Sri Lanka, India, Pakistan, Sudan, Nigeria and Somalia.

Culturally, Hollywood has often demonstrated its lack of nuance and subtlety by depicting Africans and Asians negatively in such movies as *Coming to America, Barbershop* and *Lost in Translation.* The Western media is often condescending in the way it has reported on events on both continents, continuing to reflect attitudes described by the late Palestinian-American intellectual Edward Said as "Orientalism,"[44] in which sometimes unconscious colonial attitudes and frameworks continue to guide how the West views its former "possessions." Unfortunately, several Asian scholars whom I have encountered at international conferences have also demonstrated these stereotypical views about Africa as a continent of disease and conflicts, preferring to wallow in a second-class, semi-developed status while looking to the West for acknowledgement of its progress. Asia has, of course, had its own genocidal Khmer Rouge to rival Rwanda's *génocidaires.* Many Africans have also adopted Western perceptions of an Asian paradise of tigers, blissfully unaware of the widespread poverty and corruption that still bedevil much of the continent.

The "New International Economic Order" promoted by Afro-Asian leaders in the 1970s proved in the end to be a tragic illusion. Instead, the global South finds itself in an age of the neoliberal "Washington consensus." In concluding this chapter, it is important that we offer some recommendations for more enlightened Northern security and economic policies towards the South. Northern countries must support democracy and courageous civil society activists in the South more seriously and consistently and not make exceptions that are politically expedient for short-term policy gains. Genuine democrats must be supported and brutish autocrats shunned. In Africa, regional organisations such as the AU, ECOWAS and SADC, which are badly in need of strengthening, should be generously supported. Similar organisations such as ASEAN must also be consulted more closely in regional peacemaking efforts. As we assess the legacy of Bandung, Africans and Asians still have many struggles in common and continuing ties of interdependence.

In 2001 Africa's exports to Asia stood at US$22.2 billion (out of US$134 billion worth of global exports), based on Nigerian, Angolan, Congolese and Sudanese oil; South African gold, platinum and cars; Ugandan, Rwandese and Mauritian seafood; Kenyan and Tanzanian tea; Ivorian and Malian cotton; and Botswanan diamonds. China, South Korea, India and Taiwan were the largest importers of African crude oil, Pakistan of African tea, and Japan and Singapore of African garments. But while Africa's exports to Asia represented 16 per cent of its total exports, only 2 per cent of total Asian imports came from Africa.[45] Africa currently supplies Asia, which now consumes 40 per cent of the world's oil, with much of its oil. South Africa has strong trade ties with East Asia. Japan, China and India have formulated initiatives such as the Tokyo International Conference on Africa's Development (TICAD), the Forum on China-Africa Cooperation (FOCAC) and India-NEPAD (New Partnership for Africa's Development) Cooperation.[46]

There is a strong, self-interested side to these countries' Africa policies. Japan, for example, used Africa's numerical strength of 53 UN members to lobby for support in the world body, particularly as it sought a permanent seat on the UN Security Council in 2005. Tokyo's relations with Africa were, however, dogged by the former's controversial trade ties with apartheid South Africa. The relationship has been characterised by Japan's quest for strategic energy and raw materials, as well as policies to facilitate Japanese trade and investment, which some have described as "neo-mercantilist."[47] By 1995 Japan was giving aid worth US$1.33 billion to 47 African states.[48] TICAD was held in 1993, 1998 and 2003.

But it is China's growing political, economic and security ties in Africa that have attracted the most attention. The Sino-African relationship is one of the most important developments in the geo-strategy of post-Cold War Africa. Former Chinese President Jiang Zemin visited Africa in 1996; Chinese President Hu Jintao visited the continent five times between 1999 and 2007; and more than 30 African leaders have visited China since 1997. Beijing held the first Forum on China-Africa Cooperation Summit in October 2000 with 44 African states, during which Western aid conditionalities were criticised, and after which China announced the annulment of US$1.2 billion of debt to 31 African countries. A second FOCAC Summit was held in Addis Ababa, Ethiopia, in December 2003. By 2004 Africa's exports to China had reached US$11.4 billion, Sino-African trade had grown from US$2 billion in 1999 to US$55.5 billion in 2006, Beijing offered the continent US$5 billion in loans and credit in the same year, and China had become the third largest foreign investor on the continent—at an estimated US$6.6 billion—behind the United States and Europe, having set up more than 1,000 enterprises in Africa. In November

2006, 40 African leaders and ministers trekked to Beijing for a third FOCAC Summit, where China promised to double aid to the continent, train 15,000 Africans and provide 4,000 scholarships.

Though China's trade with Africa accounts for only 2 per cent of its total global trade, its direct investment in Africa represents 16 per cent of its total global investment. What is significant about these growing ties is the diversity of Beijing's trade with Africa, ranging from oil in Nigeria, Angola, Sudan and Congo-Brazzaville (an impressive 28 per cent of China's oil imports came from Africa in 2006) to tourism; construction; wholesale; retail; energy; transport; communications; health and education in Sierra Leone, Seychelles, Ethiopia and Senegal; manufacturing in Morocco and Zimbabwe; fisheries in Gabon and Namibia; building stadiums in Mali, Djibouti and the Central African Republic; and agriculture in Zambia and Tanzania. China has also contributed peace-keepers to UN missions in Liberia and the DRC at a time when most Western governments are reluctant to send troops to Africa. Beijing has supported perma-nent African representation on an expanded UN Security Council, while solid African backing helped China secure the 2008 Olympics. But some of China's actions in Africa have not been without controversy: Beijing controversially became a large investor (40 per cent of the largest oil venture) and importer of oil from the Sudanese government, which has been accused of widespread human rights violations in Darfur. Oil was also imported from the equally controversial government of Equatorial Guinea, and arms were sold to Ethiopia and Eritrea during their bloody civil war between 1998 and 2000.[49] Beijing's insistence on a policy of "non-interference" and close ties with autocratic and/or corrupt regimes have also been criticised, as has its use in its projects in Africa of an estimated 80,000 Chinese labourers.[50] Despite these concerns, the growing relationship between China and Africa has undoubtedly been one of the most significant developments in South-South relations over the last two decades.

In order to improve security in the South more broadly, the global trading system, as represented by the inequities of the World Trade Organization and the Bretton Woods institutions—the World Bank and the IMF—must be urgently reformed in ways that give greater voice to the South. About 500 million Asians and 300 million Africans still live in extreme poverty. Many African and Asian countries will not meet the UN's Millennium Development Goals' target of halving poverty by 2015. Unfair trade practices by the industrialised North make it harder for Southern countries to grow out of poverty. Most Northern countries impose higher tariffs on agricultural goods and manufactures, the areas of comparative advantage for Southern countries. For example, in 2001 Bangladesh exported US$2.4 billion worth of goods to the United States and paid 14 per cent in tariffs, while France exported US$30 billion worth of goods to the US market and paid tariffs of only 1 per cent. During the same period, 60 per cent of imports from the South were subject to peak tariffs in Canada, the European Union, Japan and the United States. In 2001, agricultural subsidies of US$311 billion in the North exceeded the national income of sub-Saharan Africa (US$301 billion).[51]

In recognition of the profligate and pernicious effect of agricultural subsidies, the Doha trade round agreed to the elimination of these subsidies in 2001, though significantly, no timetable was set for this process. The disappointing collapse of the Doha trade round in 2005 underlined the insensitivity of the rich to alleviating the suffering of the "wretched of the earth" in the global South. Even as subsidies and tariffs cripple the South's economic prospects, the rich world has become less generous with development assistance. Between 1990 and 2001, official development assistance fell from 0.33 per cent to 0.22 per cent: way below the 0.7 per cent target set as far back as 1970. The North must continue to play a more active role in annulling the South's huge debts, which were largely accumulated by corrupt, monstrous Afro-Asian autocrats and *caudillos*, many of whom were fed with Western loans during the Cold War era. Even with raging conflicts, grinding poverty and an AIDS epidemic that threatens to wipe out large populations in the South, these governments are forced to use a large part of their export earnings on servicing debts that everyone knows can never be repaid. Scarce resources that should go towards health and education must not continue to go towards servicing unpayable debts.

In April 2005 African and Asian leaders met in Indonesia to commemorate the 50th anniversary of the Bandung Conference and to launch the New Asian-African Strategic Partnership. The agreement seeks to build a bridge between two continents across the Indian Ocean and envisages partnerships in the areas of political solidarity, economic cooperation and socio-cultural relations. The "spirit of Bandung" is kept alive today as countries such as India, South Africa and Brazil (under the auspices of the Group of 21) coordinate international trade efforts to present a more powerful and united bloc that can more effectively defend Southern interests from the protectionist excesses of the profligate North. The Afro-Asian bloc consists of 106 countries with 4.6 billion people (more than 70 per cent of the world's population) and a combined economic strength of US$9 trillion.[52] The Bandung Conference in 1955 caused a political earthquake. With reports of earth tremors in Bandung as Afro-Asian leaders met there in April 2005, it was unclear whether the 50th anniversary conference could cause the same seismic shift in the global economic landscape that had given birth to the Bandung Spirit.

Notes

1   I would like to thank Dr. Kweku Ampiah for his extremely useful comments in revising this chapter. See Kweku Ampiah, *The Political and Moral Imperatives of the Bandung Conference of 1945* (London: Global Oriental, 2007).

2   See M.K. Gandhi, *An Autobiography: The Story of My Experiments with Truth* (London, New York and New Delhi: Penguin Books, 2001).

3   See, for example, Frank-Jürgen Richter and Thang D. Nguyen, *The Malaysian Journey: Progress in Diversity* (Singapore: Times Editions, 2003).

4   See, for example, Joseph Stiglitz, *Globalization and its Discontents* (London, New York and New Delhi: Penguin Books, 2002), pp. 89–132.

5   Geoffrey Barraclough, "The Revolt Against the West," in Prasenjit Duara (ed.), *Decolonization: Perspectives from Now and Then* (London and New York: Routledge, 2004), p. 118.

6   Barraclough, "The Revolt Against the West," p. 118. See also Rupert Emerson, *From Empire to Nation: The Rise to Self-Assertion of Asian and African Peoples* (Boston: Beacon Press, 1960); Hedley Bull, "The Revolt Against the West," in Hedley Bull and Adam Watson (eds.), *The Expansion of International Society* (Oxford: Clarendon Press, 1985), pp. 117–26; and D.A. Low, "The Asian Mirror to Tropical Africa's Independence," in Prosser Gifford and Wm. Roger Louis (eds.), *The Transfer of Power in Africa: Decolonization, 1940–1960* (New Haven and London: Yale University Press, 1982), pp. 1–29.

7   Ali Mazrui, "Africa and Other Civilizations: Conquest and Counter-Conquest," in John W. Harbeson and Donald Rothchild (eds.), *Africa in World Politics: The African State System in Flux*, 3rd Edition (Boulder and Oxford: Westview, 2000), p. 126.

8   Mazrui, "Africa and Other Civilizations," p. 127.

9   Mazrui, "Africa and Other Civilizations," p. 130. See also Kader Asmal, David Chidester and Wilmot James (eds.), *South Africa's Nobel Laureates* (Johannesburg and Cape Town: Jonathan Bull, 2004).

10   See, for example, Alistair Horne, *A Savage War of Peace: Algeria 1954–1962* (New York: New York Review Books, 2006).

11   Hari Sharan Chhabra, *Nehru and Resurgent Africa* (New Delhi: Africa Publications, 1989), p. 121. For a more recent perspective, see Chris Landsberg, "Beyond the 'Cargo Cult': Learning from India's Principle-based Foreign Policy," Centre for Policy Studies, Johannesburg, Research Report no. 65, October 1998, pp. 35–51.

12   Chhabra, *Nehru and Resurgent Africa*, p. 123.

13   Ibid., pp. 151–2.

14   Ali Mazrui, "Africa and Egypt's Four Circles," in Ali Mazrui, *On Heroes and Uhuru-Worship: Essays on Independent Africa* (London: Longman, 1967), p. 96.

15   Ibid., p. 111.

16   Ibid., p. 99.

17   See, for example, J.D. Hargreaves, *Decolonization in Africa* (London and New York: Longman, 1988), pp. 156–8; Keith Kyle, *Suez: Britain's End of Empire in the Middle East* (London and New York: I.B. Tauris, 2nd Edition, 2003); and Wm. Roger Louis, *Ends of British Imperialism: The Scramble For Empire, Suez and Decolonization* (London and New York: I.B. Tauris, 2006).

18   Ali Mazrui, "Nkrumah: The Leninist Czar," in *On Heroes and Uhuru-Worship*, p. 124.

19   See Hargreaves, *Decolonization in Africa*, pp. 114–21; Mazrui, "Nkrumah: The Leninist Czar;" and Kwame Nkrumah, *Ghana: The Autobiography of Kwame Nkrumah* (London: Panaf Books, 1973).

20   See Ali Mazrui, *Towards a Pax Africana: A Study of Ideology and Ambition* (Chicago: Chicago University Press, 1967), pp. 150–1.

21   Joe Garba, *Diplomatic Soldiering* (Ibadan: Spectrum Books, 1987), pp. 188, 190.

22   Sally Morphet, "Multilateralism and the Non-Aligned Movement: What Is the Global South Doing and Where Is It Going?" Review Essay, *Global Governance* 10 (2004): 529–30.

23   Ibid., pp. 517–37.

24   See Adekeye Adebajo and Helen Scanlon (eds.), *A Dialogue of the Deaf: Essays on Africa and the United Nations* (Johannesburg: Jacana, 2006).

25   International Peace Academy/Centre on International Cooperation, *Refashioning the Dialogue: Regional Perspectives on the Brahimi Report on UN Peace Operations*, Regional Meetings, February–March 2001, Johannesburg, Buenos Aires, Singapore and London, pp. 6–11 (<www.ipacademy.org>).

26   Members included Robert Badinter, Joao Soares, Gro Harlem Brundtland, Mary Chinery-Hesse, Gareth Evans, David Hannay, Enrique Iglesias, Amr Moussa, Satish Nambiar, Sadako Ogata, Anand Panyarachun, Yevgeny Primakov, Qian Qichen, Nafis Sadik, Salim Ahmed Salim and Brent Scowcroft.

27   *A More Secure World: Our Shared Responsibility*, Report of the United Nations Secretary-General's High-Level Panel on Threats, Challenges and Change. Published by the United Nations Department of Public Information DPI/2367, December 2004. See also, *In Larger Freedom: Towards Development, Security and Human Rights For All*, Report of the UN Secretary-General, Follow-up to the outcome of the Millennium Summit, 21 March 2005, A/59/2005; and Centre for Conflict Resolution, *A More Secure Continent: African Perspectives on the UN High-Level Panel Report*, Seminar Report, Cape Town, 23–24 April 2005, available at <http://ccrweb.ccr.uct.ac.za>.

28   See African Union, Draft Recommendations at the Ministerial Committee of Fifteen on the Report of the High-Level Panel on the Reform of the UN System, 20–22 February 2005, Mbabane, Swaziland. CTTE/15/Min/ReformUN/Draft/Recomm. (I).

29   Kishore Mahbubani, "The Permanent and Elected Council Members," in David M. Malone (ed.), *The UN Security Council: From the Cold War to the 21st Century* (Boulder and London: Lynne Rienner, 2004), pp. 253, 256.

30 Ibid., pp. 253–66.

31 Brian Urquhart, *A Life in Peace and War* (New York and London: W.W. Norton & Company, 1987), p. 189.

32 This information has mostly been gleaned from Urquhart, *A Life in Peace and War*, pp. 189–208.

33 Boutros Boutros-Ghali, *Unvanquished: A US-UN Saga* (London and New York: I.B. Tauris, 1999).

34 See Stanley Meisler, "Dateline UN: A New Hammarskjold?" *Foreign Policy*, no. 98 (Spring 1995): 180–97.

35 See Adekeye Adebajo, "Pope, Pharaoh or Prophet? The Secretary-General after the Cold War," in Simon Chesterman (ed.), *Secretary or General? The UN Secretary-General in World Politics* (Cambridge, New York and Singapore: Cambridge University Press, 2007), pp. 139–57; Stanley Meisler, *Kofi Annan: A Man of Peace in a World of War* (New Jersey: John Wiley & Sons, 2007); and James Traub, *The Best Intentions: Kofi Annan and the UN in the Era of American World Power* (New York: Farrar, Straus & Giroux, 2006).

36 Maggie Farley, "Ban Struggles to Find Feet after Early Stumbles," *The Sunday Independent* (South Africa), Dispatches section: p. 14, 15 April 2007.

37 See Farley, "Ban Struggles to Find Feet after Early Stumbles."

38 See Adekeye Adebajo and Ismail Rashid (eds.), *West Africa's Security Challenges: Building Peace in a Troubled Region* (Boulder and London: Lynne Rienner, 2004).

39 See Adekeye Adebajo, Adebayo Adedeji and Chris Landsberg (eds.), *South Africa in Africa: The Post-Apartheid Era* (Scottsville, South Africa: University of Kwazulu-Natal Press, 2007).

40 Members include Indonesia, Malaysia, Singapore, the Philippines, Thailand, Brunei, Vietnam, Laos, Myanmar and Cambodia.

41 I owe a great debt of gratitude for my analysis of ASEAN to Mely Caballero-Anthony, "The Regionalization of Peace in Asia," in Michael Pugh and Waheguru Pal Singh Sidhu (eds.), *The United Nations and Regional Security: Europe and Beyond* (Boulder and London: Lynne Rienner, 2003), pp. 195–211.

42 See Amitav Acharya, *Regionalism and Multilateralism: Essays on Cooperative Security in the Asia-Pacific* (Singapore: Eastern University Press, 2nd Edition, 2003).

43 Caballero-Anthony, "The Regionalization of Peace in Asia," p. 208.

44 See Edward W. Said, "Orientalism Reconsidered," in *Reflections on Exile and Other Essays* (Cambridge: Harvard University Press, 2002), pp. 187–97.

45 See World Bank Group, *Patterns of Africa-Asia Trade and Investment: Potential of Ownership and Partnership*, October 2004.

46 See Francis A. Kornegay, "Pax AfroAsiatica? Revisiting Bandung amid a Changing World Order," Institute for Global Dialogue Occasional Paper no. 46, October 2004.

47 See Kweku Ampiah, *The Dynamics of Japan's Relations with Africa: South Africa, Tanzania and Nigeria* (London: Routledge, 1997).

48   See Scarlett Cornelissen, "Japan-Africa Relations: Patterns and Prospects," in Ian Taylor and Paul Williams (eds.), *Africa in International Politics: External Involvement on the Continent* (London and New York: Routledge, 2004), pp. 116–35.

49   See Ian Taylor, "The 'All-Weather' Friend? Sino-African Interaction in the Twenty-First Century," in Taylor and Williams (eds.), *Africa in International Politics*, pp. 83–101. See also Garth le Pere, *China through the Third Eye: South African Perspectives* (Midrand, South Africa: Institute for Global Dialogue, 2004).

50   See Garth le Pere (ed.), *China in Africa: Mercantilist Predator, or Partner in Development?* (Midrand and Johannesburg: Institute for Global Dialogue and South African Institute of International Affairs, 2006); Greg Mills and Alberto Trejos, "China and Africa—Can It Be Win-Win?" *Business Day*, 22 February 2007: 17; and Anver Versi, "China and Africa: A Meeting of Minds—and Needs," and Neil Ford, "Economic War for Africa's Loyalties begins," both in *African Business*, July 2006, no. 322: 16–21.

51   United Nations Development Programme, *Human Development Report* (Oxford: Oxford University Press, 2003), pp. 155–6.

52   See Ali Alatas, "Towards a New Strategic Partnership between Asia and Africa," keynote address at the Institute of Defence and Strategic Studies conference, *Bandung Revisited: A Critical Appraisal of a Conference's Legacy*, Singapore, 15 April 2005.

CHAPTER 6

China and the Bandung Conference: Changing Perceptions and Representations

Chen Jian

The People's Republic of China was a major participant in the Bandung Conference of 1955. The Bandung Spirit, as is well known, has played an important—and at times even central—role in Beijing's representation of its international strategies and policies. Yet how Beijing has defined Bandung and the "spirit" associated with it remains a question far from being sufficiently studied and clearly answered.

The purpose of this paper is to provide a brief historical review of Beijing's changing perceptions and representations of Bandung and its "spirit" in the past half-century. In particular, the emphasis of the paper will be on Beijing's changing representation of the Five Principles of Peaceful Coexistence,[1] the entity by which the Bandung Spirit has been substantiated. While the paper concentrates on building a historical narrative with the support of Chinese source materials available in recent years, it also aims at pursuing a genuine understanding of Bandung as a symbol and the Bandung Spirit as an underlying principle in China's changing attitudes towards the outside world.

Restraint

When the People's Republic of China (PRC) was established in 1949, Mao Zedong and the Chinese Communist Party (CCP) leadership announced that the "new China" would adopt an international policy of "leaning to one side"—the side of the Soviet Union and the socialist bloc—in a world that had been profoundly divided by the global Cold War.[2] Following this policy, the PRC and the Soviet Union signed a treaty of strategic alliance in February

1950. Eight months later, in October 1950, Mao and the Beijing leadership decided to send Chinese troops to Korea to support Kim Il-sung's North Korean communist regime, which resulted in a direct military confrontation between China and the United States that would last until July 1953.[3] In the meantime, Beijing dispatched military and political advisers to support the Vietnamese communists in a war against the French colonialists.[4] Throughout its first five years, the PRC appeared as a radical "revolutionary country" on the international scene, challenging the legitimacy of the existing international system controlled by Western imperialist powers (and the United States in particular). Indeed, Mao and his comrades made it clear that one of the primary missions of the "new China" was to destroy the "old" world in which China had been a humiliated member during modern times. The Chinese communist revolution, while aiming at eventually turning China into a land of prosperity and universal justice and equality, would serve as a model of other "oppressed" nations and would play a central role in creating a "new" world.[5]

In the context of the PRC's revolutionary foreign policy, Beijing's international discourse was dominated by a class-struggle-centred language. Beijing's attitudes towards non-Western, nationalist countries were a mixture of harsh criticism and, at times, tactics and actions designed to neutralise them in the Cold War confrontation. In the early years of the PRC, for example, in attacking such Western imperialist countries as the United States and Britain, Beijing's leaders also characterised Vietnam, Malaya, Burma, Thailand, Indonesia, the Philippines and India as being "dominated by reactionary forces" and experiencing the "oppression of imperialism."[6] Mao Zedong introduced an "Intermediate Zone" thesis in the late 1940s, in which the CCP chairman argued that between the United States and the Soviet Union there existed a vast "intermediate zone" in Asia, Africa and Europe, and that before the US imperialists could directly attack the Soviet Union they would have to first try to control the "intermediate zone" through acts of aggression aimed at countries there. While identifying the competition over the vast "intermediate zone" as of primary importance in the confrontation between the socialist and capitalist camps, Mao also claimed that it was the communists in various countries in the "intermediate zone," rather than the capitalists (even national capitalists) there, who would play a major role in checking the aggression of Western imperialist countries and their "lackeys."[7]

In 1954 and 1955, however, Chinese foreign policy experienced visible changes towards an ostensibly more modest direction. At the Geneva Conference of 1954, attended by a PRC delegation led by Premier Zhou Enlai, the Chinese took the initiative to meet with delegates from Great Britain, France, Laos and

Cambodia.[8] In late June 1954, during an interval of the Geneva Conference, Zhou Enlai travelled to India and Burma and had a series of meetings with Indian Prime Minister Jawaharlal Nehru and Burmese Prime Minister U Nu. In the joint Sino-Indian statement issued at the end of Zhou's visit, and then in the joint Sino-Burmese statement, Zhou, together with Nehru and U Nu, introduced the Five Principles of Peaceful Coexistence, also known as Pancasila.[9] Following all of this were Beijing's active promotion of the Five Principles and then its participation in the Bandung Conference of leaders from 29 countries in Asia and Africa on 18–24 April 1955. Towards the later stage of the Conference, Zhou announced that the PRC did not want to be the enemy of the United States and that Beijing was willing to "sit down" to negotiate with Washington to reduce "tensions in the Far East" and solve the problems between China and the United States.[10]

There were profound domestic and international reasons behind Beijing's changing foreign policy outlook in 1954–55. First of all, with the end of the Korean War, Beijing's leaders sensed the need to devote more of China's resources to domestic issues. In 1953–54 they were contemplating the introduction of the first five-year plan, as well as shifting China's resources to the "liberation" of the Nationalist-controlled Taiwan.[11] After five years of sharp confrontation with the United States and the West, many leaders in Beijing perceived that for the purpose of promoting the socialist transformation and reconstruction at home, China needed a more stable outside environment. The Chinese leaders thus saw the Geneva and Bandung Conferences as opportunities to improve China's international image. They obviously believed that a reconciliatory and positive Chinese approach would help strengthen Beijing's new claim to peaceful coexistence as the foundation of the Chinese foreign policy.[12] At this moment, Mao Zedong also endorsed this relatively moderate approach in the PRC's international strategies and policies.[13]

Second, the CCP leadership saw China's presence at the Geneva and Bandung Conferences as a valuable opportunity to boost the country's international prestige and reputation. This was particularly important for Mao and the CCP not only for apparent international reasons but also because of subtle domestic considerations. Since the birth of the People's Republic, "We the Chinese people have stood up"—the announcement that Mao made at the PRC's formation—had played a central role in legitimising the revolutionary programmes Mao tried to carry out in China. In 1954 and 1955, when Mao and his comrades were eager to "construct the foundation of a socialist society" in China, they fully understood that if they were able to present a strong case of advancement in the PRC's international status to China's ordinary people—

who, informed by their own unique "victim mentality,"[14] had been so prone to the revival of China's central position in the world—they would occupy a more powerful position to promote the party's mass mobilisation plans at home. Thus, China's active role at the Geneva and Bandung Conferences became a crucial test case that would have a profound impact upon Mao's continuous revolution and China's domestic development.

Beijing's endorsement of the Five Principles, however, was conditioned by the PRC's revolutionary foreign policies in an overall sense. In theoretical terms, Beijing's leaders, in accordance with the Leninist thesis on imperialism, believed that crises, revolutions and wars were inevitable in the "Age of Imperialism." Therefore, as they viewed it, the principle of peaceful coexistence could be applied only to the relationships between socialist countries, between socialist countries and nationalist countries, and between nationalist countries. In defining the Bandung Spirit, Beijing's leaders treated it primarily as a mentality of compromise that should be adopted in managing relations among non-Western countries. By doing do, Beijing virtually excluded such Western countries as the United States as possible target countries for the implementation of the spirit.[15] In the meantime, Beijing's leaders also tried to bring the Five Principles as a reference for directing relations between socialist countries.[16] Also related to the Chinese discourse of the Five Principles was the continuous propaganda that Beijing was a natural ally of the oppressed peoples of the world in their struggles for national liberation.

It was against this background that when the Polish and Hungarian crises erupted in October 1956, Beijing's leaders, in attempting to help the leaders in Moscow to control the crisis in Poland, raised the question of establishing a pattern characterised by more "equal" relationships within the socialist camp—especially between Moscow and other socialist countries. In particular, they criticised Moscow's "big power chauvinism" as a legacy of the Stalin era. Liu Shaoqi and Deng Xiaoping, the heads of the CCP delegation visiting Moscow at that time, repeatedly argued for the need for Moscow to respect the desires for independence of other East European communist countries, as well as to follow the principles of Pancasila in handling state-to-state relations with those countries. Largely because of the pressure from the Chinese, the Soviet leader Nikita Khrushchev and his colleagues agreed to issue a "Declaration on Developing and Enhancing the Friendship and Cooperation between the Soviet Union and other Socialist Countries" on 30 October. In this statement, issued for governing the basic principles underlying the relationships among socialist countries, Moscow promised to follow a pattern of more equal exchanges with other communist states and parties.[17]

The CCP leadership's advocacy of the Five Principles as the guideline for relations among socialist countries was accompanied by its strong opposition to Moscow's attempt to use the same principles in its dealings with the West. When Khrushchev, in the context of his de-Stalinisation efforts, discussed the necessity and possibility of pursuing "peaceful coexistence" with the United States and other Western capitalist countries, Beijing immediately expressed strong reservations. In November 1957 Mao Zedong visited Moscow to attend celebrations for the 40th anniversary of the Russian Bolshevik Revolution. At a meeting of leaders of communist and workers' parties from all socialist countries, Mao emphasised that the communists should not be frightened by the prospect of a nuclear war started by the imperialists but should realise that such a war, although carrying a high price, would bring the imperialist system to its grave.[18] Mao's statement was an apparent and deliberate challenge to Khrushchev's emphasis on "peaceful coexistence" with Western imperialist countries, and it inevitably worried Moscow's leaders. When Khrushchev and his colleagues made it clear that they were unwilling to yield to such Maoist discourse, the relationship between Moscow and Beijing was in trouble.

The PRC's relatively moderate foreign policy in the mid-1950s ended abruptly in 1958 when the "Great Leap Forward," one of the most dramatic and radical episodes of Mao's "continuous revolution," swept across China. Mao's decision to order the Chinese People's Liberation Army to bombard the Nationalist-controlled Jinmen Island played a central role in promoting the extraordinary domestic mass mobilisation associated with the Great Leap. Yet the specific reason and, related to it, timing of the shelling were internationally oriented. In July 1958 a group of young nationalist officers led by Abdel Karim Kassim staged a coup in Iraq, resulting in the establishment of a new regime friendly to the socialist bloc. In response, US marines landed in Lebanon and British paratroopers in Jordan. Despite China's distance from the Middle East, Beijing angrily protested the US-British intervention there. While millions of ordinary Chinese held protest demonstrations and rallies in Beijing, Shanghai and other major cities, the PRC government openly announced that it firmly opposed Washington's and London's imperialist behaviour in the Middle East and supported the newly born Republic of Iraq.[19] Then, under the banner of "supporting the Arabic people's anti-imperialist struggle in the Middle East," Mao ordered the Chinese People's Liberation Army to shell Jinmen. When American President Dwight Eisenhower ordered the reinforcement of US naval units in East Asia and the use of US naval vessels to help the Nationalists protect Jinmen's supply lines, a serious crisis erupted between Beijing and Washington. As Mao had not informed Moscow in advance of his decision to shell Jinmen, the Soviet leaders were shocked by Beijing's behaviour, and the Chinese-Soviet alliance was further weakened.[20]

Beijing's claim of the PRC being a major supporter of the Five Principles was further challenged in 1959, when a series of conflicts emerged between China and India. In March 1959 an anti-Chinese, anti-communist revolt erupted in Tibet. When Beijing used force to suppress the rebellion and when the Dalai Lama, Tibet's religious and political leader, took refuge in India, serious tension emerged in Sino-Indian relations. Throughout the 1950s, relations between China and India had been characterised by friendship and, oftentimes, high-level cooperation. In the autumn of 1959 there were two border clashes between Chinese and Indian garrisons, and the long-existing yet hitherto well-controlled Chinese-Indian border disputes immediately made international headlines.[21] Consequently, the end of the 1950s witnessed increasing tension between the PRC's continuous endorsement of the Five Principles discourse and its revolutionary international behaviour.

Revolution

Entering the 1960s, China experienced dramatic changes both domestically and internationally. Early in the 1960s, in the wake of the disastrous failure of the Great Leap Forward, the Beijing leadership adjusted its radical domestic policies. With Mao retreating to the "second line," Liu Shaoqi and Deng Xiaoping adopted a series of more moderate and flexible domestic policies—such as allowing the peasants to maintain small plots of land for their families—designed for economic recovery and social stability.

Within the context of these domestic changes came the softening of the tone of Beijing's representation of China's international policies. In addition to making efforts in 1960–61 to repair the damage in China's relationship with the Soviet Union, Beijing's leaders also tried to improve the PRC's relations with other countries—in particular, its non-communist neighbours. Thus, in January 1960 and October 1961, the PRC government, through making significant concessions and conducting constructive negotiations, signed treaties with Burma and Nepal respectively to settle China's border disputes with them.[22] In the meantime, Beijing also endeavoured to improve relations with New Delhi. In April 1960 Chinese Premier Zhou Enlai took the initiative to visit New Delhi and tried to seek compromises on the disputes over Chinese-Indian borders. Although no substantial agreement was reached in the meetings between Zhou and Nehru, the tension between the two Asian countries was placed under control for the moment.[23] Beijing's leaders emphasised that all of these developments were indications of China's willingness to carry out the Five Principles and to pursue a relationship characterised by "mutual respect" and "peaceful coexistence" with its neighbours.[24]

Yet this period of relatively moderate policies was short-lived. Mao was unwilling to give up either his revolutionary plans at home and abroad or his position as China's paramount leader. When the Chinese economy showed signs of recovery in 1962, Mao quickly called upon the whole party "never to forget class struggle," at a Party Central Committee meeting in October 1962.[25] Then, on a series of occasions from late 1962 to 1964, Mao repeatedly emphasised that China was facing an international environment full of crises, arguing that the international reactionary forces headed by the US imperialists were preparing to wage a war against China. Mao therefore contended that it was necessary for China to get prepared, both politically and militarily, to face this serious challenge.[26]

Among CCP leaders, voices favouring a more moderate foreign policy did not disappear immediately. For example, in the spring and early summer of 1962, Wang Jiaxiang, the head of the Party's External Liaison Department, submitted to the party's top leadership a series of reports on international affairs, in which he argued that China should base its international policies more on the Five Principles. In particular, Wang contended that China should avoid involving itself in another Korea-style military confrontation with the United States.[27] But Mao, after returning to the "first line" in the party's central leadership, quickly characterised Wang's ideas as an attempt to make China conciliate with imperialists, revisionists and international reactionaries, while at the same time reducing China's support to those countries and peoples fighting against imperialists. He stressed that the policy of "three conciliations and one reduction" came at a time when some leading CCP members had been frightened by the international reactionaries and were inclined to adopt a "pro-revisionist" policy line at home. He further emphasised that his own strategy and policy, by contrast, was to fight against the imperialists, revisionists and reactionaries all over the world and, at the same time, to increase support to anti-imperialist forces in other countries.[28] All of this inevitably caused Beijing's propaganda to return to a radical and revolutionary language, emphasising that it was impossible for the "new China" to pursue "peaceful coexistence" with the imperialists and their reactionary lackeys.

These developments occurred at a time when China's relations with India were deteriorating, along with continuing tensions on the borders between the two countries. Beijing's leaders were facing a dilemma trying to formulate a strategy to deal with the crisis situation with India. From a security perspective, since the PRC had been involved in a total confrontation with the United States since the early 1950s, and since Beijing's solidarity with Moscow had begun to disintegrate in the late 1950s, it was inconceivable for Beijing's leaders to allow China to engage in another confrontation with India. Furthermore, given India's crucial and influential position among non-Western countries, it was even less desirable for Beijing's leaders, who had consistently claimed that the PRC was a natural ally of the "oppressed nations and peoples" in the non-Western world, to get into a direct military showdown with New Delhi. Not surprisingly at all, Beijing had maintained a low-key and non-confrontational approach towards the Chinese-Indian dispute until late 1962.

In October 1962, when Nehru ordered Indian troops to expel the Chinese from the controversial territory, however, Beijing's leaders completely abandoned their policy of restraint. On 20 October Chinese troops started a large-scale "military campaign for self-defence" along China's long borders with India. In a few weeks, the Chinese not only repulsed the Indian offensive but even shattered the Indian resistance. By 20 November it was evident that the Chinese had already won the war, and the Chinese troops, if Beijing so wanted, were in a position to invade India's interior, or, as many military observers believed, even to attack New Delhi. At this moment, Beijing suddenly announced a unilateral ceasefire beginning on midnight 22 November, and the Chinese troops were ordered to retreat to areas 20 kilometres behind the actual control line between the two sides in November 1959. The Chinese-Indian border war thus ended.[29]

Mao was the central figure behind the decision to use force against India. When the situation on the Chinese-Indian borders deteriorated in the second half of 1962, Mao was the first among top CCP leaders to argue that Chinese troops were "absolutely not to yield to the pressure of the invading Indian troops."[30] Early in October 1962, when top CCP leaders were discussing how to deal with the crisis with India, Mao pointed out that it was necessary for the Chinese troops not only to repulse the invading Indian troops but also to give them a "bitter strike." On 18 October the Chinese Military Commission formally ordered Chinese troops to begin the "Chinese-Indian Border Campaign of Self-defence," emphasising that the Chinese military operation concerned the "reputation and prestige of our country and our army" and therefore China must achieve a glorious victory.[31]

What was revealed here was a crucial factor that would define the orientation of Chinese foreign policy during the rest of the 1960s. When Mao was striving to galvanise strength and momentum for the highest phase of his "continuous revolution" programmes, the "Great Proletarian Cultural Revolution," he attached more importance to international issues with the hope that international tension would be used as a source of domestic mobilisation. This was an indication that since such Maoist revolutionary programmes as the Great Leap Forward had brought disastrous consequences to China and the Chinese people, Mao and his close associates would have to rely heavily on presenting China's international achievements (in other words, re-emphasising "We the Chinese people have stood up") as an effective strategy to maintain and enhance the legitimacy of the Chinese communist state. Thus, in such events as China's border war with India, Mao was eager to stress that it was China's resolute struggles against the various reactionary forces (including the "reactionary forces" in India) that had helped enhance the PRC's international prestige and reputation as the model of a true revolutionary country. The message, first and foremost, was designed to appeal to the Chinese people's sentiment of revolutionary nationalism.

Not surprisingly, after 1962–63 Beijing's international discourse increasingly highlighted the central role that China would play in promoting revolutionary movements in Asia, Africa and Latin America. Ever since the victory of the Chinese revolution in 1949, the CCP leadership had believed that China's experience had established a model for the struggles of other oppressed peoples, and that the significance of the Chinese revolution went far beyond China's boundaries. But in the 1950s and early 1960s, Beijing's interpretation of China's international role was still subordinated to the "two camps" theory, according to which the centre of the world revolution remained in Moscow. With the emergence of the Sino-Soviet split in the early 1960s, and especially following the radicalisation of Chinese politics at home and abroad, Beijing changed its tone, publicly alleging that the centre of the world revolution had moved from Moscow to Beijing. Applying China's experience of "encircling the cities by first liberating the countryside" to the entire world, Beijing viewed Asia, Africa and Latin America as the "world's countryside." China, by virtue of its revolutionary past, was entitled to play a leading role in promoting revolutionary struggles against the "world cities."[32] As a result, tension inevitably emerged between the Five Principles and this international discourse dominated by a language of rebellion and revolution.

All of this occurred while the split between China and the Soviet Union was rapidly widening. Along with the escalation of the great Sino-Soviet polemic debate—in which both Beijing and Moscow openly and emotionally questioned each other's loyalty to Marxism-Leninism—how to define the Five Principles (and the coverage and implications of "peaceful coexistence" in particular) increasingly occupied a central position in the mutual criticism of Beijing and Moscow. In a series of attacks that Beijing waged against Khrushchev and his fellow Soviet leaders in 1963–64, the Chinese communists argued that the Five Principles in general and the principle of peaceful coexistence in particular should and could only be defined and carried out with strict restrictions. Under no circumstances, argued Mao and other CCP theorists, should these principles be interpreted as if it were possible for prolonged, let alone permanent, "peaceful coexistence" to be pursued between socialist/communist countries and other progressive forces in the world on the one hand, and the imperialists and their reactionary "running dogs" in various countries on the other. In criticising what they labelled as Khrushchev's "shameless betrayal" of the true principles of the "proletarian world revolution," Mao and the CCP leadership repeatedly contended that Moscow was making a mistake by seeking détente and "peaceful coexistence" with Washington. Beijing's leaders emphasised, "we will never pursue 'peaceful coexistence' with the US imperialists and their lackeys. ... It is our historical duty to fight against them and to bury them. On this issue of basic principle, we are fundamentally different from the leaders of the Soviet Party."[33]

Interpretation of the Five Principles along this radical line also led Mao and his fellow CCP leaders to define the tradition of the Bandung Conference and the spirit associated with it in revolutionary ways. This was most clearly revealed in Beijing's attitudes towards the second conference by leaders of Afro-Asian countries. As a gathering designed to follow the model of the Bandung Conference of 1955, the second Afro-Asian Conference was scheduled to be convened in Algeria in June 1965, in commemoration of the 10th anniversary of the Bandung Conference. From the time that the Conference was being prepared, Beijing firmly opposed Soviet participation, even in the capacity of "observer." Beijing also did everything possible to restrict the influence that India was to have on the Conference, arguing that the Conference must be held in compatibility with the spirit of promoting "revolution" and "national liberation" in Asia and Africa, and that India, as a "lackey" of Western imperialists, should not be allowed to occupy a major position at the Conference. It is apparent that Beijing, in accordance with Mao's revolutionary ideas, intended to turn the second Afro-Asian Conference into an institution of "anti-imperialism" and "anti-revisionism." Finally, the Conference was called off after Algerian leader Ben Bella was overthrown in a coup in June 1965.[34]

When the "Great Proletarian Cultural Revolution" swept across China's cities and countryside after summer 1966, Beijing's revolutionary and unyielding policies in international affairs reached a new height. This was fully reflected in the CCP leadership's attitude towards the issue of whether or not the Vietnamese communists should enter into negotiations with Washington. Since the early stage of the United States' military escalation in Vietnam, Beijing's leaders repeatedly advised their Vietnamese comrades that they should—and could only—achieve the final victory in the war by defeating the "U.S. imperialists and the Saigon puppet regime" on the battlefield.[35] In many conversations with the Vietnamese leaders in 1966–68, Beijing's leaders advised Hanoi to stick to the line of military struggle, repeatedly emphasising that "what could not be achieved on the battlefield would not be achieved at the negotiation table."[36] In the meantime, Beijing firmly rejected any attempt by Moscow or other "revisionist parties" to use the theme of "supporting the Vietnamese people" to create any "united action" against the United States within the international communist movement.[37]

Consequently, by the late 1960s, "peaceful coexistence" as a positive political term had been marginalised in Beijing's international discourse. In the meantime, China had become one of the most isolated countries in the world, facing serious security threats from all directions—the north (the Soviet Union), the west (the United States), the east (Taiwan, Japan and South Korea) and the south (India).

Rapprochement

The late 1960s and early 1970s witnessed a major turning point in China's international relations. The grave security situation that China was facing in the late 1960s, combined with the fading status of Mao's enterprise of "continuous revolution" (indeed, following the failure of the "Cultural Revolution," Mao's programmes of transforming China's state and society were increasingly losing the "inner support" from China's ordinary people), created the context in which the Sino-American rapprochement occurred.[38] In February 1972 American President Richard Nixon visited China. This event reshaped the world, which had been profoundly divided by the global Cold War. As far as Sino-American relations are concerned, it ended the total confrontation between the PRC and the United States that had lasted for almost a quarter-century, opening a new chapter in the development of relations between the world's most populous nation and its most powerful.

In preparing conditions for the Sino-American rapprochement, Beijing for the first time changed its definition of the Five Principles, so that the principle of peaceful coexistence and the Bandung Spirit could be used to justify the PRC's pursuit of a new relationship with the world's number one imperialist country—the United States. On 17 September 1968, less than one month after the Soviet invasion of Czechoslovakia, the US State Department dispatched a message to Beijing via the PRC Embassy in Poland proposing a resumption of the Sino-American ambassadorial talks in Warsaw that had been interrupted since early 1968. To the "amazement" of the Americans, Beijing not only gave a generally positive response within two days but also claimed in the response that "it had always been the policy of the People's Republic of China to maintain friendly relations with all states, regardless of social system, on the basis of the Five Principles of Peaceful Coexistence."[39]

After a series of secret contacts and exchange of messages—some of which were conveyed through Pakistani President Yahya Khan—China's intention to pursue improving relations with the United States was made open in April 1971, when Beijing invited an American table tennis team to visit China. Following the dramatic "ping pong diplomacy," in late May 1971 the CCP leaders approved the policy of pursuing a rapprochement with Washington, contending that this would be beneficial in the long run to the causes of revolutions in the world (including in the United States).[40] In July 1971 Nixon's national security adviser, Henry Kissinger, secretly visited Beijing and, through talks with Chinese Premier Zhou Enlai, paved the way for Nixon's visit to China. In the discussion, Zhou repeatedly emphasised that "equality," "mutual respect" and "peaceful development" should serve as the principles governing the relationship between the two countries.[41]

Towards the end of Nixon's visit, China and the United States signed the Shanghai Communiqué. Largely due to the insistence of the Chinese, the communiqué included a paragraph referring to the Five Principles: "The two sides agreed that countries, regardless of their social systems, should conduct their relations on the principles of respect for the sovereignty and territorial integrity of all states, non-aggression against other states, non-interference in the internal affairs of other states, equality and mutual benefit, and peaceful coexistence. International disputes should be settled on this basis, without resorting to the use or threat of force. The United States and the People's Republic of China are prepared to apply these principles to their mutual relations."[42] The Five Principles thus formally occupied a central position in China's representation of its relations with the United States.

The Sino-American rapprochement dramatically shifted the balance of power between the two conflicting superpowers—the United States and the Soviet Union—in the Cold War. In the meantime, it also completely changed China's international environment. While policy makers in Washington found it possible to allocate more of the United States' resources and strategic attention to dealing with the threats posed by the Soviet Union, Moscow's leaders, having to confront the West and China simultaneously, seriously overextended the Soviet Union's strength and power. In a deeper sense, though, Beijing's cooperation with Washington and confrontation with Moscow even changed the essence of the global Cold War. Since its beginning in the late 1940s, the Cold War had been characterised by a fundamental confrontation between two contending ideologies—liberal capitalism versus communism. The great Sino-Soviet split buried the shared consciousness among communists and communist sympathisers all over the world that communism was a solution to the problems created by the worldwide process of modernisation, leading the global Cold War in the 1970s and 1980s to continue more in *realpolitik* ways, rather than primarily on ideological terms.[43]

Consequently, beginning in the early 1970s, international politics—especially from Beijing's perspective—became dominated by a specific "triangular structure." Taking the "Soviet threat" as an overriding concern, Beijing and Washington gradually established a quasi "strategic partnership." Political leaders and military planners from the United States and the PRC frequently consulted their counterparts from the other side regarding important regional and global political and security issues.[44] It was against this background that Beijing's representation of the Five Principles—as well as the theoretical justification of the representation—experienced another significant change in the early 1970s with Mao Zedong's introduction of his "Three Worlds" theory.

As discussed earlier, in the late 1940s Mao Zedong put forward his "Intermediate Zone" theory, in which he argued that in the post-war international politics there existed a vast "intermediate zone" that was not directly controlled by either of the two superpowers yet had been identified as the main target of competition by the two superpowers. Mao believed that China also belonged to the "intermediate zone," a view that he held persistently even after the PRC entered a strategic alliance with the Soviet Union.

With the collapse of the Sino-Soviet alliance and the initiation of the Sino-American rapprochement, Mao found both the space and the necessity further to develop a new theoretical framework that would not only make sense of the PRC's changed international policies but also, and more importantly, provide crucial legitimacy to the CCP chairman's fading enterprise of "continuous revolution" at home. This formed the background against which Mao's "Three Worlds" notion gradually came into being.

In a series of talks with foreign visitors in 1973–74, Mao presented his vision of a world that had been divided into "three worlds." On 22 February 1974, in a meeting with Zambian President Kenneth David Kaunda, Mao stated: "The United States and the Soviet Union belong to the First World. The middle elements, such as Japan, Europe, Australia and Canada, belong to the Second World. We are the Third World … The United States and the Soviet Union have a lot of atomic bombs, and they are richer. Europe, Japan, Australia and Canada, of the Second World, do not possess so many atomic bombs and are not so rich as the First World, but richer than the Third World ... All Asian countries, except Japan, belong to the Third World. All of Africa and also Latin America belong to the Third World."[45]

On 10 April 1974, Deng Xiaoping, head of the Chinese delegation attending that year's United Nations General Assembly, publicly presented Mao's "Three Worlds" notion. Deng emphasised that the "First World" was made up of the two superpowers, the Soviet Union and the United States, "the two largest international oppressors and exploiters" and the "main war origins in the contemporary era." However, in comparison, the Soviet Union was even more dangerous than the United States. The "Second World" was composed of capitalist/developed countries in Europe and Asia (i.e., Japan), which, while facing the threat from the two superpowers trying to control them, demonstrated in their policies the legacies of their own past as colonial powers. The "Third World" was formed by the vast majority of developing countries in Asia, Africa and Latin America, which, in a general sense, favoured the "tendency of revolution" and opposed "the tendency of war," thus representing the "force playing a major role in promoting progress in the world."[46]

It is apparent that there were striking similarities in perceptions of how the structure of the world should be defined between Mao's "Three Worlds" notion and his "Intermediate Zone" thesis: both posed fundamental challenges to the existing world order, and both envisioned China as a central actor in bringing about changes in the world. But there were also significant differences between the two. The "Intermediate Zone" thesis, despite its Maoist feature, was formatted around the discourse of "international class struggle" in its representation. In comparison, what formed the foundation and the primary concern of the "Three Worlds" notion was the issue of economic development. In presenting it, Mao and his fellow Chinese leaders still adopted some of the "class struggle" language (such as describing the "First World" nations as international "oppressors" and "exploiters"). But as far as the notion's basic problematique is concerned, it already highlighted the importance of "development" as a question of fundamental importance that China and other "Third World" countries must encounter. Although Mao never thought of introducing a grand strategy characterised by "reform and opening to the outside world," it is through his emphasis on the issue of "development" that he—although not necessarily intentionally—created the much-needed space for the post-Mao Chinese leadership to adopt a new grand strategy that would take development, rather than revolution, as its central mission.

In terms of its impact on the practice of Chinese foreign policy, the "Three Worlds" notion also provided the necessity and created the foundation for Beijing to redefine the Five Principles as well as the Bandung Spirit in China's external relations. For the first time in the history of the PRC, Beijing began to give some universality to the Five Principles, allowing them to surpass the doctrine of "international class struggle" to become a more fundamental guideline in international affairs. In his presentation at the UN General Assembly, for example, Deng Xiaoping emphasised that the Five Principles should be treated as being of universal power in governing the political and economic relations between all nations—regardless of their size, level of development, and political, social and economic system. In particular, he stressed that "international economic affairs should be commonly managed by all nations in the world, and should not be monopolised by one or two superpowers."[47] Thus, even before Mao's death, Beijing had already made it clear that the definition and implementation of the Five Principles should be related to reforming the "political and economic order in the world."

After Mao's death in September 1976, Deng Xiaoping quickly emerged to become China's paramount leader. In the late 1970s and early 1980s, Deng managed to abandon Mao's class-struggle-centred discourse and practice of "continuous revolution," placing the modernisation of China's industry, agriculture, national defence, and science and technology at the top of his agenda. Following his pragmatic "cat theory"—"black cat or white cat, so long as it catches mice, it is a good cat"—Deng allowed economics to take precedence over politics, hoping that an improvement in people's living standards would help bring legitimacy back to the communist state.[48]

Along with these domestic changes, the Chinese government under Deng's leadership further changed its definition of the Five Principles and how the principles might be implemented. In the late 1970s and early 1980s, Beijing's leaders changed their fundamental estimation of the danger involved in a new world war. Since the 1950s, Mao and the Beijing leadership persistently claimed that because of the existence of imperialism and "social imperialism," a new world war—one that most likely would involve the use of nuclear weapons—could only be delayed, but not avoided. Beijing's leaders held this view until the late 1970s, and it had effectively prevented Beijing from giving more general significance to the Five Principles of Peaceful Coexistence. With the introduction of Deng's modernisation programmes, the Chinese leadership gradually discarded this assessment. In accordance with the changing evaluation of the world situation, Beijing increasingly emphasised the universality of the Five Principles as a guideline in international affairs. In October 1984 Deng emphasised, "by applying the Five Principles of Peaceful Coexistence, some hot spots causing international disputes and confrontation can be eliminated."[49]

Consequently, starting in the late 1970s, Beijing also dramatically reduced and finally stopped its support to revolutionary/radical nationalist states and movements in other parts of the world. In the meantime, it adopted a new opening approach in China's external relations by managing to give up some of its key ideological biases to improve relations with other prominent world powers, by applying the redefined Five Principles, in both the West and the East. By the late 1980s, when China's official ties with the United States, Britain, France, West Germany and Japan were developing smoothly, its relations with the Soviet Union had also improved significantly.

The most profound change during this period was Beijing's adoption of a new opening approach towards the capitalist-dominated "world market." Throughout the Maoist era, China maintained only minimal exchanges with other countries. Starting in the late 1970s and early 1980s, Deng took several important steps, including the dispatch of Chinese students to study abroad, promoting China's international trade, and welcoming foreign investments in China, to open China's door to the rest of the world.[50] Consequently, as the global Cold War approached its end in the late 1980s, China—as a country, economy and society—was drastically different from the China under Mao.

Reformism

China's process of "reform and opening" encountered a challenge of the most serious nature in the late 1980s and early 1990s, when the Cold War ended with the collapse of the Soviet Union and the Soviet-led communist bloc. The development associated with China's "reform and opening" was a major factor that triggered the chain effect eventually leading to the collapse of the Soviet Union and the Soviet bloc. China's "reform and opening" process up to the late 1980s had been carried out exclusively in the economic field, leaving the political system dominated by the CCP's one-party reign virtually untouched. Consequently, the huge gap between the political stagnation and the rapid economic and social changes brought about by reforms caused deep tension between China's state and society, as well as within Chinese society, finally resulting in the Tiananmen tragedy—the popular protests in Beijing and the government's bloody suppression of the protesters—in June 1989.

In the meantime, the Soviet Union's strategic overextension as a result of having to confront the West and China at the same time had exhausted its resources and power. More importantly, communism—which was most beautiful while not a political philosophy in action—repeatedly failed the tests of people's lived experience. Ordinary citizens in the Soviet Union, as well as in other communist countries in Eastern Europe, had long withdrawn their "inner support" for communism as a vision and way of life that would bring about a society of "universal justice and equality" in the future. Consequently, despite the Soviet leader Mikhail Gorbachev's courageous efforts towards *glasnost* and *perestroika*, the Soviet empire was too ailing to be saved from total disintegration. In December 1989 the Berlin Wall, which had existed as the real and symbolic dividing line between the East and West for almost three decades, was destroyed by the uprising masses. Within two short years, the Soviet Union itself also disappeared.

On the grand scale of history's development, the collapse of the Soviet Union and the end of the Cold War symbolised one of the greatest transformations in international politics. With the United States ascending to the position of sole superpower in world affairs, a host of new issues—or, old issues that had been overwhelmed by other "more important" concerns during the Cold War—emerged to define the agenda of international relations. For many in the United States and the West, the end of the Cold War initially looked like "The End of History."[51] But it quickly turned out that international communism's failure did not necessarily mean liberal capitalism's ultimate victory. This is particularly true as far as China and East Asia are concerned. The communist regime in China—together with those in North Korea, Vietnam and Laos—survived (at least in name) the end of the Cold War. In the case of China, the end of the Cold War even helped create a new space and new ways for Beijing to enter the existing international system. Thus, the Five Principles and the Bandung Spirit also were given new meanings in China's representation of its vision of the post-Cold War international system and structure.

To be sure, the legacy of 1989 was hugely negative to China. By using military force to conduct a bloody suppression of the people, the Chinese communist government had created an image of itself as the "Beijing butcher" among the international community. The human rights issue in China would be constantly highlighted as a target of widespread international criticism. Furthermore, the collapse of the Soviet Union and the end of the Cold War had effectively deprived China of the strategic advantage of being treated as the United States' "tacit ally" due to the shared perception of the "Soviet threat." The post-Cold War world was indisputably dominated by the United States' military and material supremacy as well as its capacity to dictate the mainstream discourse (as fashioned in the universality of "American-style democracy"). China, in continuing its own course of development, found it necessary to establish an identity that would allow it to appear as an "insider" in the US/West-dominated international system while, at the same time, emphasising its unique contributions to the world's peace, stability and prosperity.

It was against this background that Beijing further emphasised the universality of the Five Principles and the Bandung Spirit in its representation of China's vision of the post-Cold War world order. Increasingly, Beijing's championing of the Five Principles became associated with the perceived need to establish a "new world political and economic order"—one that would counterbalance the United States' exclusive dominance in shaping the discourse governing international relations in the post-Cold War era.

As early as the late 1980s, even before the collapse of the Soviet Union and the end of the Cold War, Beijing's leaders were already contemplating how best to define the "international system" with which China would increasingly be connected as a result of the "reform and opening" process. In presenting his consideration of this crucial question, senior Chinese leader Deng Xiaoping introduced the idea of pursuing a "new international political and economic order" on the basis of widely adopting the Five Principles of Peaceful Coexistence. Deng contended that the "new order" should be characterised by ending the "politics of hegemony" or the "politics of contending blocs" and should be supported by solving all problems between nations (particularly those with shared borders) through the Five Principles of Peaceful Coexistence. In further justifying the necessity and feasibility of pursuing such a "new order," Deng argued that in the next several decades it would not be a question of "peace or war" but, rather, a question of "development" that would determine the "new order" in the world. Deng emphasised that this was an issue that must be dealt with "on the grand level of the development of human history."[52] A noteworthy feature of Deng's statement was that even before the end of the Cold War, Deng had already identified the issue of development as one of primary importance in China's external relations, including in Beijing's pursuit of a "new political and economic order" in the world.

The period immediately after 1989 represented one of domestic and international adjustments for China. The urgent challenge facing the Chinese communist state seemed to be its own survival. To the surprise of many observers (including China experts) in the West, after a three-year period of stagnation and internal adjustment, China's process of "reform and opening to the outside world" regained strength and momentum after 1992 following Deng's (who was already in his late 80s) spring 1992 trip to China's southern provinces.[53] While the regime in Beijing remained characterised by the CCP's one-party reign, the Chinese economy had developed at an unprecedented speed until 1997, registering a growth rate in China's gross national product of around 10 per cent annually. After 1997, despite the fallout of Asia's financial crisis, China's GNP has maintained an annual growth rate of above 7 per cent, picking up speed when the impact of the crisis started to wane. The post-Cold War age has thus witnessed China's rapid rise as a significant world economic power.

This story of success provided the Chinese communist state with a much-needed basis on which to reclaim some of its lost legitimacy. However, it also brought about new challenges to China internationally. As China's economic development was not accompanied by progress in political democratisation, the persistent dominance of political authoritarianism in China often kept Beijing on the defensive in the face of criticism from the international community. China's human rights record, as many—especially international human rights watchers—view it, has not just lacked improvement, but has worsened from time to time. Moreover, along with the growth of China's economic power, there emerged the notion highlighting the "China threat"—at the centre of it was the worry that the expansion of China's economic power would eventually make it a dominant regional power, or even a hegemonic world power.

Thus we see an interesting—indeed, almost ironic—phenomenon in China's general attitude towards the outside world during the post-Cold War age. On the one hand, China has become increasingly incorporated into the world market and international community as a result of the continuation of the "reform and opening" process; on the other hand, China has become increasingly sensitive over how best to define the norms and codes of behaviour underlying the existing international order—in particular, China has become extremely sensitive towards the unilateralist and hegemonic leadership style of the United States in world politics and economy.

Against this background, Beijing's leaders—from Jiang Zemin to Hu Jintao—have continued to use Deng's language concerning the necessity of pursuing a "new political and economic order" in the world, and endeavouring to give new meanings to the Five Principles and the Bandung Spirit. They have done so in the apparent hope that this high-profile discourse will, on the one hand, allow China to claim itself as an "insider" in the US/West-dominated international system, and, on the other, will provide China with a tool to check and balance the US-dominated unilateral world order.

Throughout the mid- and late 1990s and, especially after the start of the 21st century, Beijing's representation of the Five Principles embodied some old features—such as giving particular emphasis to "mutual respect for sovereignty and territorial integrity," "non-interference in other countries' internal affairs," and "equal and mutual benefit." It also included some new considerations, especially as revealed by Beijing's efforts to construct a closer connection between the need to adopt the Five Principles and the constructive role played by the United Nations.

China's attitude towards the United Nations showed important and interesting changes during the Cold War. From the early 1950s to the early 1970s, the People's Republic of China was excluded from the UN and its Security Council as the result of China's UN seat being occupied by the Nationalist government in Taiwan. Beijing thus consistently characterised the UN as an instrument of the US imperialists and their "running dogs." After the PRC entered the UN in October 1971 (following the expulsion of the Nationalist government), Beijing's attitude towards the UN appeared to be twofold. While acknowledging that the majority of UN members were Third-World countries and that the UN could serve as a forum to reflect their voices, Beijing also emphasised that it was the First World—namely, the two superpowers—that controlled the UN.

Beijing's attitude towards the UN changed significantly during the post-Cold War age. As an integral part of China's efforts to enter the existing international community while at the same time adhering to its own identity, Beijing's leaders increasingly found that the UN (along with several other international institutions) could serve as a useful stage and forum for China. Thus, beginning in the 1990s, Beijing's leaders emphasised on many international occasions that, taking the Five Principles as the foundation, the UN should play a central role in constructing the world's "new political and economic order."

Despite the overwhelming emphasis during the post-Cold War period that Beijing's leaders have given to the Five Principles of Peaceful Coexistence, on one issue—Taiwan—they have consistently and firmly rejected the idea of renouncing military force as a possible means to achieve reunification between the mainland and Taiwan.

Underlying Beijing's inflexible policy towards Taiwan is the impact of a deepening legitimacy crisis facing the Chinese communist state in the post-Cold War era. From a historical perspective, the CCP has justified its one-party reign by emphasising two of the Chinese communist revolution's fundamental missions: that the revolution would create in China a new, communist society characterised by universal justice and equality; and that it would change China's weak country status and revive its central position on the world scene. Mao's revolution, while failing to end political privilege in Chinese society, succeeded in creating an egalitarian situation (though accompanied by poverty) in China's economic life. The post-Mao "reform and opening" process, in changing the economic poverty left over by Mao, has created sharp divisions between the rich and poor within Chinese society, thus undermining Maoist egalitarianism both as an ideal and as a social reality. As a consequence, the legitimacy of the Chinese communist regime is seriously called into question.

Under these circumstances, the Chinese communist state must attach more importance to the Chinese revolution's second mission in an effort to legitimise its existence. Consequently, appealing to the victim mentality among the Chinese people, a central myth of the communist narrative of modern Chinese history—without the CCP's successful revolution, China would have remained a weak, corrupt and divided country with no status on the world scene—has been made the single, most important justification for the existence of the CCP's one-party reign. As a result, maintaining China's unification and sovereignty becomes an issue of utmost importance for the CCP, and Taiwan represents a crucial test case in this regard.

Thus, we see a serious dilemma that China has been facing in the post-Cold War era: In China's domestic affairs, the "reform and opening" process has brought about a profound transformation in China's economy, society and population; but that transformation is yet to be carried farther into the political field. The imbalance here, in the final analysis, reflects a profound and ongoing legitimacy crisis that the Chinese "communist" state has been facing. When this is reflected in China's international behaviour, it has formed an important reason to restrict China from becoming a complete "insider" of the international community.

Entering the 21st century, Beijing's perception and definition of the Five Principles of Peaceful Coexistence became more comprehensive, further reflecting China's need to appear as an "insider" in the existing international system while, at the same time, having the space and rights to reform the system. This was most clearly demonstrated in July 2004, when the PRC government held official activities commemorating the 50th anniversary of the introduction of the Five Principles. Wen Jiabao, the premier of the PRC government, emphasised that the Five Principles were "an important political underpinning for world peace and security" as well as "an important embodiment of the spirit of the Charter of the United Nations." He further contended that the UN should be taken as "the most universal, most representative and most authoritative international organisation in today's world." Accordingly, "the UN Charter, which crystallised mankind's political wisdom in the 20th century, should find in the Five Principles an important embodiment of its spirit." (One must remember here that China as a permanent member of the UN Security Council has veto power.) Wen further emphasised that the "old security concepts centred around military alliances and arms build-ups did poorly to keep the world a safe place," and that "the Cold War mentality must be done away with in favour of a new security concept featuring mutual trust, mutual benefit, equality and cooperation, so that security be achieved through dialog and stability through cooperation." In particular, he stressed the importance for big powers (obviously with the United States as his reference) to respect—and certainly not to violate—the sovereignty and territorial integrity of other countries.[54] All of this, according to Beijing's leaders, should be viewed as the foundation for establishing a new and more reasonable international order in the 21st century.

Reconstitution

In the past half-century, the Bandung Conference and the Five Principles have occupied a crucial position in China's international relations. While it seems that Beijing has consistently based the Bandung Spirit on the Five Principles of Peaceful Coexistence in the past 50 years, the actual strategy/policy implications of the "spirit" (including how the Five Principles should be defined and implemented) changed over space and time in China's international relations. In the mid-1950s, when the Bandung Conference was convened in the heyday of the Cold War, Beijing took the Conference as an important forum for breaking up its isolation on the international scene—especially among the countries in Asia and Africa—while, at the same time, creating a new discourse of international norms that would allow the "new China" to challenge the existing international system and institutions. In the 1960s, in the context of the rapid radicalisation of China's society and politics associated with the emergence of the "Great Proletarian Cultural Revolution" and the gradual disintegration of the Sino-Soviet alliance and the "socialist camp," Beijing attached new, revolutionary meanings to the Bandung Spirit. It endeavoured to transform the Afro-Asian Conference into a Beijing-dominated institution of anti-imperialism and anti-revisionism. In the 1970s, accompanying its rapprochement with Washington and worsening confrontation with Moscow, Beijing developed the novel "Three Worlds" theory and extended the coverage of the Five Principles to include such major Western imperialist countries as the United States.

With the unfolding of a new era of "reform and opening to the outside world," the post-Mao Chinese leadership—from Deng Xiaoping to Jiang Zemin and Hu Jintao—transformed China from a "revolutionary country" and an outsider of the existing international system into a kind of "status quo country" and a quasi "insider" of the international community. Consequently, since the late 1970s and early 1980s, Beijing's definition of and attitude towards the Bandung Spirit and the Five Principles have experienced profound changes.

The Chinese leadership abandoned completely the "international class struggle" theory and "revolutionary" features in its representation of the Bandung Spirit and the Five Principles. In the meantime, Beijing's leaders have transformed the Chinese discourse associated with Bandung into a more universal guideline in international relations that all nations should observe, thus making it a crucial component of China's efforts to create a "new world order," one that has—from a Chinese perspective—a genuine diversity and multipolarity as compared with the US-dominated unilateral world order prevailing in the post-Cold War age.

The Bandung Conference was held more than 50 years ago—in April 1955. Yet the Five Principles and the Bandung Spirit associated with it—although having been repeatedly defined and redefined—remain a highly influential discourse and, at times, institution, in international affairs entering the 21st century. In China's case, with its continuous growth as a regional and world power, it can be anticipated that Beijing will hold tight onto its "power" to define and interpret the Five Principles and the Bandung Spirit, thus claiming a more prominent position on the world scene.

Notes

[1]   The Five Principles, or Pancasila, included (1) mutual respect for sovereignty and territorial integrity, (2) non-aggression, (3) non-interference in other countries' internal affairs, (4) equal and mutual benefit, and (5) peaceful coexistence. They were introduced in a joint statement by Indian Prime Minister Jawaharlal Nehru and Chinese Premier Zhou Enlai in New Delhi in June 1954.

[2]   Mao Zedong, "On People's Democracy," in *Mao Zedong xuanji* (Selected Works of Mao Zedong) (Beijing: Renmin, 1965), vol. 4, p. 1477.

[3]   For discussions, see Chen Jian, *China's Road to the Korean War: The Making of the Sino-American Confrontation* (New York: Columbia University Press, 1994); Shu Guang Zhang, *Mao's Military Romanticism: China and the Korean War, 1950–1953* (Lawrence: University Press of Kansas, 1995).

[4]   For accounts and discussions of China's involvement in the First Indochina War, see Chen Jian, *Mao's China and the Cold War* (Chapel Hill: University of North Carolina Press, 2001), chap. 4; Zhai Qiang, *China and the Vietnam Wars* (Chapel Hill: University of North Carolina Press, 2000), chaps. 1–2.

[5]   See, for example, Mao Zedong, "On People's Democratic Dictatorship," "The Bankruptcy of Historical Idealism" and "The Chinese People Have Stood Up," in *Mao Zedong xuanji*, vol. 4, pp. 1473–86, 1519–20; vol. 5, pp. 342–6. See also Zhou Enlai, "Our Foreign Policies and Our Tasks," in *Selected Works of Zhou Enlai*, vol. 2 (Beijing: Foreign Languages Press, 1989), pp. 94–102, see pp. 94–6.

[6]   See, for example, Liu Shaoqi to Stalin, "Report on Strategies of National Revolutionary Movements in East Asia," 14 August 1949, *Jianguo yilai Liu Shaoqi*

wengao (Liu Shaoqi's Manuscripts since the Founding of the People's Republic), vol. 1 (Beijing: Zhongyang wenxian, 2005), pp. 50–3.

7   Mao Zedong, "Talks with the American Correspondent Anna Louise Strong," in *Mao Zedong xuanji*, vol. 4, pp. 1191–2; Mao Zedong's conversation with Liu Shaoqi and Zhou Enlai, 21 November 1946, CCP Central Archive; see also *Mao Zedong nianpu* (A Chronology of Mao Zedong), vol. 3, pp. 150–1; Lu Dingyi, "Explanations of Several Basic Problems Concerning the Postwar International Situation," *Renmin ribao* (People's Daily), 4 and 5 January 1947. (Lu was the chief of the CCP Central Committee's Propaganda Department, and this article was revised and approved by Mao before publication.)

8   For discussions, see Chen Jian, "China and the Indochina Settlement of the Geneva Conference of 1954," in Mark Lawrence and Fredrik Logevall (eds.), *The First Vietnam War: Colonial Conflict and Cold War Crisis* (Cambridge: Harvard University Press, 2007), pp. 240–62, 346–9; Zhai, *China and the Vietnam Wars*, chap. 2.

9   For Chinese accounts of Zhou Enlai's visits to India and Burma, and his meetings with Nehru and U Nu, see Xue Mouhong *et al.*, *Dangdai zhongguo waijiao* (Contemporary Chinese Diplomacy) (Beijing: Zhongguo shehui kexue, 1988), pp. 79–81.

10 Ibid., pp. 81–9; Pei Jianzhang *et al.*, *Zhonghua renmin gongheguo waijiao shi, 1949–1956* (A Diplomatic History of the People's Republic of China, 1949–1956) (Beijing: Shijie zhishi, 1994), pp. 231–51.

11 For a more detailed discussion of Beijing's changing policies towards Taiwan in 1953–54, see Chen, *Mao's China and the Cold War*, pp. 167–70.

12 Wang Bingnan, *Zhongmei huitan jiunian* (Recollections of the Nine Years Sino-American Talks) (Beijing: Shijie zhishi, 1985), pp. 5–6; Zhou Enlai, "Report on Diplomatic Issues," 12 August 1954, Fujian Provincial Archive, 101–5–5, 54.08.12.

13 Mao's relationship with Zhou Enlai and his "peace initiative" in 1954–55 was a complicated one. Although Mao supported the "peaceful coexistence" foreign policy at the time, he regretted it in the summer of 1958, when the Great Leap Forward was emerging in China. For a more detailed discussion, see Chen, *Mao's China and the Cold War*, p. 343.

14 For a definition and discussion of the Chinese "victim mentality," see ibid., pp. 12–3.

15 On several occasions in the mid-1950s, Chinese leaders stated that China was willing to "coexist peacefully" with Western capitalist countries. At the same time, Mao contended, "Although Britain and the United States also talk about peaceful coexistence, they merely take this as lip service, and if they are asked to take true action on this, they will desist." Therefore, emphasised Mao, the Five Principles should be taken as "fitting the situation and conditions of most countries in Asia and Africa." See, for example, Mao Zedong's conversation with U Nu, 11 December 1954, *Mao Zedong waijiao wenxuan* (Selected Diplomatic Papers of Mao Zedong) (Beijing: Zhongyang wenxian and Shiji zhishi), 1994, pp. 186–7.

16 See, for example, Pang Xiaozhi and Jin Chongji *et al.*, *Mao Zedong zhuan, 1949–1976* (A Biography of Mao Zedong, 1949–1976) (Beijing: Zhongyang wenxian, 2003), p. 742.

17 See Chen, *Mao's China and the Cold War*, chap. 6; Shi Zhe, *Zai lishi juren shenbian: Shi Zhe huiyilu* (At the Side of Historical Giants: Shi Zhe's Memoir, revised edition) (Beijing: Zhongyang wenxian, 1998), pp. 549–62.

18 Mao Zedong, "Speech at the Moscow Conference of Communist and Workers' Parties," in *Jianguo yilai Mao Zedong wengao* (Mao Zedong's Manuscripts since the Founding of the People's Republic) (Beijing: Zhongyang wenxian, 1987–98), vol. 6, pp. 635–6.

19 *Renmin ribao*, 17 July 1958; Xu Dashen (chief ed.), *Zhonghua renmin gongheguo shilu* (A Factorial History of the People's Republic of China), 10 vols. (Changchun: Jilin Renmin, 1994), vol. 2, part 1, p. 215.

20 Chen, *Mao's China and the Cold War*, chap. 7.

21 On 25 August 1959 there was a bloody accident between Chinese and Indian border garrisons at Longju, which is located north of the McMahon Line of the Sino-Indian border's eastern section. Reportedly, one Indian soldier was killed and one was wounded. In less than two months, on 21 October, a more serious clash occurred at the Kongka Pass, located on the Sino-Indian border's western section, resulting in a dramatic deterioration in Sino-Indian relations. For an informative account of the Longju and Kongka Pass incidents, see Xuecheng Liu, *The Sino-Indian Border Dispute and Sino-Indian Relations* (Lanham: University Press of America, 1994), pp. 26–8.

22 Xue *et al.*, pp. 145–50.

23 Ibid., pp. 182–3.

24 See Li Ping and Ma Zhisun *et al.*, *Zhou Enlai nianpu, 1949–1976* (A Chronological Record of Zhou Enlai, 1949–1976) (Beijing: Zhongyang wenxian, 1998), vol. 2, pp. 281–2, 440.

25 Mao Zedong's remarks on and revision of the communiqué of the Tenth Plenary Session of the CCP's Eighth Central Committee, 26 September 1962, *Jianguo yilai Mao Zedong wengao*, vol. 10, pp. 195–8; for discussions, see Roderik MacFarquhar, *The Origins of the Cultural Revolution*, vol. 3, "The Coming of the Cataclysm," 1961–1966 (New York: Columbia University, 1997), chap. 12; see also Cong Jin, *Quzhe fazhan de suiyue* (The Years of Tortuous Development) (Zhengzhou: Henan renmin, 1989), pp. 505–24.

26 Zheng Qian, "The Nationwide War Preparations before and after the CCP's Ninth Congress," in *Zhonggong dangshi ziliao* (CCP History Materials), no. 41 (April 1992), p. 205; and Cong, ibid., pp. 502–4.

27 Wang Jiaxiang's report to the CCP Central Committee (29 June 1962). The original of the document is kept at Chinese Central Archives. An abridged version of the report is published in *Wang Jiaxiang xuanji* (Selected Works of Wang Jiaxiang) (Beijing: Renmin, 1989), pp. 446–60.

28 *Jianguo yilai Mao Zedong wengao*, vol. 10, pp. 188–9; Cong, *Quzhe fazhan de suiyue*, pp. 576–7, 579.

29 Editorial Group, *Zhongyin bianjie ziwei fanji zuozhan shi* (A History of Operations in the War for Self-defence on the Sino-Indian Borders) (Beijing: Junshi kexue, 1994), see chaps. 4 and 5.

30 Han Huanzhi *et al.*, *Dangdai zhongguo jundui de junshi gongzuo* (The Military Affairs of Contemporary Chinese Army) (Beijing: Zhongguo shehui kexue, 1989), vol. 2, p. 616.

31 Editorial Group, *Zhongyin bianjie ziwei fanji zuozhan shi*, pp. 179–80.

32 This idea was first openly suggested by D.N. Aidit, the chairman of the Indonesian Communist Party, and was soon widely adopted by Beijing.

33 See, for example, the nine editorial essays by the editorial boards of *Renmin bibao* and *Hongqi* (Red Flag) that were published by the CCP mouth-organs and very widely circulated between 6 September 1963 and 14 July 1964. In particular, see the two essays titled "Two Lines on the Questions concerning Peace and War" and "Two Fundamental Opposing Policies towards Peaceful Coexistence."

34 Xie Lifu (ed.), *Xin zhongguo waijiao wushi nian* (Half Century of New China's Diplomacy) (Beijing: Shijie zhishi, 1999), chap. 50; Xiong Xianghui, "The Cancellation of the Second Asian-Afro Conference and Zhou Enlai's Style of Diplomacy," in *Xin zhongguo waijiao fengyun* (The Experience of New China's Diplomacy) (Beijing: Shijie zhishi, 1996), vol. 2, pp. 168–99.

35 See, for example, Odd Arne Westad, Chen Jian, Stein Tonnesson, Nguyen Vu Tung and James G. Hershberg (eds.), *77 Conversations between Chinese and Foreign Leaders on the Wars in Indochina, 1964–1977* (Washington, D.C.: The Cold War International History Project at the Wilson Centre, 1998), Working Paper 22 (hereafter Westad *et al.*), p. 92.

36 See, for example, *Zhou Enlai waijiao huodong dashi ji* (A Chronicle of Important Events in Zhou Enlai's Diplomatic Activities) (Beijing: Shijie zhishi, 1993), p. 524; see also transcripts, Zhou Enlai's conversations with Pham Van Dong, 13 and 19 April 1968, ibid., pp. 123–9.

37 See Wu Lengxi, *Shinian lunzhan, 1956–1966: zhongsu guanxi huiyilu* (Ten-year Polemic Debate, 1956–1966: A Memoir on Sino-Soviet Relations) (Beijing: Zhongyang wenxian, 1999), pp. 913–21; Cong, *Quzhe fazhan de suiyue*, pp. 607–8; Masaru Kojima (ed.), *The Record of the Talks between the Japanese Communist Party and the Communist Party of China: How Mao Zedong Scrapped the Joint Communiqué* (Tokyo: The Central Committee of the Japanese Communist Party, 1980).

38 For a more detailed discussion of how the grave security situation in China combined with the declining of Mao's "continuous revolution" to form the context in which the Sino-American rapprochement finally occurred, see the analysis in Chen, *Mao's China and the Cold War*, chap. 9, pp. 239–45.

39 John H. Holdridge, *Crossing the Divide: An Insider's Account of Normalization of U.S.-China Relations* (Lanham, 1997), p. 25. Reportedly, it was Mao Zedong

himself who approved Beijing's quick and positive response. See Gong Li, *Mao Zedong waijiao fengyun* (A Record of Mao Zedong's Diplomacy) (Zhengzhou; Zhongyuan nongmin, 1996), p. 207.

[40]   "CCP Politburo's Report on Chinese-American Talks," 29 May 1971, in Song Yongyi (ed.), *Wenhua dageming wenku*, part I, 29 May 1971.

[41]   Memcon, Kissinger and Zhou, 9 July 1971, 4:35–11:20 p.m., Top Secret/Sensitive/ Exclusively Eyes Only, Box 1033, China HAK Memcon, July 1971, National Archive.

[42]   *Renmin ribao*, 28 February 1972.

[43]   In turn, this change in the essence and orientation of the Cold War also created an important condition to facilitate China's own process of "socialisation" in its relationship with the international system. In retrospect, this was the beginning of China's graduate transformation from an "outsider" to an "insider" of the existing international system.

[44]   Two important cases demonstrating the quasi "strategic partnership" between Beijing and Washington were Vietnam's invasion of Cambodia in 1979 and the Soviet Union's invasion of Afghanistan in 1980. Beijing's and Washington's reactions to these two crises were highly compatible. They both condemned Hanoi and Moscow, both emphasised that there existed deep interconnections between the events in Cambodia and Afghanistan, and both provided the various resistance movements/groups in these two countries with military, political and other kinds of support.

[45]   *Mao Zedong waijiao wenxuan*, pp. 600–1.

[46]   *Renmin ribao*, 11 April 1974.

[47]   Ibid.

[48]   For a critical survey of Deng Xiaoping's "reform and opening" policies in China, see Maurice Meisner, *The Deng Xiaoping Era: An Inquiry into the Fate of Chinese Socialism, 1978–1994* (New York: Hill and Wang, 1996); Harry Harding, *China's Second Revolution: Reform After Mao* (Washington, D.C.: The Brookings Institution, 1987); Merle Goldman, *Sowing the Seeds of Democracy in China: Political Reform in the Deng Xiaoping Era* (Cambridge: Harvard University Press, 1994).

[49]   Tian Zengpei (ed.), *Gaige kaifang yilai de zhongguo waijiao* (Chinese Diplomacy since the Reform and Opening) (Beijing: Shijie zhishi, 1993), p. 14.

[50]   For discussions, see Harding, *China's Second Revolution*, chap. 6; Bruce Cumings, *The Political Economy of China's Turn Outward*; William R. Feeney, "Chinese Policy toward Multilateral Economic Institutions," in Samuel Kim (ed.), *China and the World: New Directions in Chinese Foreign Policy* (Boulder: Westview Press, 1989), chaps. 9 and 10.

[51]   This was the title of Francis Fukuyama's famous book published in the early 1990s.

[52]   CCP Central Institute of Historical Documents (ed.), *Deng Xiaoping sixiang nianpu* (A Chronological Record of Deng Xiaoping's Idea) (Beijing: Zhongyang wenxian, 1998), pp. 412–3.

53   During the trip, Deng Xiaoping emphasised the crucial importance for China to continue "reform and opening to the outside world." Most important of all, Deng approved the idea of a "socialist market economy," thus opening the door for China to become further integrated into the international community.

54   *Renmin ribao*, 29 June 2004.

CHAPTER 7

Appraising the Legacy of Bandung: A View from India

Rahul Mukherji[1]

This paper attempts to explain the reasons for the decline in India's interest in Afro-Asian solidarity in the aftermath of the Bandung Conference between 18 and 24 April 1955 and its revival in the 1990s. Jawaharlal Nehru could not revive the spirit of Bandung after 1955. In the 1980s, efforts by India to revive its relationship with Southeast Asia did not meet with a warm response. The question of Bandung's legacy is especially pertinent, as India's "Look East Policy" had met with success in the aftermath of the Cold War. This policy coincided with India's shifting its development strategy from an autarchic self-reliant strategy of economic development to one that would be more comprehensively based on global economic integration. It also occurred after the end of the Cold War, at a time when India's relations with the United States had improved substantially after the demise of the Soviet Union.

This paper makes two central arguments. First, strategies of regionalism in Asia, which were based on economic integration of the region, needed partners that desired such integration. If states emphasised a model of development based on a closed economy, regional initiatives would not succeed. Second, regional integration had a strategic face. There was greater likelihood of economic co-operation among strategic friends. Bandung norms such as consensus building, dialogue, non-interference and informality, which may have aided regionalism in Southeast Asia, were not of much use in promoting India's integration with Asia in the absence of a conducive economic and strategic setting.[2]

India's tryst with East and Southeast Asia remained subdued until the end of the Cold War, for economic and strategic reasons. The legacy of the East India Company, the large Indian market, and the dominant Indian development ideology of the 1950s and 1960s stressed the need for an inward-oriented route to development. These factors reduced India's need for economic partners. Second, as the world got divided into military blocs in the 1950s and 1960s, India was not on the side of those countries that were closer to the United States and embraced global economic integration as a route to development. The United States and Japan became actively involved with the development of like-minded countries in East and Southeast Asia. Despite India's non-alignment, its proximity with respect to the USSR was viewed with suspicion and distrust by the United States and its friends. India could not become part of the co-prosperity sphere that drove economic development in East and Southeast Asia.

I shall first posit arguments about regionalism by considering two important reasons for the success of preferential economic arrangements in Asia. In the next section, I will evaluate the consequence of these arguments for assessing the legacy of Bandung for India. The final section will sum up the lessons that could be learnt from the legacy of Bandung and will argue that the region needs to avoid the contradictions that characterised the relationship between India and East Asia during the period between 1955 and the end of the Cold War.

Two Reasons for Regionalism in East Asia

This section will posit the two propositions deployed for explaining the reasons for India's lacklustre integration with Asia, despite the legacy of Bandung. The first proposition suggests that regional strategies can work if countries believe in the benefits of global economic integration. If countries such as India are sceptical about the benefits of global economic integration, there will be little incentive for them to push economic activity beyond their boundaries. The second factor impacting India's urge to come closer to Asia was the strategic setting. The Bandung norms facilitated the rise of regionalism in Southeast Asia (chapter 1). This regionalism developed in response to the perceived threat of a common enemy—communism—at a time when these countries were convinced about the benefits of trade. India, on the other hand, was closer to the enemy camp—the USSR. The next section will demonstrate why the absence of a conducive strategic and commercial setting rendered the legacy of Bandung less relevant for India for a long time, even though Jawaharlal Nehru was one of the pioneers of the movement that culminated in the Bandung Conference.

The Economic Factor

The desire to reap the gains of comparative advantage via regional trade and investment can be a source of economic regionalism. Costs of regional commerce can be cut by evolving a regional regulatory framework that is transparent and can be monitored. Such a regime can include regulatory mechanisms related to harmonised product standards, low tariffs and non-tariff barriers, easy access to port and customs facilities, acceptable rules of origin,[3] transparent production subsidies, and national treatment for foreign service providers.[4] However, countries such as India, which believed that the global economic system was exploitative, reduced their dependence on such measures until the early 1990s.[5]

An example will demonstrate the relationship between India's pro-trade policy and the success of this commercial policy. Indo-Sri Lankan trade did not pick up between 1977 and 1990, even though Sri Lanka had embraced global economic integration after 1977. A clear statement of an Indian strategy of promoting competitiveness was born only after 1991. By 1996, thanks to the success of India's globalisation, India became Sri Lanka's pre-eminent source of imports, a fact that spurred a free trade agreement between the two countries in 1998. It took just five years into the economic liberalisation for India to beat Japan to second place as a source of Sri Lanka's imports. Illegal trade between India and Pakistan, and India and Bangladesh, were robust, despite the trade barriers.[6]

This logic of integration worked well in East and Southeast Asia. A majority of the countries in this region reaped the benefits of global economic integration via an informal type of economic regionalism. Intra-regional trade as a proportion of total trade in East Asia rose from 36 per cent in 1980 to 50 per cent in 1994. For the Asia-Pacific region as a whole, the figures were 59 per cent and 74 per cent respectively.[7] In the 1950s Japan led the way in showing how export orientation with state direction was conducive to development. This was followed by the second wave of growth in South Korea, Taiwan and Singapore from the 1960s; and by a third wave of export-oriented industrialisation in countries such as Malaysia, Thailand, the Philippines and Indonesia. China adopted the same strategy in the late 1970s, Vietnam in the mid-1980s, and India only in the early 1990s. Japanese aid to the region increased from US$502 million in 1975 to US$3.6 billion in 1998. Foreign direct investment inspired by Asian production networks built by Japan played an important role in the development story. The magnitude of such investment increased from US$4.1 billion in 1985 to US$69.9 billion in 1998. The East Asian economic crisis did not produce beggar-thy-neighbour policies that would hurt countries within the region affected by the crisis. According to one estimate, Japan provided the region with more than US$80 billion in aid, and China did not depreciate its currency to hurt the competitiveness of the countries afflicted by the financial crisis.[8]

Some might puzzle over the fact that East Asia did not have formal mechanisms of regional governance of the kind that had facilitated commerce within Europe. Europe, after all, had a common currency and negotiated as one player within the World Trade Organization. Intra-regional trade as a proportion of the total trade between members of the ASEAN countries hovered around 20 per cent between 1967 and 1994.

Asian regionalism has been viewed as an inclusive, open and informal regionalism. It has been based on geographical proximity and economic complementarities rather than on supranational institutions, which required states to renounce sovereignty. Chapter 1 argues that this informality is a trait that has been characteristic of regionalism in Asia since the Bandung Conference of 1955. Economic integration among the ASEAN and the APEC countries showed how open the region was. It was dependent on US and Japanese capital and markets. It was based, in general, on a commitment to non-discrimination and a willingness to include new members or partners who could contribute to the Asian growth story.[9]

India did not participate in the process of global economic integration until 1991. Its lack of dependence on world markets precluded the need for it to participate in regional or global strategies for promoting interdependence. Bandung norms were not sufficient to spur India's integration with Asia in the absence of a commercial need. It was only after 1991, when India had come to embrace trade as a route to development that it began to take its Look East Policy seriously.

The Political Factor

The second factor that spurs regionalism, nay even economic regionalism, is cordial security relations among the concerned countries. This section demonstrates the validity of this proposition, and the next one illustrates, through a historical description of India's relations with Asia, how valid that proposition was for an understanding of India's integration with Asia. The Bandung Spirit for India needed to be predicated on a certain kind of security relations, which was marred by the Cold War.

Are security considerations, quite separate from considerations of comparative advantage, important for deciding the extent of trade with certain countries? The pursuit of relative power and wealth are intimately related to the question of gaining more from international rules compared with other states in the system. This pessimistic environment for international economic management has been used to argue that trade between a large country and a small one is especially dangerous for the small country, because the large one can exploit the dependence of the weak one in bilateral or regional settings. Albert Hirschman showed how Germany used its preferential bilateral trading arrangements with its Eastern neighbours to make them vulnerable. This was put to good use on the eve of World War II, when these countries had nowhere to go to find substitute sources of imports and exports that came from Germany.[10]

This proposition is inadequate for comprehending the roots of economic interdependence in Asia. Small countries such as South Korea, Taiwan and Singapore built up their trade with large countries such as the United States. Even within the ASEAN region, Singapore and Brunei were much smaller than Malaysia or Indonesia. The majority of the states in East Asia followed either a state-directed export-oriented policy or a laissez faire trade policy, which emphasised the importance of wealth creation through trade rather than dependence and vulnerability.

How could states in East Asia focus on comparative advantage when considerations of vulnerability and dependence characterised many other parts of the world? Scholarship in international political economy has tested the hypothesis that trade is more likely among allies, especially with one dominant power with an interest in collective security, rather than among adversaries. The dominant power has the resources and the interest to promote the institutions of trade. Trade among allies enhances the aggregate political and military power of states, which have a common goal in securing themselves against a common enemy. Vulnerability and relative gains are less a predicament within an alliance or security community than among adversaries. They increase the security of the collective with respect to those who can exploit the vulnerability of like-minded states.[11]

Statistics and historical evidence reveal that trade is greater among allies than among adversaries. The United States wished to reconstruct Europe and Japan and maintain the Canadian economy, to fight communism after the end of World War II. Dean Acheson was of the following view in the 1940s: "The preservation and development of sound trading relationships with other countries of the free world is an essential and important element in the task of trying to build unity and strength in the free world."

Denial of trade benefits to adversaries is equally important. By the early 1950s trade between the United States and the Eastern bloc was negligible. The United States had a stake in South Korea's prosperity, as this would increase its security against the North and the Soviet Union. It pushed South Korea towards this export-led growth, and the two countries developed a very special economic and trade relationship based on strategic factors. The United States' economic relations with China improved after its relations with the USSR became strained.[12]

How does the story of East Asia fit into the theory that suggests a relationship between alliances and trade? Asian prosperity, which began with Japan and subsequently engulfed ASEAN and China, was promoted through US initiatives. Second, these countries were anti-communist at the time when they became part of the co-prosperity sphere. Even though the relationships of all ASEAN countries with the United States were not similarly intimate, the ASEAN countries were all united against communism and were firmly opposed to the rise of Vietnam in Indochina. Much has been written about the evolution of norms within the ASEAN countries, which stressed non-interference and avoidance of conflict among the member countries of the region.[13] A common purpose could evolve partly due to the opposition to communism and the rise of Vietnam in Indochina.[14] The antidote for communist insurgency in East Asia was economic development through a strategy of export-oriented development.

The next section will demonstrate that security relations between India and countries in Asia that were either a part of the US alliance or aligned as a group against communism were strained during the Cold War. This happened despite Jawaharlal Nehru's bold attempts to transcend the power politics of blocs. The Bandung Spirit for India could not overcome the Cold War dilemmas. India's vigorous engagement with Asia had to wait until the end of the Cold War.

The Legacy of Bandung: India in Asia

The Political Factor

This section demonstrates the validity of the proposition that cordial security relations were essential for the efflorescence of the Bandung Spirit. Nehru tried hard through a variety of conferences, which culminated in the Bandung Conference, to use conference diplomacy as a weapon against the power politics of blocs. He achieved limited and transient success, because India's relations with China deteriorated quickly after the Bandung Conference. Second, many countries in East and Southeast Asia veered closer to the United States, while India's security relations with the USSR became cordial. The Cold War had thus taken a toll on the relevance of the Bandung Conference for India. India's substantial integration with Asia had to wait until the end of the Cold War.

India attempted to build an Asian solidarity on two important pillars at Bandung in April 1955. These were decolonisation and non-alignment. India had convened a successful conference on Indonesia in December 1948. As the decolonisation of Asian states progressed, India opposed a bipolar world with two separate spheres of influence. It needed to convince post-colonial states of the merits of its policy of non-alignment with respect to power blocs. India's wish was that countries of Asia and Africa would form a solidarity based on cooperation and development that would not require either of the superpowers for security.

Faith in Asian civilisation and values turned out to be a third—though much less effective—source of Asian solidarity. Jawaharlal Nehru opined that Asia had a glorious past and that the time for Asia had arrived again, as colonialism had been dealt a mortal blow. Indian culture had made an impact in Southeast Asia through Hindu and Buddhist cultural influences in the region. Nehru was enamoured by the continuity and depth of Chinese civilisation and had asserted that the two great countries had a dense and deep interaction, which was interrupted only by the colonial interlude. Asian cultural superiority and identity could play a role in galvanising the region once again.[15]

Such notions of pan-Asianism were viewed with scepticism by many countries in the immediate aftermath of colonialism in Asia. Perhaps the most important occasion for expressing Asian solidarity was the Asian Relations Conference held in New Delhi in 1947. Even at the height of Asian solidarity in 1947, Sino-Indian differences over Tibet emerged in this conference. The Chinese protested against a map that showed Tibet as a separate state. Delegates from Burma and Malaysia were worried that Asian domination might turn out to be worse than Western domination. Neither China nor India could concede leadership to the other party. The next proposed conference to be held in China in 1949 had to be abandoned. The Arabs were not interested in participating in such a conference. This conference mechanism for developing Asian solidarity had to be wound up by 1957.

In the early 1950s, Nehru enunciated the idea of an Afro-Asian area of peace. He had defined it as an area that did not wish war, or one that wished for peace and cooperation. It would work towards removing poverty and backwardness. The Afro-Asian bloc was not a homogenous bloc and was often opposed to the prickly Indian leadership of V.K. Krishna Menon in the United Nations. The African nations could not support India's candidacy for election to the Economic and Social Council, thus enabling Japan to get elected.

The cornerstone of Asian solidarity that remained for Nehru to exploit during the period preceding the conference in Bandung in April 1955 was to keep Asia out of the Cold War bipolar politics of the blocs. For this to happen, states in Asia needed to trust each other so that they would not desire the intervention of the superpowers. This would get increasingly difficult due to competition between the United States and the communist world for supremacy in Asia. To give an example, Carlos Romulo of the Philippines became deeply interested in the conference idea after the success of the Indian initiative on Indonesia, which was designed to fight the Dutch intervention in 1948. Romulo had planned a conference in Baguio in 1949, which would kindle the spirit of the conference on Indonesia. India opposed this conference on the grounds that it might turn into an anti-communist platform. Discussions took place between Romulo, Syngman Rhee and Chiang Kai-shek, all of whom were considered to be close to the United States. India hesitatingly agreed to a low-key participation in the Baguio Conference after the names of Syngman Rhee and Chiang Kai-shek were dropped from the list of conference invitees.

A few Asian countries had security concerns due to the communist insurgency. At the Colombo Powers Conference of April 1954,[16] both Ceylon and Pakistan raised the issue of the communist threat. Pakistan also raised the issue of Kashmir. They wished to declare communism as the major threat facing the region. It was only after considerable opposition from India and Indonesia that the watered-down resolution sought to condemn interference by communist and non-communist states alike. The situation evolving in Indochina was viewed with concern. The participants agreed to go ahead with the conference in Bandung in April 1955. The Colombo Powers Conference met for the last time in 1956.

US arms aid to Pakistan in 1954 was a significant setback for India's policy of non-alignment.[17] While the official US view was that this aid was not against India, there were hints that it was to teach India a lesson for its neutralism. In 1951 John Foster Dulles undertook a fact-finding tour of Asia and omitted India from the list of countries he visited. The United States opposed India's inclusion in the Far Eastern Political Conference in 1953. Burma was also excluded from this conference because of its close ties with India. When India was unceremoniously invited at the last moment, it declined the offer. It worried that the treaty being negotiated by the United States would only promote its sphere of influence in Asia.[18]

Nehru became dependent on China for asserting the importance of an Asian bloc, which would base its behaviour on the principle of peaceful coexistence. Within months of the US aid to Pakistan, Zhou Enlai visited India and reaffirmed the Five Principles of Peaceful Coexistence. Nehru and Zhou signed a joint declaration in New Delhi in June 1954. India had hoped that the Five Principles of Peaceful Coexistence embodied in the Pancasila Agreement between India and China, where India accepted China's sovereignty over Tibet, would become a model for promoting peace in the newly emergent nations.[19] This agreement was timely as it came a year before the Bandung Conference.

If states could coexist peacefully by abiding to certain principles, there would be little need for superpowers in Asia.

One of the successes of Bandung for Nehru was India's ability to temporarily discourage Cambodia and Laos from entering the US alliance, even though they felt insecure with respect to developments in South Vietnam. Zhou Enlai was invited to Bandung at Nehru's insistence. And, Beijing and Hanoi were encouraged to pledge themselves to the Pancasila principles of peaceful coexistence. Nehru saw an opportunity in Bandung to lobby Asian countries against the Southeast Asian Treaty Organization. He played a critical role in convincing Cambodia and Laos about China's commitment to the Pancasila principles. Prince Norodom Sihanouk of Cambodia visited New Delhi for 12 days in March 1955. By the end of the visit he was convinced of the Pancasila route to peace. This visit was significant because it occurred after Dulles's visit to Cambodia and barely weeks before the Bandung Conference. Dulles had earlier tried to convince Sihanouk of Cambodia's need to join the US alliance.

Sihanouk's Delhi visit was followed by the visit of Pham Van Dong, the foreign minister of the Democratic Republic of Vietnam in April 1955, just ten days before the Bandung Conference. Van Dong pledged allegiance to the Pancasila principles and agreed to aid the work of the International Control Commission, chaired by India. The commission had the mandate to look into the problem of Indochina at that time. U Nu of Burma, Nehru and Van Dong traveled together to Bandung from Rangoon in April 1955.

Nehru's success in Bandung lay in his ability to get Zhou, Van Dong, U Nu and Sihanouk together to pledge allegiance to the Pancasila principles of coexistence. Laotian Prime Minister Katay Sasorith observed that if the Five Principles, especially those related to non-interference and non-aggression, were observed, it would solve many problems in international relations. Zhou reassured the Thai delegation about China's strict adherence to the Five Principles. Later, he went to lunch with Sihanouk and assured him of the same. Nehru had a private meeting with Zhou, Sasorith, Van Dong and Sihanouk, where he raised the concerns of Laos and Cambodia. Zhou and Van Dong gave assurances of non-interference in Laos and Cambodia. The group came out with a remarkably harmonious joint statement.[20]

Zhou's charm impressed even pro-US heads of state such as Mohammed Ali of Pakistan, Prince Wan of Thailand and Romulo of the Philippines. There was a general feeling at the Conference that China did not present the kind of danger that they had expected. The diplomacy of tying Pancasila to non-alignment depended heavily on the Chinese acceptance of the principles. It was a temporary source of comfort for anti-communist countries in the region. Faith in the principles of Pancasila reduced their need to rush to the United States for help in the short run.

The Conference was a source of discomfort for Nehru despite his success in bringing adversarial communist and anti-communist countries together at Bandung. Many felt that Zhou's friendly demeanor won the day, while Nehru's leadership was viewed with suspicion. It was Nehru rather than Zhou who faced a barrage of criticism from countries such as Turkey, Iraq, the Philippines, Siam, Pakistan and Ceylon. Nehru was hardly called upon to mediate between China and the rest. Even though Ceylon and Pakistan brought in Cold War issues by openly condemning communist colonialism, they were on friendly terms with Zhou. Nehru could not entertain Iraqi Fadhil Jamali's proposal of forming a third bloc of developing countries.[21] Acutely aware of Zhou's ability to exploit conference diplomacy to China's advantage, Nehru became sceptical about future conferences of this sort. Neither Nehru nor the Congress Party wished to do China's bidding by facilitating Chinese participation.

There were two views about Pancasila in Indian politics. Nehru's, which had the more sympathetic press coverage, was that Pancasila was the best way to fight superpower politics and create an autonomous political space for the post-colonial world. There was another powerfully articulated view of the socialists within the Praja Socialist Party, which suggested that Pancasila was too big a price to pay for Chinese support of India's quest for international order. Acharya Kripalani, an exponent of this view, argued that Pancasila was a deal that implied acceptance of Chinese sovereignty over Tibet without obtaining any clear concessions for India on the border question. Chinese incursions into territories that India considered its own had ensued since 1954.[22]

The paradox of Pancasila in Sino-Indian relations was that the two countries, which had not even settled their own borders, were trying to push for a relationship based on mutual trust. Relations between the two countries were aggravated by Chinese activities in Tibet and the escape of the Dalai Lama to India.[23] Nehru was quite aware of the irreconcilable border differences, which had discouraged him from discussing these issues with Zhou either in China or in India. Curiously enough, Nehru had faith in Pancasila despite this knowledge. He did not bring matters regarding border incidents to the Parliament until August 1959. India's defence preparedness with respect to China left much to be desired. The death knell to Pancasila was spelled out in a letter written by Zhou to Nehru in September 1959, in which Zhou alleged that Indian demands with respect to the border amounted to formal recognition of British imperial aggression against China. China practised a consistent policy of forward movements into India between 1959 and 1961. Despite this, and clear evidence about China's intentions, India neither negotiated the border nor adequately prepared for war. The Chinese aggression of October–November 1962 resulted in a humiliating situation for the Indian Army. This defeat was one reason that made India re-think its need for a greater level of defence preparedness with respect to its neighbour.[24]

The logic of the Cold War was now clearly reflected in Asia. The ASEAN nations united as a group of states that believed in non-interference and anti-communism.[25] The fall of Sukarno and coming to power of General Suharto in Indonesia aided the formation of a pro-US group of states in Southeast Asia, which included Malaysia, Indonesia, Thailand, the Philippines and Singapore. They began to participate in market-oriented development to check communism, aided by the United States and Japan. Various proposals, such as the Zone of Peace, Freedom and Neutrality (ZOPFAN, 1971) and the Treaty of Amity and Cooperation (1976), expressed this urge. The ASEAN countries became united in their opposition and did not recognise the Heng Samrin government in Kampuchea (earlier Cambodia), which had come to power with Vietnamese support. Thailand provided refuge to the defeated forces of Pol Pot. Japan, South Korea and Taiwan were firmly in the US camp. China's relations with the United States improved considerably after the Nixon visit, and China drew closer to ASEAN.

India continued to be sceptical of countries that veered closer to the United States, and it sought security guarantees from the USSR. India's Treaty of Friendship and Cooperation with the USSR in 1971 coincided with ASEAN's proposal for the ZOPFAN. While India welcomed ZOPFAN as an assertion of independence within Southeast Asia, the Indo-Soviet Treaty was viewed with scepticism in Southeast Asia. India's dependence on Soviet military hardware only grew over time.

All this did not augur well for India's relations with anti-communist countries in Asia during the Cold War. ASEAN countries had resented India's signing the Treaty of Friendship and Cooperation with the Soviet Union in 1971. Despite Singapore's having supported India in the 1965 war, India did not respond to the former's request for help in setting up its army. India showed indifference and hostility towards Malaysia's invitations in 1975 and 1980 to Kuala Lumpur to participate in a dialogue with ASEAN. Even the chances of improved Indo-ASEAN relations during the Janata Party's rule (1977–79), in the aftermath of the Congress Party's first electoral debacle, did not bear results. India's position was complicated by the situation in Indochina when Samrin came to power in Kampuchea. In 1979 Indian delegates travelling to ASEAN countries were viewed as trying to persuade these countries to recognise the

Vietnam-backed Samrin government. India wished to strengthen Vietnam vis-à-vis China and showed its support to the USSR. The Soviet invasion of Afghanistan was also a dampener for relations between India and Southeast Asia. Consequently, the visits by Prime Minister Indira Gandhi and Foreign Minister P.V. Narasimha Rao in 1981 to mend Indo-ASEAN relations did not meet with success. Neither could Rajiv Gandhi's prime ministership yield results, largely due to the differing positions on Vietnam.

The Cold War had taken its toll on Asian solidarity. India and Vietnam had veered closer to the Soviet position, while most other countries had veered closer to the United States. The security of Asia was not considered the security of a collective that included India. Certain Asian countries that became participants in a quest for collective security and global economic interdependence, and pursued development through export promotion, were unfavourably disposed towards the USSR. Consequently, India had to stay out of the Asian co-prosperity sphere.[26]

The end of the Cold War was therefore a landmark opportunity for India and ASEAN to come together with respect to their strategic concerns. No longer would the United States, Japan or countries of Southeast Asia worry about India's taking opposing strategic sides. India's military cooperation with the United States and countries of Southeast Asia had become significant. India was invited to the ASEAN Regional Forum in 1996, a year after it was made a full dialogue partner of ASEAN. Indonesia, Malaysia and Singapore have held joint naval exercises near the Andamans since late 1991. India supplied Malaysia with training and spare parts for its Russian MiG-29 aircraft. Singapore was the one foreign country with access to training facilities at Cochin's Southern Naval Command. It also used India's missile testing range at Chandipur. The defence cooperation agreement signed by the two countries in October 2003 was significant. Thai pilots were trained to fly Sea Harriers in India. Vietnam was likely to seek India's help in upgrading its Russian MiG-21 fighter aircraft. The navies of India and Indonesia jointly patrolled the Straits of Malacca. Even the Philippines expressed an interest in the Indian Navy. A fascinating facet of India's naval diplomacy was the coming together of the navies of the Bay of Bengal, including Bangladesh, India, Sri Lanka, Indonesia, Malaysia, Singapore and Thailand, near the Andaman Islands in a congregation that was aptly christened Milan, or "confluence" in Sanskrit.[27]

The Economic Factor

This section demonstrates the validity of the first proposition discussed above, that is, the desire to reap the gains of comparative advantage via regional trade can be a source of regionalism. As long as India was pledged to a closed-economy model of development, there was little need for it to improve relations with Southeast and East Asia. All this changed after India's embrace of economic liberalisation, which pushed it to vigorously explore markets and investment. India's economic relations with its eastern neighbours were quite lacklustre until 1991 but picked up quickly thereafter, when bold economic reforms favouring competitiveness were initiated. The legacy of Bandung could not be enlivened until the onset of economic reforms in India. And the second Bandung Conference, in 2005, was quite a contrast to the first one.

The ideological and strategic battles at Bandung were not about the relative success of closed economies. It turned out that those countries that had opted out of the Soviet sphere also held a more positive view of global economic interdependence. India, on the other hand, was neither anti-communist nor a believer in the benefits of trade for a long time. This became clear immediately after independence, when debates raged about the role of trade in India's development. The Bombay Plan, suggested by the business house of the Tatas, which took a relatively benign view of trade, was rejected. India, on the other hand, believed that trade in the post-colonial world would perpetuate both dependence and poverty and destroy India's manufacturing potential.

India opted instead to borrow from a Soviet planning model of 1928, believing that Indian conditions of the 1950s were similar to those of the Soviet Union in the late 1920s. India needed to generate savings and investment from within the large Indian economy, and to use imports only for the domestic production of consumer durables. This was consistent with the literature in development economics supporting import-substituting industrialisation (ISI), which argued that countries needed to protect their markets for a while before they could compete with the rest of the world. Without learning and network externalities created within a protected market, firms in these countries would never be able to compete with the rest of the world. India's exports were discouraged by the country's ISI, with an overvalued exchange rate that made exports exorbitantly expensive; stringent licensing conditions for imports and for manufacturing in all sectors; and financial incentives for domestically oriented manufacturing. In 1966 India devalued its currency under pressure from the donors during a balance of payments crisis but reverted to the most stringent autarchic policy between 1969 and 1974. Even the first oil shock was inadequate to change India's mind. India's share of manufacturing exports of the world fell from 0.84 per cent in 1962 to 0.54 per cent in 1992.

The late 1970s was a period when the government of India initiated a critical rethink of its past policies. Various reports of the government of India stressed the need for exports and efficiency considerations. It was only in the early 1980s that some gradual changes favouring efficiency and export promotion were introduced. Rajiv Gandhi introduced bolder measures in the mid-1980s, but these could not succeed as desired because of a political economy biased in favour of ISI. The most important development of the 1980s was that reformist technocrats with a shared consensus regarding the inadequacies of import substitution had arrived within the Indian policy-making elite.

India had to wait for the balance of payments crisis of 1991, when the executive team of Prime Minister Rao and Dr Manmohan Singh initiated far-reaching reforms of the Indian economy. The crisis was the pivot around which the convinced technocrats could overturn the earlier bias in the political economy favouring ISI. The story of 1991 was, therefore, a remarkable contrast to the devaluation under US pressure in 1966. These reforms, which were home-grown, covered areas such as trade policy, exchange rate management and industrial licensing to begin with. They subsequently came to involve other areas, such as privatisation of loss-making state assets and the introduction of competition and private capital in infrastructure areas such as telecommunications, power, banking, airlines and a host of services that were considered critical for India's global competitiveness. India was also actively seeking foreign capital through foreign direct and portfolio investment. Despite the gradual pace of India's reforms, the commitment to economic reforms has been steady.[28]

India's decision to engage in global economic interdependence generated the need for trading partners. India's Look East Policy ran parallel to its economic liberalisation program.[29] ASEAN countries had expressed reservations about India's joining ASEAN in 1987. Finance Minister Singh went to Malaysia and Singapore in April 1991, soon after the balance of payments crisis. This was the Finance Minister's first trip abroad. Prime Minister Rao travelled to Japan in 1992. In his historic lecture at Singapore's Institute of Southeast Asian Studies in 1994, Rao defined the role of the non-resident Indian for fostering the development of the motherland.

Proactive Indian diplomacy at the end of the Cold War transformed ASEAN-Indian relations.[30] India was offered the status of a sectoral dialogue partner in 1992, and in December 1995 India, China and Russia were given the status of full dialogue partners. India and Singapore signed the Comprehensive Economic Cooperation Agreement, which became operational from 1 August 2005. This is the first free trade agreement signed by India. The agreement is expected to lead to a mutual elimination of tariffs, with Singapore making greater concessions to begin with. Second, there is recognition of national treatment in the service sector and easier mobility of service personnel across the two countries.[31] Third, India hopes that these provisions will not only help it to launch commerce in East and Southeast Asia but also to attract significant foreign investment. Cooperation among the best Indian institutions, such as the Indian Institute of Technology in Mumbai and the Indian Institute of Science (Bangalore), and Singapore institutions has been stressed.[32]

South Korea has been a successful investor in India. Daewoo and Hyundai raised their investment in India from US$12 million in 1994–95 to US$333 million in 1996. In June 2005 the Korean steel manufacturer Posco signed an understanding with the government of Orissa agreeing to invest US$12 billion in the state for mining and producing iron and steel. Japan's foreign investment in India is much less, even though its Overseas Development Assistance to India is substantial (US$4.2 trillion).

India's economic relations with China have undergone a transformation, despite politically contentious issues such as the boundary dispute and the question of Tibet. Prime Minister Atal Bihari Vajpayee's visit to China in 2003 was a major breakthrough in commercial terms. Bilateral trade, which was US$3 billion at the end of 2000, was US$13 billion in 2004. India enjoyed a trade surplus of US$1.78 billion. There were expectations that the volume of Sino-Indian trade could reach US$30 billion by the end of the decade. Premier Wen Jiabao's visit to India in April 2005 gave a stimulus to the task of pushing a free trade agreement with India.[33]

The Bandung Conference of April 2005 was a study in contrasts. The end of the Cold War had a salutary effect on the summit. Countries of Asia and Africa could come together on issues such as development and a greater voice in international relations. Trade and development were not in dispute, but the Western control over natural resources of the South was decried. The post-colonial world had, among its members, both great manufacturing powerhouses as well as countries that could supply raw materials. The important question was whether they could create enough commercial and cultural ties among themselves and reduce barriers to commercial exchange.

Indian Prime Minister Dr Manmohan Singh's call for a more democratic version of globalisation found many supporters. Pakistan did not participate in an anti-India campaign. India's relations with China were cordial. Singh's humble, erudite and dignified interventions won for him and for India the presidency of the New Afro-Asian Strategic Partnership. It was agreed that there would be a second conference after four years in South Africa. The United States did not seem to view this solidarity for progress as being antithetical to its interests.[34]

Lessons from Bandung

India struggled with a policy of non-alignment, which was supposed to provide it with some autonomy from superpower politics during the Cold War. It was especially concerned with keeping the United States out of Asia. Many countries in Asia were worried about the threat of communism and wished for either US support or the creation of a third bloc of post-colonial states that could accept India's leadership. India was in favour of neither and offered instead the Pancasila principles of peaceful coexistence. The 1954 Sino-Indian agreement on the Pancasila principles pointed towards a model of peace based on the practice of non-interference, non-aggression and harmonious coexistence. If two large countries with territorial differences could live peacefully on the basis of principled behaviour, this could be a lesson for others. India's limited success lay in getting China and the states of Indochina to commit to the Pancasila principles. Countries such as Cambodia and Laos momentarily stayed out of a Cold War alliance system, a fact that would have marred the Bandung Spirit. This temporary withholding of the Cold War in Asia, with respect to a few countries, could be viewed as India's success in pushing for a normative order, despite the Cold War. Nehru tried quite hard to keep Asia out of the Cold War, even though his success was rather transient.

In the long run, non-alignment and Pancasila failed to create an Asian security community consistent with India's vision. Pancasila could not produce an Asian security community independent of the United States. The security community that evolved among countries of Southeast Asia had the blessings of the United States. India was isolated from the anti-communist group because it veered closer to the USSR. Second, India was not committed to promoting its trade as an engine of growth until 1991. It was content with a development strategy that would generate a surplus within a closed economy. It therefore needed neither security nor economic linkages with Southeast and East Asia, which had cordial relations with the United States.

The alliance against communism in Southeast and East Asia developed production and trade networks with the help of US and Japanese support, in the form of access to capital and markets. The United States' success ultimately lay in the fact that anti-communist Asia became a robust area of growth in the world economy. Trade and investment networks developed more spontaneously among states that united in their fight against communism. The story of economic development in Southeast and East Asia lent support to the proposition that trade relations among states that did not pose a security threat were likely to be more robust than those that posed a security concern. India did not participate in the Asian growth story until 1991, as long as the Cold War lasted.[35]

What were the imperatives for India's Look East Policy in the post-Cold War era, and why was it succeeding? Both the security and economic considerations impeding India's engagement with Asia changed after 1991. The Cold War had ended, and India had evolved a policy of constructive engagement with the United States and the rest of Asia. India had also found benefit from exploiting international trade and capital as components of its strategy of economic development. It was now natural for India to look eastwards towards the rest of Asia for trade and capital, once the scepticism about its close ties with communism and global economic integration had been removed. This strategy produced tangible results. India secured a place as a dialogue partner of ASEAN. Indian Prime Minister Singh was elected president of the New Afro-Asian Strategic Partnership in April 2005. And India signed its first Comprehensive Economic Cooperation Agreement with Singapore in June 2005. The agreement could serve as a model for other economic partnerships in the future.[36] India was also invited to the East Asian summit in December 2005.

India, Southeast Asia and China needed to ensure that security concerns did not obstruct production networks from going beyond ASEAN and China in the direction of South Asia. Hegemonic initiatives that heightened insecurity in the region needed to be checked. The positive sum in Asian economic interdependence, which was driven by production networks in the region, needed to be boosted. The end of the Cold War and India's globalising growth strategy offered this possibility. Asia's economic regionalism, which was less institutionalised and yet more open than European regionalism, offered the hope that it could become an inclusive way to strengthen multilateralism in the post-Cold War world. India would welcome Asian regionalism as a way to generate a genuine multilateral and democratic international economic and political order.

Notes

[1]   I am grateful to Evelyn Goh, Amitav Acharya, Sumit Ganguly and Partha N. Mukherji for suggestions and discussion. I thank See Seng Tan for his prodding and patience. Anjali Mukherji provided timely editorial advice. Siddharth Mukherji and Anvita Bhuvan helped with various aspects of the research. The Institute of South Asian Studies, National University of Singapore, chipped in with valuable resources that aided the completion of this paper. The errors that remain are the sole responsibility of the author.

[2]   For an excellent description of the salience of the Bandung norms in promoting Southeast Asian regionalism, see chapter 1 in this volume.

3   Product standards often impede trade even when customs and non-tariff barriers are low. Standards often allow countries to define products and services in a way that might be tough to achieve in foreign countries. Oftentimes, such standards in goods and services trade exist only for protectionist reasons. For example, if you need a US degree to be a chartered accountant in the United States when such training is available elsewhere, this raises the cost of becoming a chartered accountant in the United States for talented people all over the world. Second, regional or bilateral arrangements have rules of origin, which are designed to ensure that a third country does not use a free trade arrangement to sell its goods or services within a member country. Such rules ensure that a certain amount of value addition should take place within a member country before a good can be exported to another member country.

4   National treatment for service providers suggests that foreign firms providing services in a particular country should enjoy all the privileges enjoyed by domestic firms.

5   See, for example, Vinod Aggarwal and Rahul Mukherji, "India's Shifting Trade Policy: South Asia and Beyond," in Vinod K. Aggarwal and Min Gyo Koo (eds.), *Asia's New Institutional Architecture: Evolving Structures for Managing Trade and Security* (New York: Springer Verlag, 2008).

6   Sanjib Pohit and Nisha Taneja, "India's Informal Trade with Bangladesh," *The World Economy* 26, no. 8 (August 2003): 1187–214.

7   East Asia included Brunei, Indonesia, Malaysia, the Philippines, Singapore, Thailand, China, Hong Kong, Japan, South Korea and Taiwan. Asia-Pacific included these 11 economies plus the United States, Canada, Mexico, Australia, Chile, New Zealand and Papua New Guinea, which were members of the Asia-Pacific Economic Cooperation.

8   Ming Wan, "Economic Interdependence and Economic Cooperation: Mitigating Conflict and Transforming Security Order in Asia," in Muthiah Alagappa (ed.), *Asian Security Order* (Stanford: Stanford University Press, 2003), pp. 280–310, see pp. 281–9.

9   Stephen Haggard, "Regionalism in Asia and the Pacific," in Mansfield and Milner, *The Political Economy of Regionalism*, pp. 20–49, see pp. 43–8.

10   David A. Baldwin, *Paradoxes of Power* (New York: Blackwell Publishers, 1989), pp. 188–93; Kenneth N. Waltz, *Theory of International Politics* (Reading: Addison-Wesley, 1979), chap. 7; Albert O. Hirschman, *National Power and the Structure of Foreign Trade* (Berkeley: University of California Press, 1945[1980]), p. 18.

11   Edward D. Mansfield and Rachel Bronson, "Alliances, Preferential Trading Arrangements, and International Trade," *American Political Science Review* 91, no. 1 (March 1997): 94–107; Edward D. Mansfield and Rachel Bronson, "The Political Economy of Major Power Trade Flows," in Mansfield and Milner, *The Political Economy of Regionalism*, pp. 188–208.

12   Mansfield and Bronson, "Alliances, Preferential Trading Arrangements, and International Trade," pp. 104–5.

178 *Rahul Mukherji*

13 Amitav Acharya, "Collective Identity and Conflict Management in Southeast Asia," in Emanuel Adler and Michael Barnett (eds.), *Security Communities* (Cambridge: Cambridge University Press, 1998), pp. 198–227; Amitav Acharya, *Constructing a Security Community in Southeast Asia: ASEAN and the Problem of Regional Order* (London: Routledge, 2001).

14 Michael Leifer, *ASEAN and the Security of South-East Asia* (London: Routledge, 1989), pp. 1–19.

15 Christophe Jaffrelot, "India's Look East Policy: An Asianist Strategy in Perspective," *India Review* 2, no. 2 (April 2003): 35–68.

16 The Colombo Powers included Ceylon, Burma, India, Indonesia and Pakistan.

17 Sumit Ganguly, *The Origins of War in South Asia* (Boulder: Westview Press, 1994).

18 Sisir Gupta, *India and Regional Integration in Asia* (Bombay: Asia Publishing House, 1964), pp. 28–63.

19 These principles were as follows: (1) mutual respect for sovereignty and territorial integrity, (2) non-aggression, (3) non-interference in the domestic affairs of other states, (4) mutual help, and (5) pacific coexistence.

20 D.R. SarDesai, *Indian Foreign Policy in Cambodia, Laos and Vietnam* (Berkeley: University of California Press, 1968), pp. 52–74.

21 Congress socialists and the British Labour Party leader Aneurin Bevan had made such a suggestion in the past.

22 Gupta, *India and Regional Integration in Asia*, pp. 63–8.

23 The rivalry over maps had emerged in 1947 when India had shown Tibet as an independent country.

24 Gupta, *India and Regional Integration in Asia*, pp. 68–84.

25 D.R. SarDesai, "South-East Asia in Independence," in M.D. David and T.R. Ghoble (eds.), *India, China and South-East Asia* (New Delhi: Deep and Deep Publications, 2000), pp. 140–3.

26 Kripa Sridharan, *The ASEAN Region in India's Foreign Policy* (Aldershot: Dartmouth Publishing Company Limited, 1996), chaps. 2–6; Sridharan, "Regional Perceptions of India," in Frederic Grare and Amitabh Mattoo (eds.), *India and ASEAN: The Politics of India's Look East Policy* (New Delhi: Manohar, 2001), pp. 65–89; Man Mohini Kaul, "ASEAN-India Relations during the Cold War," in Grare and Mattoo, *India and ASEAN*, pp. 43–88. Also see Ganganath Jha, *South-East Asia and India: A Political Perspective* (New Delhi: National Book Organization, 1986).

27 Baladas Ghoshal, "India's Relations with ASEAN," *World Focus*, New Delhi (September 2004): 3–6; G.V.C. Naidu, "India and Southeast Asia: Look East Policy," *World Focus* (New Delhi), September 2004; Vijay Sakhuja, "Cooperative Security in the Straits of Malacca: Policy Options for India," *ORF Issue Brief*, no. 2 (New Delhi, Observer Research Foundation, August 2005), pp. 1–5.

28 Rahul Mukherji, "India's Aborted Liberalization – 1966," *Pacific Affairs* 73, no. 3 (Fall 2000): 375–92; Rahul Mukherji, "Privatization, Federalism and Governance," *Economic and Political Weekly* 39, no. 1 (3 January 2004): 109–13; Rahul Mukherji,

"Economic Transition in a Plural Polity," in Rahul Mukherji (ed.), *India's Economic Transition: The Politics of Reforms* (New Delhi: Oxford University Press, 2007).

29   Isabelle Saint-Mezard, Frederic Grare and Amitabh Mattoo (eds.), *Beyond the Rhetoric: The Economics of India's Look East Policy* (New Delhi: Manohar, 2003), pp. 20–43.

30   Rahul Sen, Mukul G. Asher and Ramkishen S. Rajan, "ASEAN-India Economic Relations: Current Status and Future Prospects," *Economic and Political Weekly* 39, no. 29 (17 July 2004): 3297–308.

31   National treatment in service trade is akin to zero duty in manufacturing trade. National treatment ensures that a foreign service provider gets all the benefits that are available to domestic service providers.

32   India's exports to ASEAN countries grew from US$1 billion to US$3.4 billion between 1991 and 2001. Its imports between 1992 and 2001 grew from US$1.3 billion to US$4 billion. Between 1991 and 1998, ASEAN investments in India were to the tune of US$2.5 billion. See also Kaul, "ASEAN-India Relations during the Cold War," pp. 58–63.

33   Alka Acharya, "India-China Relations: Beyond the Bilateral," *Economic and Political Weekly* 40, no. 14 (2 April 2005): 1421–4.

34   Financial Times Information, "Afro-Asian Cooperation," *The Statesman* (India), 1 June 2005.

35   John Ravenhill, "Economic Cooperation in Southeast Asia," *Asian Survey* 35, no. 9 (1995): 850–66.

36   Jayan Jose Thomas, "India-Singapore CECA: A Step Towards Asian Integration?" *ISAS Insights*, no. 6 (Singapore, Institute of South Asian Studies, September 2005), available at <http://www.isasnus.org/events/insights/6.pdf>.

CHAPTER 8

Indonesia and the Bandung Conference: Then and Now

Dewi Fortuna Anwar

Indonesia held a major celebration to mark the Golden Jubilee Commemoration of the Asian-African Conference, more popularly known as the Bandung Conference, in April 2005. An Asian-African summit with the theme of "Reinvigorating the Bandung Spirit: Working Towards a New Asian-African Strategic Partnership" took place in Jakarta on 22–23 April, followed by a 50th anniversary celebration in Bandung on 24 April. The Asian-African Summit was co-sponsored by Indonesia and South Africa, and 106 countries were invited, including a number of non-aligned countries from Latin America. Preparations for the Summit began with the holding of the Asian-African Sub-Regional Organisations meetings, co-hosted by Indonesia and South Africa, first in Bandung in July 2003 and then in Durban, South Africa, in August 2004.[1]

The Bandung Conference, which took place in April 1955, was a major milestone in the resurgence of Asian and African nations for a number of reasons. First, this conference was the first ever formal gathering of Asian and African states, most of which had only just become independent after long periods of living under European colonial rule. Before independence, the foreign policy and international interaction of most of these countries had been carried out by their colonial masters, which were oriented more towards their respective metropolitan powers. Interactions amongst the subjected peoples of the different colonies at the formal level were generally not encouraged, though there were relatively free movements of people between Indonesia and Malaya during this period. Second, at the time of the Conference many countries in Asia and Africa were still under colonialism and struggling to gain their independence, faced with racial discrimination and segregation, and without a voice in the international arena. Third, the Bandung Conference took place at a time when the Cold War was beginning to make its impact felt, when countries in Asia and Africa were treated as pawns in the global conflict between the US-led Western bloc and the Soviet-led Eastern bloc. Fear of being dragged into the superpower conflict and used as proxies, and an even greater fear of the threat of the weapons of mass destruction that could be unleashed in the event of a global war, provided the background for the historic meeting in Bandung.

If nothing else, the Bandung Conference marked the desire of the peoples of Asia and Africa, long separated by colonial rule, to become reacquainted with each other and to draw strength from a new-found sense of solidarity in facing their common problems, both at home and in the international arena. In fact, the Asian-African Conference achieved much more than that, for from that time on one could observe the development of more concerted international efforts by Asian and African nations to end colonialism and support the movements for self-determination of the subjected peoples in these two regions. Even more significant, the Conference and its outcomes signalled the desire and confidence of Asian and African countries to play a more autonomous role in international politics that transcended the Cold War ideological divide.

The Final Communiqué of the 1955 Bandung Conference enunciated the common stance adopted by the participants, including their strong opposition to, and rejection of, colonialism, racism, the use of force in settling disputes and the presence of weapons of mass destruction. Even more significant, and having a more lasting impact, was the adoption of the Ten Principles (*Dasa Sila*) of international relations, which, among others, emphasised the principle of peaceful coexistence.[2] The Final Communiqué stated, "Free from mistrust and fear, and with confidence and goodwill towards each other, nations should practice tolerance and live together in peace with one another as good neighbours and develop friendly cooperation on the following principles:

1. Respect for fundamental human rights and for the purposes and principles of the Charter of the United Nations;
2. Respect for the sovereignty and territorial integrity of all nations;
3. Recognition of the equality of all races and of the equality of all nations large and small;
4. Abstention from intervention or interference in the internal affairs of another country;
5. Respect for the right of each nation to defend itself singly or collectively, in conformity with the Charter of the United Nations;

     a.   Abstention from the use of arrangements of collective defence to serve any particular interests of the big powers;

     b.   Abstention by any country from exerting pressures on other countries;

6.   Refraining from acts or threats of aggression or the use of force against the territorial integrity or political independence of any country;

7.   Settlement of all international disputes by peaceful means, such as negotiation, conciliation, arbitration or judicial settlement as well as other peaceful means of the parties' own choice, in conformity with the Charter of the United Nations;

8.   Promotion of mutual interests and cooperation;

9.   Respect for justice and international obligations."[3]

It is important to note that though a number of the Conference participants were members of US military alliances, such as Turkey, Pakistan, the Philippines and Thailand, whose rights to be parties to such an alliance were recognised, the Bandung Principles prohibited these collective arrangements from being used to serve the interests of the big powers. The result of the Bandung Conference clearly served as an embryo for the emergence of the Non-Aligned Movement, formally established in Belgrade in September 1961, whose membership encompassed countries in Asia, Africa, Europe and Latin America. Starting with the Bandung Conference, the new states in Asia and Africa, which on their own were too small or too weak to have their voices heard, let alone to exert influence on the big powers, together became an important voice in international politics, particularly as their numbers grew.

For Indonesia the 50th anniversary of the Bandung Conference provided a momentum not only to revisit past achievements, but more importantly to reinvigorate its foreign policy after a period of uncertainty and domestic preoccupations. The 1955 Asian-African Conference was the first major international event held by the Republic of Indonesia. Its achievements in giving birth to the Bandung Spirit and as a precursor of the Non-Aligned Movement constituted a high point in Indonesia's foreign policy, against which all later achievements would be measured. Indonesia's role in hosting the Bandung Conference and the principles that it stood for have generally been regarded as the best articulation and manifestations of the country's free and active foreign policy doctrine. As will be seen below, however, the interpretations and implementation of this foreign policy doctrine have evolved with time.

The Historical Significance of the Bandung Conference for Indonesia

The first Asian-African Conference was the brainchild of Indonesia's Prime Minister Ali Sastroamidjojo of the Indonesian Nationalist Party (PNI), whose first cabinet lasted from July 1953 to July 1955. The proposal to organise a conference of the newly independent states of Asia and Africa was first put forward by the Indonesian Prime Minister during the first meeting of the so-called Colombo Powers. At the invitation of the Prime Minister of Ceylon, the Prime Ministers of Burma, India, Indonesia, Pakistan and Ceylon met in Colombo between 28 April and 2 May 1954 in an attempt to influence the course of the Geneva Conference, which was then taking place to resolve the Indochina conflict. Sastroamidjojo suggested that the five Prime Ministers' meeting in Colombo should jointly sponsor a large and high-level conference of the independent states of Asia and Africa, to be held in Indonesia. A gathering of the Asian and African states was considered necessary to coordinate these countries' responses to the unfolding Cold War tensions, particularly as a number of these states had entered into military alliances with the big powers. The conference was expected to contribute to the relaxation of the Cold War tensions on the two continents, as well as acting as a rallying point for the continuing struggle of Asians and Africans against colonialism.[4]

Although the initial responses to Sastroamidjojo's idea were cool, as the other leaders felt at the time that Indonesia was still facing enormous internal problems, Nehru became an enthusiastic supporter after Zhou Enlai, the Prime Minister of the People's Republic of China, visited New Delhi in June 1954. Nehru and Zhou announced the Pancasila, or Five Principles of Peaceful Co-existence, and Nehru became convinced that China was sincere in its desire to develop peaceful relations with neighbouring countries. The Asian-African Conference proposed by the Indonesian Prime Minister would provide an ideal opportunity to bring China out of its isolation.[5] The Prime Ministers of the Five Colombo Powers met in Bogor in late December 1954, and it was agreed that a conference would be held in Bandung for a week beginning 18 April 1955. A joint secretariat was established for the Conference, chaired by Indonesia, in which all sponsoring powers were represented. Besides the five sponsoring countries, 24 other countries from independent or almost independent states of Asia and Africa agreed to attend and to be represented at a ministerial level.[6]

The significance of the Bandung Conference for Indonesia can probably be divided into two major areas, namely, domestic politics and foreign policy.

While some of the political impacts of the Bandung Conference were mostly felt in the period between 1955 and 1965, the Ten Principles or Dasa Sila agreed upon at the Conference, which informed the so-called Bandung Spirit, have continued to influence Indonesia's foreign policy outlook and conduct till the present day.

Since 1948 Indonesia had formally adhered to the doctrine of a "free and active" foreign policy, signifying that it would not take sides in the Cold War division between the Western and the communist blocs. Instead, Indonesia would chart its own course in international relations, based on its own considerations of its national interests.

Throughout the multiparty Parliamentary Period (1950–57), however, foreign policy in general and the orientation of Indonesia's external relations in particular were highly contested issues among the competing political parties and elites. This period saw the rise and fall of no less than seven governments in rapid succession, as no single party could form a majority government. A number of political parties and leaders wished to pursue a moderate foreign policy and closer relations with Western powers, particularly with the United States, as a means to weaken communism at home and support a more development-oriented domestic agenda. Others espoused a more revolutionary foreign policy to strengthen Indonesia's independence, complete the decolonisation process and heighten nationalism. The development-minded group of political elites had been referred to by Herbert Feith as the "administrators," while those who espoused a more revolutionary internal and external policy to mobilise the public behind a more vigorous nationalism were referred to as the "solidarity-makers."[7]

The United States had been trying to persuade Indonesia to join in the anti-communist alliance that Washington was then trying to forge, which was aimed at containing China and at preventing communist forces from gaining political power in newly independent countries such as Indonesia, among other goals. Towards this end Washington tried to tie its economic aid and military assistance to these countries to an acceptance of US political and security objectives. Indonesia had on the whole rejected US pressures to align itself with Washington, except for a brief period in the early 1950s. During the Sukiman Cabinet (April 1951–February 1952), dominated by politicians from the Islamic Masyumi Party who were pronouncedly anti-communist, Indonesian Foreign Minister Subardjo secretly signed an agreement in Washington, DC, in January 1952, in which Indonesia would agree to receive economic and military assistance from the United States under the terms of the 1951 Mutual Security Agreement. Disclosures of this agreement, however, caused controversies that led to the fall of the Sukiman government the following month.[8] From then onward, no Indonesian government would take the political risk of formalising a security tie with the United States.

Prime Minister Ali Sastroamidjojo's proposal to hold an Asian-African conference was not only intended to serve the purposes stated, but also to distinguish his administration from the previous pro-US government. Even more important, the Prime Minister espoused a more vigorous nationalism as a means to bolster domestic support for the PNI-led government, by uniting people behind an inspiring ideal of Third World solidarity against colonialism and imperialism. The Bandung Conference could be seen as the first manifestation of Indonesia's free and active foreign policy, and served as a good example of what Herbert Feith referred to as "solidarity-making" activities. Even Sastroamidjojo's political opponents had to mute their criticisms of the Conference as wasteful in the face of the enthusiasm and pride of the general public for Indonesia's role as an emerging Third World leader. Moreover, Indonesia's championing of the general struggle against colonialism also served the Sastroamidjojo government's view that Indonesia's own revolution had not been completed, a view that was most strongly propagated by President Sukarno, the founder of the PNI.

Besides the obvious gain for the Sastroamidjojo government, Indonesia also obtained two important diplomatic victories from the holding of the Bandung Conference. The first was the signing of the Dual Nationality Agreement between China and Indonesia, and the second was the support of the Conference participants for Indonesia's claim on West Irian. Under the Dual Nationality Agreement, signed by Prime Minister Zhou Enlai and Indonesian Foreign Minister Sunario, people of Chinese descent living in Indonesia would have to make an active choice to become Indonesian or Chinese nationals. This was then considered an unprecedented concession from China, since by allowing ethnic Chinese living in Indonesia to choose their citizenship China had to waive her traditional claim that all ethnic Chinese were her nationals. At the same time, Indonesia made China agree to a treaty that would make it more difficult for ethnic Chinese to become Indonesian citizens.[9] The signing of the Dual Nationality Agreement signalled the growing warmth in the relations between Jakarta and Peking.

Equally important, the Final Communiqué of the Bandung Conference included an affirmation of support for Indonesia's claim on West Irian.[10] Under the terms of the December 1949 Round Table Conference in The Hague, in which sovereignty over the Netherlands East Indies was formally transferred to the Republic of Indonesia, the province of West Irian was not included in the transfer. Throughout the 1950s and early 1960s, the struggle to free West Irian from Dutch control dominated Indonesia's foreign policy and coloured its relations with the major powers. Indonesia scored an important diplomatic triumph by obtaining the support of Asian and African countries in its attempt to resolve the dispute over West Irian through negotiations, which the Netherlands was reluctant to do. The Final Communiqué stated, "The Asian-African Conference, in the context of its expressed attitude on the abolition of colonialism, supported the position of Indonesia in the case of West Irian based on the relevant agreements between Indonesia and the Netherlands." Furthermore, "The Asian-African Conference urged the Netherlands Government to reopen negotiations as soon as possible, to implement their obligations under the above-mentioned agreements and expressed the earnest hope that the United Nations would assist the parties concerned in finding a peaceful solution to the dispute." Support from the Asian and African countries, particularly from China, undoubtedly contributed to Indonesia's increasingly radical stance over the West Irian issue in the years ahead, when negotiations and the vote in the United Nations failed to bring the desired result for Indonesia.

The Bandung Conference, however, had more far-reaching historical consequences for Indonesia. Indonesia's neutralist foreign policy had not pleased the Eisenhower government in Washington. US Secretary of State John Foster Dulles regarded neutralism in the Cold War as immoral. Although the American Ambassador in Jakarta Hugh Cumming (11 October 1953–3 March 1957) did not view President Sukarno's socialist tendency with alarm, President Dwight D. Eisenhower, John Foster Dulles and CIA Director Allen Dulles believed that Sukarno was leaning towards communism.[11]

As early as 1953 the United States was already concerned about the possible "loss" of Indonesia to communism, as it had "lost" China. Before his departure for Indonesia the new US ambassador, Hugh Cumming Jr., was apparently told by Eisenhower and Secretary of State Dulles that, using the analogy of China, Washington would prefer to see the break-up of Indonesia rather than see a territorially united Indonesia fall into communist hands. As quoted by Kahin and Kahin, Cumming recorded the Secretary of State as saying: "The territorial integrity of China became a shibboleth. We finally got a territorially integrated China—for whose benefit? The Communists … As between a territorially united Indonesia which is leaning and progressing towards Communism and a break up of that country into racial and geographical units, I would prefer the latter as furnishing a fulcrum which the United States could work later to help them eliminate Communism in one place or another, and then in the end, if they so wish arrive back again at a united Indonesia."[12]

The primary objective of US policy in Indonesia, according to NSC 171/1, was to "prevent Indonesia from passing into the communist orbit." Washington also believed that the domestic communist influence in Indonesia was then a much greater threat than the external communist influence. The United States regarded the anti-communist Masyumi and the Socialist Party of Indonesia as natural allies of Washington, while the PNI and Sukarno were viewed as being soft on communism, if not fellow travellers. Eisenhower and Secretary of State Dulles, therefore, viewed the PNI-dominated Ali Sastroamidjojo government with great suspicion.[13]

State Secretary Dulles was strongly opposed to Indonesia's initiative in organising and hosting the Asian-African Conference. Sukarno's fiery anti-colonial rhetoric and call for the rebirth of a new Asia and a new Africa, which should stand united to promote world peace based on the principles of equality and mutual tolerance of fundamental differences, contradicted the US policy of trying to contain communism, and only served to strengthen Washington's antipathy towards Sukarno. While not all of the Conference participants were non-aligned, the Conference did strengthen the neutralist tendencies of some.[14]

Even more alarming to the US government, which then pursued the policy of isolating China, Prime Minister Zhou Enlai, as Nehru had hoped, succeeded in overcoming the suspicions and hostilities of several Asian countries represented at the Bandung Conference. In the eye of the participants of the Conference, the United States was put on the defensive over its China policy, especially the ongoing Formosa Straits crisis.[15] In 1954 the United States established the Manila Pact, a military alliance between the United States, Britain, France, Australia, New Zealand and three Asian countries—Pakistan, the Philippines and Thailand—aimed at containing communism in the region. Indonesia openly opposed the alliance, and instead initiated a new grouping of Asian and African nations that sought to pursue a more independent course of action in regional and global politics. As Andrew Roadnight observed, "the Bandung Conference was seen by the Administration, as a challenge to the Manila Pact and represented, for the CIA, yet another example of Sukarno's fraternisation with the Communist Chinese—he was, as the CIA agent responsible for Indonesia put it, 'in the process of selling his charisma, if not his soul, to the communists'."[16]

The growing rapport between the Indonesian government and communist China, which was evident during and after the Bandung Conference, was viewed as an increasing threat by Washington. As mentioned earlier, Indonesia and China signed the Dual Nationality Agreement, which was regarded as an important concession by Peking towards Jakarta. At the conclusion of the Bandung Conference Zhou was an official guest of the Indonesian government, and the following month Prime Minister Ali Sastroamidjojo made an official visit to China. While only two years earlier Indonesia had leaned closer to Washington and stalled on sending an ambassador to Peking, after the Bandung Conference the situation changed quite dramatically. Feith noted, "as the US government saw it, Indonesia had moved fast from a friendly neutralism to one which was pregnant with hostility."[17] The US government became even more convinced that Indonesia was moving towards communism when the Indonesian Communist Party (PKI) came fourth with 16.4 per cent of the vote in the parliamentary elections, the first ever democratic elections in Indonesia, held in September 1955.[18]

Historians have generally agreed that Sukarno was never a communist, but rather a nationalist who was strongly anti-colonialism and imperialism.[19] Sukarno did not initially display any animosity towards the United States, which he had hoped would exert pressure on the Netherlands to resolve the West Irian issue through negotiations. The United States, however, did not wish to alienate the Netherlands, which was a valuable NATO ally, so Washington refused to accede to Indonesia's requests. Sukarno's increasingly trenchant anti-Western rhetoric and flirtation with China and the Soviet Union did not necessarily mean that he was leaning towards communism, but was partly probably an attempt to put pressure on the United States to push the Netherlands towards the negotiating table.

Sukarno's foreign policy, however, in addition to his domestic balancing act of patronising the PKI to balance the anti-communist military, was seen by the Eisenhower government as being too dangerous to be allowed to continue unchecked. The history of the US clandestine activities against Indonesia during the Eisenhower administration has now been made public and is beyond the scope of this paper. Suffice it to say that from 1955 onwards the Eisenhower government began to intervene directly in Indonesian politics, such as by giving financial support to the PNI's political opponents during the 1955 parliamentary elections. The United States also became directly involved in supporting the regional rebellions that broke out in 1958.[20] The US intervention in Indonesian politics, particularly its support for regional rebellions, would have major long-term repercussions on Indonesia's domestic politics and views of the big powers.

Although the Bandung Conference also talked about the need to promote economic and technical cooperation amongst the participating countries, there was no real development in this area due to their common lack of capacity. Notwithstanding their anti-colonial stance, participants of the Bandung Conference, as can be seen from the Final Communiqué, also recognised the need to attract foreign capital, which mostly came from the Western developed countries. There was no attempt to institutionalise the outcomes of the Bandung Conference. Instead, the most lasting legacy of the Asian-African Conference was the birth of the "Bandung Spirit," which signified Third World solidarity in promoting global peace, justice and the collective rights of the developing countries.

The Bandung Spirit and the outcomes of the Conference provided Sukarno with the platform and the mission to expound his nationalist and revolutionary zeal on a wider global stage. Indonesia's initiative and success in holding the first ever Asian-African conference put Indonesia on the world map, while Sukarno emerged as a leading spokesman for the developing nations of Asia and Africa in their struggle against continuing marginalisation, injustice and interventions at the hand of the big powers. From the time of the Bandung Conference until Sukarno's downfall in 1965, Indonesia pursued an activist and internationalist foreign policy, what was later referred to as a "Light House" foreign policy.

Probably even more important than Sukarno's tireless struggle to bring an end to colonialism worldwide and at home, his activist foreign policy and his role as a leading spokesman for the newly independent countries of Asia and Africa served important domestic political ends. Foreign policy became an important rallying cry that could unite the contending political forces in Indonesia, and pride over Indonesia's global role helped to shore up support for Sukarno during that precarious time in Indonesia's political development.

After the defeat of the vote on West Irian at the United Nations in 1956, however, and the involvement of the United States in the regional rebellions of 1957–58, Indonesia pursued a more radical foreign policy. The Bandung Spirit, which emphasised adherence to the United Nations Charter, mutual tolerance, non-interference in each other's internal affairs and the peaceful resolutions of conflict, gave way to a more confrontationist foreign policy. Beginning in 1959 Indonesia prepared to liberate West Irian by force,[21] and by 1963 Jakarta had launched a confrontation against Malaysia.[22] Sukarno's anti-colonial rhetoric became even more strident, and by the early 1960s he had organised the "Conference of the New Emerging Forces" and called on the "New Emerging Forces" of Asia and Africa to confront the "Old Established" forces of colonialism and imperialism (meaning the West). Sukarno even tried to pull Indonesia out of the United Nations, and Indonesian foreign policy veered to the left, becoming closer to communist China. This was a factor that contributed to Sukarno's downfall in October 1965.

Indonesia's Current Perspectives on the Bandung Conference

Throughout the years Indonesians have generally looked to the achievement of the first Asian-African Conference with unalloyed pride. The Bandung Conference, as already mentioned earlier, has been regarded as the finest articulation of Indonesia's free and active foreign policy principle. Indonesia's roles as a leading spokesman of Asian and African states on the global stage and as a founding member of the Non-Aligned Movement have become intrinsic to Indonesia's national identity, and provided the framework within which Indonesia's foreign policy would be conducted.

The Bandung Principles have been constantly referred to in important documents relating to Indonesia's foreign relations and in various regional and international organisations in which Indonesia is a member. Resolution No. II/MPR/1993 of Indonesia's People's Consultative Assembly on Indonesia's foreign relations stated, "Indonesia's role in settling international problems, particularly those threatening peace and contrary to justice and humanity shall be continued and intensified in the spirit of the Ten Principles of Bandung." In her address at the Thirteenth Conference of Heads of State or Government of the Non-Aligned Countries in Kuala Lumpur in 2003, Indonesian President Megawati Sukarnoputri again referred to the Bandung Spirit: "I am of the view that the spirit of Asia-Africa launched almost 50 years ago in the Asia-Africa Conference in Bandung, which then became the precursor of the Movement's inception, is in fact still valid and relevant. The Bandung spirit, whose cores are solidarity, friendship and cooperation, continue to be solid and effective foundation upon which we base our collective endeavour in resolving world order and better relations among nations."[23]

The establishment of ASEAN also referred to the Bandung Principles as its guideline. The reference to foreign military bases in the region not to be used against the member states clearly echoes one of the principles agreed upon in Bandung. More recently, the Indonesian Minister of Foreign Affairs again referred to the Bandung Principles in his argument that Southeast Asian countries should pay more attention to human rights. In his speech at a workshop on the ASEAN Regional Mechanism on Human Rights, Hassan Wirajuda said, "It is always worth reminding that the first principle of the Ten Principles of Bandung, to which ASEAN subscribes, reads '*Respect for fundamental human rights and the principles of the Charter of the United Nations.*' Indeed, the Final Communiqué of the 1955 Asia-Africa Conference in Bandung dedicated one chapter specifically for human rights and self-determination."[24] Indonesia is pushing for the inclusion of the promotion and protection of human rights as part of the ASEAN agenda, under the ASEAN Security Community formula.

Nevertheless, while Indonesia constantly refers to the Bandung Spirit and the Ten Principles of Bandung in its foreign policy, after the demise of Sukarno there was not much interest in pursuing Asian-African cooperation in more concrete terms. In fact, with the establishment of the New Order under President Suharto, Indonesia abandoned its high-profile or "Light House" foreign policy in favour of a more modest and low-profile role in promoting regional cooperation. Instead of trying to represent the developing countries in the fight against colonialism and imperialism, Indonesia's foreign policy under Suharto was primarily aimed at helping to attract international capital and foreign assistance for the country's economic development and to promote regional stability within which domestic development could take place. Notwithstanding continuing lip-service reference to Asian-African solidarity and the Non-Aligned Movement, Indonesia's foreign policy had become much more pragmatic and oriented more towards a few countries in the Asia-Pacific region and the developed countries that had played a prominent role in Indonesia's economic development. From being too close to the communist camp under Sukarno, Indonesia moved closer to the Western camp during the later period of the Cold War, which to some extent compromised Indonesia's credibility in the Non-Aligned Movement among the more radical members.

Domestic criticisms of Indonesia's low-profile role and that Indonesia was losing its international position through its neglect of its historic link to the larger Asian and African regions had partly contributed to Indonesia's commitment to making its chairmanship of the Non-Aligned Movement in 1992–94 a success. More important, however, the success of its economic development and the end of the Cold War had made it possible for Indonesia once again to assume a leading role in the Non-Aligned Movement by emphasising the importance of economic and technical issues. In contrast to the Cold War confrontational policy, it was now possible for Indonesia to promote North-South dialogue and South-South cooperation, or to pursue close cooperation with both developed and developing countries.

Indonesia's foreign policy resurgence towards the later period of the New Order was, however, short-lived due to the onset of the economic crisis. Between 1997 and 2002 Indonesia became more inward-looking as it tried to deal with various crises at home, paying scant attention even to ASEAN. Indonesia's weakening position due to its political instability, economic crisis and internal conflicts severely tarnished the country's international image and diminished its position as the first amongst equals in ASEAN.

The celebration of the 50th anniversary of the Bandung Conference, when Indonesia held an Asian-African Summit with the theme "Reinvigorating the Bandung Spirit: Working Towards a New Asian-African Strategic Partnership" in Jakarta on 22–23 April 2005, followed by a celebration in Bandung on 24 April, probably meant several things for Indonesia. The stated purpose of the

Summit was to reinvigorate the Bandung Spirit by developing more concrete cooperation between the countries of Asia and Africa in a new strategic partnership. Both Asia and Africa have developed a number of regional organisations, which have also established links with countries and organisations in other parts of the world. Yet links between Asia and Africa have remained limited, despite the hope expressed at the first Bandung Conference. The organisers of the second Asian-African summit hoped that countries in these two regions, which constitute the largest number of countries in the United Nations, could benefit from closer economic and political cooperation.

The revitalisation of the Bandung Spirit, with its emphasis on promoting peace and respecting diversity, was also regarded as timely in the face of the decline of the multilateral processes under the United Nations. Indonesia had been one of the more outspoken critics of the US unilateralism and invasion of Afghanistan and Iraq. The second Asian-African Conference reiterated the Ten Bandung Principles and the United Nations Charter as the governing principles for resolving international conflicts. The "Declaration on the New Asian-African Strategic Partnership," issued at the conclusion of the Bandung Summit on 24 April 2005, clearly stated: "We emphasise the importance of multilateral approaches to international relations and the need for countries to strictly abide by the principles of international law, in particular the Charter of the United Nations. As Asia and Africa represent the majority of the community of nations, we reaffirm the need to support and strengthen multilateralism in order to address global issues, including reforming multilateral institutions."[25]

Unlike the first Asian-African Conference, which acted primarily as an inspiration for Third World solidarity in the struggle against colonialism and autonomy in international relations, the second conference emphasised the need for practical cooperation that would bring Asia and Africa closer together. The leaders meeting in Jakarta and Bandung agreed on "the establishment of a New Asian-African Strategic Partnership (NAASP) as a framework to build a bridge between Asia and Africa covering three broad areas of partnership, namely political solidarity, economic cooperation, and socio-cultural relations."[26] The political commitment as enunciated in the declaration has been followed up by a "Joint Ministerial Statement on the New Asian-African Strategic Partnership Plan of Action" for the three broad areas of cooperation.

Equally important for Indonesia, the golden jubilee of the Asian-African Conference provided it with an opportunity to carry out a more activist foreign policy. The Asian-African Summit in April 2005 was the first major international conference organised by Indonesia since the onset of the financial crisis. With its return to political stability, Indonesia is clearly ready to embark on a more high-profile foreign policy once again. From 2002, when it held the chairmanship of ASEAN, Indonesia again tried to exercise a more vigorous role in ASEAN by introducing the ASEAN Security Concept. Just as in 1955, when the first Asian-African Conference gave birth to the Bandung Spirit and paved the way for the establishment of the Non-Aligned Movement, Indonesia hoped that the 2005 Asian-African Summit would lead to a new revitalised era in the relations between the two regions to advance their common interests.

As stated by President Megawati in 2003 at the first Asian-African Sub-Regional Organisations Conference, which met in preparation for the 50th anniversary celebration of the Bandung Conference:

> [T]he vision of human dignity that president Sukarno espoused here in Bandung, almost five decades ago, when he inaugurated the Asian-African Conference, has been largely unfulfilled … because most of the six billion world population still live in poverty. There can be no peace in the world until there is comprehensive justice. When 20 percent of the human race control 80 percent of the wealth, and 80 percent must live on 20 percent of the wealth, it is very justifiable for us Asians and Africans to be united … We have to build a bridge of cooperation that spans the Indian Ocean and connects our two continents in a New Strategic partnership.[27]

Indonesia's success in holding successive general elections, including the first ever direct election of the President and Vice President in 2004, its improved political stability and economic recovery, albeit still at a modest rate of growth, has certainly given Indonesia a renewed confidence in pursuing a more assertive foreign policy. Indonesia's initiative in holding the summit has also received accolades from different quarters. One enthusiastic ASEAN observer went so far as to note the following:

> Indonesia is rising with incredible speed. The world's largest Muslim nation has transformed itself into a proactive catalyst for change in both the regional and international arena under the leadership of President Susilo Bambang Yudhoyono … The (Asian-African) summit will mark a new benchmark for Indonesia's regional and international identity, unlike previous meetings that were heavy on fanfare and light on substance.[28]

In his first foreign policy speech, President Susilo Bambang Yudhoyono made it clear that he remained committed to the principle of an independent and active foreign policy, which, he argued, "has shown a remarkable degree of resilience and adaptability."[29] While reiterating that an independent and active foreign policy entails "independence of judgment" and "freedom of action,"

Yudhoyono argued "the necessity of a constructive approach in the conduct of foreign policy." As Yudhoyono said, Indonesia should not take an independent course of action just for the sake of being different, or end up taking a wrong turn or become marginalised, or be active for its own sake. He further argued, "constructivism helps us to use our independence and activism to be a peace-maker, confidence-builder, problem-solver, bridge-builder."

Clearly brushing aside Indonesia's relatively lacklustre foreign policy in recent years, Yudhoyono in the same speech highlighted Indonesia's past diplomatic achievements:

> We are proud of our diplomatic heritage. Indonesia convened the historic Asian-African Conference in 1955. We are a founding member of the Non-Aligned Movement. We are a founding member of ASEAN. We were at the forefront of the international law of the sea. We helped the peace settlement in Cambodia and in Southern Philippines. We are helping to manage potential conflicts in the South China Sea. We helped design the ASEAN Security Community. We have always been active in shaping regional order. And recently, we hosted the historic second Asian-African Summit in Jakarta.

It is also important to note that the political changes that have taken place in Indonesia, in particular the transition to democracy, have been reflected in the country's foreign policy outlook. In his speech at the opening of the Asian-African Summit in Jakarta on 22 April 2005, Yudhoyono argued that while the battle cry in 1955 was "Freedom," in 2005 the battle was for "human dignity" and the quest for "good governance." He also argued that the Strategic Partnership for Asia and Africa "should also serve as an instrument for the promotion of a just, democratic, accountable and harmonious society" as well as "to promote and protect human rights and fundamental freedoms." Indonesia's influence as the chairman of the second Asian-African Conference can probably be discerned from the principles adopted as the basis for the New Asian-African Strategic Partnership, which almost echoed Yudhoyono's opening speech. These include "Promotion of a just, democratic, transparent, accountable and harmonious society" and "Promotion and protection of human rights and fundamental freedoms, including the right to development." The inclusion of these principles, which have become priorities in post-Suharto Indonesia, is noteworthy if one takes into account the fact that a number of countries present at the second Asian-African Conference have tended to be hostile to these principles.

At the same time, Indonesia has begun to look at the economic potential of African countries, which it tended to ignore in the past, and to try to widen cooperation beyond government-driven activities. The government asked the

Indonesian Chamber of Commerce to host an Asian-African Business Summit in Jakarta, in conjunction with the 50th anniversary of the Bandung Conference. The two-day summit, on 21–22 April 2005, brought together high-level business representatives from the two regions. The "Jakarta Joint Declaration on Enhancing Cooperation for Progress between Asian-African Business Community," issued at the conclusion of the summit, agreed on a number of practical measures to strengthen South-South cooperation and to increase direct trade between Asia and Africa. These include the exchanging of information about each other's potential through the establishment of Asian-African Business Centres, setting up a working group to identify viable areas of economic cooperation and harmonise policies, and strengthening commitment to multilateralism and cooperation in international fora. The Asian-African Business Summit also agreed to organise an Asian-African Business Conference every two years, involving the public, academia and business sectors to intensify future cooperation and enhance trade and investment opportunities in the two regions.

Notes

[1]　Background information on the Asian-African Summit 2005 and the Golden Jubilee Commemoration of the Asian-African Conference 1955 is available at <http://www.asianafricansummit2005.org/history.htm>.

[2]　China and India had earlier enunciated the Five Principles of International Relations, known as Pancasila (as mentioned in the previous chapters). The Bandung Conference, however, elaborated on these Five Principles so that the Final Communique in fact outlined Ten Principles of International Relations, more popularly known in Indonesia as *Dasa Sila Bandung*. In Indonesia, "Pancasila" refers only to the Indonesian State Ideology, adopted in August 1945, ten years before the Bandung Conference. (The Five Principles, or Pancasila, as Indonesia's State Ideology are as follows: belief in one God, humanity, national unity, democracy and social justice).

[3]　The Final Communiqué of the Asian-African Conference is available at <http://www.asianafricansummit2005.org/history_final.htm>.

[4]　Herbert Feith, *The Decline of Constitutional Democracy in Indonesia* (Ithaca and London: Cornell University Press, 1978), p. 387.

[5]　Ibid.

[6]　The only country that declined the invitation was the white-governed Central African Federation. The two Koreas, Outer Mongolia, Israel and South Africa were not invited (ibid., p. 388). The countries participating in the first Asian-African Conference were the five sponsoring countries—Burma, Ceylon, India, Indonesia and Pakistan—plus 24 other countries: Afghanistan, Cambodia, the People's Republic of China, Egypt, Ethiopia, Gold Coast, Iran, Iraq, Japan, Jordan, Laos, Lebanon,

Liberia, Libya, Nepal, the Philippines, Saudi Arabia, Sudan, Syria, Thailand, Turkey, Democratic Republic of Vietnam, State of Vietnam and Yemen.

[7] In his book *The Decline of Constitutional Democracy in Indonesia* (cited above), Herbert Feith divided the style of the Indonesian political leaders during the 1950s into two categories: the "solidarity-makers" and the "administrators." The "solidarity-makers," exemplified by President Sukarno, believed that the Indonesian revolution was not yet over as West Irian had not been liberated from Dutch control, and that to create a strong sense of national unity the government must promote a strong sense of nationalism and pursue policies that would unite the politically fragmented nation behind the government. The "administrators," exemplified by Vice President Hatta, an economist, believed that after obtaining independence Indonesia must achieve political stability and economic development, and to achieve these Indonesia should develop cooperation with the developed countries, including the United States and the former colonial powers.

[8] Ibid., pp. 198–9. See also Robert J. McMahon, *Colonialism and Cold War: The United States and the Struggle for Indonesian Independence, 1945–49* (Ithaca and London: Cornell University Press, 1981).

[9] Ibid., p. 300.

[10] Ibid., p. 303.

[11] Audrey R. Kahin and George McTurnan Kahin, *Subversion as Foreign Policy: The Secret Eisenhower and Dulles Debacle in Indonesia* (New York: The New Press, 1995), pp. 76–7.

[12] Kahin and Kahin, *Subversion as Foreign Policy*, p. 75. See also Andrew Roadnight, *United States Policy towards Indonesia in the Truman and Eisenhower Years* (Basingstoke and New York: Palgrave MacMillan, 2002), p. 106.

[13] Roadnight, ibid.

[14] Ibid.

[15] A chartered Air India plane carrying eight members of the Chinese delegation, a Vietnamese and two European journalists to the Bandung Conference crashed under mysterious circumstances after taking off from Hong Kong on 11 April 1955. The Chinese government claimed that it was an act of sabotage carried out by the United States and Taiwan. See William Blum, "Indonesia 1957–1958. War and Pornography," in William Blum, *Killing Hope: US Military and CIA Interventions since World War II* (Monroe, Maine: Common Courage Press, 2003).

[16] Roadnight, *United States Policy towards Indonesia*, p. 126.

[17] Feith, *The Decline of Constitutional Democracy*, p. 391.

[18] Kahin and Kahin, *Subversion as Foreign Policy*, p. 75.

[19] John D. Legge's *Sukarno: A Political Biography* (London: Allen Lane, Penguin Press, 1972) is the best scholarly biography on Sukarno to date.

[20] See Kahin and Kahin, *Subversion as Foreign Policy*; Blum, "Indonesia 1957–1958;" Roadnight, *United States Policy towards Indonesia*, p. 106.

21   Indonesia tried to buy arms from the United States to fight against the Dutch, but the proposal was turned down by the United States since it did not want its weapons to be used against its own ally. Indonesia then turned to the Soviet Union, which granted the request. After the United States saw that its policy towards Indonesia, especially *vis-à-vis* West Irian, had pushed Indonesia even closer to the communist camp, the new Kennedy government tried to broker a peaceful settlement between Indonesia and the Netherlands. An agreement was reached in 1962.

22   Indonesia objected to the establishment of Malaysia, which incorporated the British Borneo territories and Singapore, seeing in it an attempt by the British to retain their presence in the region and to encircle Indonesia. See J.A.C. Mackie, *Konfrontasi: The Indonesia-Malaysia Dispute, 1963–1966* (Kuala Lumpur: Oxford University Press, 1974).

23   Address by the President of the Republic of Indonesia at the Thirteenth Conference of Heads of State or Government of the Non-Aligned Countries, Kuala Lumpur, 24 February 2003.

24   Keynote speech by H.E. Dr. N. Hassan Wirajuda, Republic of Indonesia Minister for Foreign Affairs, at the Fourth Workshop on the ASEAN Regional Mechanism on Human Rights, Jakarta, 17 June 2004.

25   "Declaration on the New Asian-African Strategic Partnership," <http://www.asianafricansummit2005.org/statements_declaration.htm>.

26   Ibid.

27   Remarks by the President of the Republic of Indonesia at the First Asian-African Sub-Regional Organisations Conference, Bandung, 29 July 2003.

28   Kavi Chongkittavorn, "Indonesia Takes Its Place among the Movers and Shakers," *The Nation*, 28 March 2005.

29   Speech by H.E. Dr. Susilo Bambang Yudhoyono, President of the Republic of Indonesia, before the Indonesian Council of World Affairs, Jakarta, 19 May 2005.

CHAPTER 9

Bandung 1955 and Washington's Southeast Asia

Michael J. Montesano[1]

Ambiguities, Tensions and Complications in the US Approach to Southeast Asia

With the destructive, aberrational purges of the McCarthy era behind it, official Washington could during the last three or four decades of the 20th century draw on an exceptionally deep roster of talented East Asia hands. Among the men and women on that roster, whose preparation contrasted so sharply with that of Washington's cadre of Southeast Asianists, few had the opportunity to be in the right place at the right time so often as James Lilley. Dispatched as the CIA's man in the new United States Liaison Office in China by James Schlesinger and Henry Kissinger in 1973 and appointed director of the American Institute in Taiwan by Ronald Reagan nine years later, the China-born Lilley also served as ambassador to Seoul at the time of the 1987 protests that launched South Korea's democratic transition and to Beijing at the time of Tiananmen in 1989. China, where his father had begun work for Standard Oil in 1916, and Sino-American relations were the focus of Lilley's long career in government. He aptly exemplifies the mature, sophisticated approach of the US government to East Asia, its political economy and its security dilemmas from the 1960s onwards.

During that period, Southeast Asia was treated in most respects as a world apart from East Asia's largest state, the People's Republic of China. In the decades before Washington first "declared" him to Beijing as an intelligence officer, however, Lilley pursued US interests *vis-à-vis* China far from the limelight, and above all in Southeast rather than East Asia.[2] The late 1950s and early 1960s found him working from the CIA's "stations" in Manila and then Phnom Penh. In each post, the essence of Lilley's mission was what would later be termed "geopolitical." To counter Beijing's operations in the Philippines and Cambodia and develop sources of information on events inside a People's Republic of China from which the CIA was otherwise cut off, that is, Lilley played his own part in Washington's broad-based prosecution of the Cold War in Asia. For all its global significance, however, Lilley's work engaged him constantly and intensively with the local and the regional in both the Philippines and Cambodia. Each posting required that he understand the character and dynamics of the local Chinese population, that he develop contacts among its leaders, and that he master the flow of people and information between Southeast Asian Chinese communities and China.[3]

The career of James Lilley reveals the contours of Washington's approach to Southeast Asia in the decades following the 1955 Bandung Conference of Asian and African nations not by following them but rather by cutting across them. From the vantage point of 2005, the early Southeast Asian detour in the career of this American China-hand in the decade after Bandung highlights the ambiguities, tensions and complications in Washington's understanding of and strategy in Southeast Asia. No effort to grasp either US involvement in Southeast Asia during the past half-century or the ultimate legacy of Bandung for the United States is complete without an appreciation of those ambiguities, tensions and complications. At least three among their number merit mention here; subsequent sections of the chapter treat each of the three in more detail.

To start, Lilley's own day-to-day work in Southeast Asia not only juxtaposed the local and the geopolitical in almost surreal—and, in the end, not terribly effective—fashion, but it also belied the central tenet of Washington's policy towards Southeast Asia at the time. Politically, militarily, economically, culturally and intellectually, that policy aimed to draw as sharp a line as possible between Southeast Asia and China, as well as to deny or obscure the fundamental importance of linkages with China in the internal workings of Southeast Asian states. Yet, rather than merely combating PRC influence in the Philippines and Cambodia, the CIA assigned Lilley to study those linkages and to make them a useful tool in his own work. This very work affirmed the salience of exactly that which US policy sought to deny.

Second, insofar as Bandung belongs above all to the history of the Non-Aligned Movement, it ought to figure as a non-event in official Washington's view of global, not to mention Southeast Asian, affairs. Washington had little interest in charting the high points of non-alignment; that the movement's achievements might actually inform US foreign policy during the Cold War would have struck most on the banks of the Potomac as inconceivable, above all in relation to Southeast Asia.

But Bandung's history belongs not only to the history of non-alignment. It also, and perhaps more significantly, belongs to that of the international community's long and ongoing effort to negotiate a relationship with and place for post-1949 China. This effort was one that Washington—albeit with occasional dramatic changes of course, frequently irreconcilable priorities, and decidedly mixed results—approached with the greatest seriousness. The United States' participation in this effort saw it deploy innumerable young spies and, eventually, many able ambassadors, such as James Lilley, to Asia. More than anything else, this chapter argues for recognition of Bandung's status as a forgotten preface to the story of their labours and the labours of the government that they represented to work out a viable Sino-American relationship.

Third, the Asian statesmen who conceived of, hosted and participated in the Bandung Conference understood it as an event of global or, at risk of anachronism, geopolitical rather than regional or Southeast Asian import. Nonetheless, the Conference's Southeast Asian setting, its subsequent strong association with one of the giants of modern Southeast Asian history, and the list of Southeast Asian states included in (and excluded from) the Conference gave Bandung—just like Lilley's effort to use Manila and Phnom Penh as perches from which to observe China—an undeniably Southeast Asian character. This chapter stresses the place of Bandung in the region's history. That stress makes manifest the relevance of the Conference to US foreign policy, with its often-overlooked basis in regional rather than global concerns.

No less during the Cold War than historically or more recently, drawing a line between China and Southeast Asia was an exercise in futility. In its clear regional dimension, Bandung presented an opportunity to affirm China's connection to Southeast Asian affairs. If it proved an opportunity in which the United States had no interest at the time, the United States would a decade and a half after the Conference change its mind.

Rather than breaking new empirical ground, this chapter takes the form of an interpretive essay. It draws on a range of well known, conventional sources to sketch in bold strokes an impression of Washington's approach to Southeast Asia from an alternative perspective. This perspective differs from dominant, essentially Cold War perspectives in its incorporation of Bandung 1955 and its implications for the region into the story of US-Southeast Asian relations. While not denying the validity or usefulness of those other perspectives outright, the chapter argues that they lead observers to pay insufficient attention to dynamics within Southeast Asia itself. It suggests that continued attention to those dynamics remains basic to understanding present and future Sino-American interactions in the region.

Viewing Bandung in Southeast Asian Perspective: China and the Region

Concerns specific to Southeast Asia motivated the Bandung Conference from the moment of its conception. For all their interest in global questions of decolonisation and neo-colonialism, capitalist-communist rivalry in international affairs, and solidarity among the new nations of Asia, Africa and perhaps beyond, the representatives of Burma, India, Ceylon, Pakistan and Indonesia whose April 1954 meeting at Colombo set concrete plans for Bandung in motion also had the region very much on their minds. Among their Southeast Asian concerns, the troubles of Indochina figured most prominently.[4]

As called to order just a year after the Colombo meeting, the Bandung Conference included among its 29 participants representatives of no fewer than eight Southeast Asian states: Burma, Indonesia, Thailand, the Democratic Republic of Vietnam (North), the State of Vietnam (South), Cambodia, Laos and the Philippines.[5] Of course, official representatives of the colonial regimes of neither British Malaya nor the Straits Settlements were welcome at the Conference.[6] It nevertheless proved unprecedented as a multilateral forum for countries in Southeast Asia. Not only did Bandung gather representatives of every independent Southeast Asian state, but those states' high proportion among participating states also gave the Conference unmistakable significance for the region. Further, even to the degree that Bandung's ostensible focus lay on much broader concerns, in both domestic politics and international relations Southeast Asia represented a microcosm of the broadest global challenges of the mid-1950s.[7]

While very much the brainchild of Premier Ali Sastroamidjojo of Indonesia, and despite the only minimal participation in the Conference of that country's president and ultimate host,[8] Bandung could not escape association with Sukarno. This association, both at the time of the Conference and especially later on, underlined the significance of the Conference for the modern history of Southeast Asia more than for the course of non-alignment. There is real irony here, for—relative to anti-imperialist, even anti-Western, nationalism— a cause so parochial as Southeast Asian regionalism held little interest for Sukarno.[9] His welcome speech to Indonesia's guests at Bandung reflected the universalist, and certainly extra-regional, scope of Sukarno's priorities.[10] At the same time, his commitment to the big idea, to the global rather than regional cause, cut both ways for Southeast Asia. If it reflected the thoroughgoing lack of interest among the president and the diplomats closest to him in the regional processes that the post-1965 New Order Indonesia of General Suharto would so

influentially shape, it also called attention to the potential international importance of Southeast Asia's largest country and of Southeast Asia itself.

The Bandung Conference was held, after all, in Southeast Asia rather than
in South Asia or Africa. If others very soon eclipsed Sukarno as leading lights
of the Non-Aligned Movement,[11] in retrospect that shift only brought into
sharper relief the particular "spirit" of the mid-1950s in Southeast Asia and the
charismatic figure who most embodied it. Reference to subsequent developments
reinforces this effect: the Suharto regime's active participation in ASEAN-style
Southeast Asian regionalism can hardly be divorced from the circumstances of its
inception, in the sinister ouster of Sukarno and the violence that attended that
ouster. Finally, if poorly understood and too often maligned, Sukarno figures
along with Ho Chi Minh far more importantly as one of the two great figures
in the history of 20th-century Southeast Asia than as a father of successful non-
alignment in world affairs.

As in the case of Sukarno and Southeast Asia, Bandung remains permanently associated with Zhou Enlai and the then young, unknown and feared
People's Republic of China. Bandung proved very much Zhou's show.[12] From
early in the preparatory process, Ali Sastroamidjojo had pitched Bandung as a
way to promote the PRC's international engagement.[13] A conference in Southeast
Asia suited the latter's purposes well, for the reassertion of a prominent Chinese
role in Southeast Asian affairs had by the mid-1950s emerged as a priority for
Beijing. The 1954 Geneva Conference on Indochina saw its diplomats pursuing
interests on at least three levels—the national, the global and the regional. As
well as national self-defence and a global role among the great powers, Geneva
had offered the PRC an opportunity to re-emerge as a player on the Southeast
Asian stage.[14] For all the emphasis at Bandung on the global significance of a
conference of Asian and African nations, that gathering represented a second
such regional opportunity for Beijing. In his first speech to the gathering, China's
Premier-*cum*-Foreign Minister Zhou Enlai made clear his determination to
make good use of that opportunity. In addition to the Conference's grand global
themes of peaceful coexistence and Afro-Asian solidarity, that speech went out
of its way to banish the PRC's Southeast Asian neighbours' concerns over its
intentions and ambitions.[15]

In at least two more concrete ways, Zhou furthered the PRC's regional
interests at Bandung. First, he reached formal agreement with Indonesia on the
termination of dual-national status for Chinese resident there, an issue whose
significance elsewhere in Southeast Asia he had noted in his opening speech.[16]
Second, he launched what has proved an astonishingly durable friendship between
the PRC and Prince Sihanouk of Cambodia.[17]

If that friendship transcended the personal and emerged as a factor of persistent, fundamental significance in regional affairs during a full half-century, the Sino-Indonesian agreement likewise had an importance exceeding its ostensible purpose. At least one leading historian of the PRC's foreign relations, Chen Jian, argues in his contribution to this volume that Beijing regarded the treaty in broad strategic terms. It calculated that its ability to reach a settlement with Southeast Asia's largest country on a difficult issue, one that had troubled not just Indonesia but also its neighbours, would enhance its image across the region as a whole.[18]

In his contribution to the present volume, Itty Abraham argues convincingly for Bandung as a triumph of the nation-state in a decolonising world.[19] In disavowing the PRC's legal relationship with Indonesia's Chinese, then, Zhou went beyond mere image-building. He suggested a state-to-state basis for relations between the PRC and its Southeast Asian neighbours, premised on mutual respect for sovereignty and on normal interactions between putatively equal legal entities.

Appreciation of Bandung in Southeast Asian perspective and recognition of renewed Sino-Southeast Asian contacts as, in their own right, a variant of the Bandung Spirit only place into sharper relief US lack of enthusiasm for the Conference of Asian and African nations. For not only did the Conference's global ideals of non-alignment and peaceful coexistence run counter to Washington's basic policy goals in the era of Dwight D. Eisenhower and John Foster Dulles, but its regional significance also challenged the United States' conception of and design for a post-1949 Southeast Asia.

Ignoring Bandung: Washington's Southeast Asia

For a number of reasons, this legacy of the Bandung Conference for the United States has received little emphasis. First, and as suggested above, appreciation of Bandung as an event of Southeast Asian, at least as much as global, significance requires a conscious shift in perspective. It does not require denial of the importance of Bandung in the geopolitics of the Cold War and the history of the Non-Aligned Movement. But Bandung had a rather different meaning in the regional perspective from its meaning in those broader contexts. In that Southeast Asian perspective it proved, above all, a moment that suggested the renewed relevance and even the salience of historical linkages with China in the economic, political and social affairs of Southeast Asia. Second, that moment passed quickly; those linkages appeared soon to wane into irrelevance. But the more recent, unmistakable and accelerating resumption of Sino-Southeast Asian ties presents a strong case for adoption of this regional perspective on Bandung today. Third, and most basic, the apparent irrelevance of China to Southeast Asia did not, to borrow from John S. Furnivall, "just happen." It resulted, rather, from a concerted definition of Southeast Asia that not only wrote China out of but also denied its organic connection to regional affairs in nearly all their dimensions.

Appreciation of this process of definition in turn casts the importance of Bandung for Washington in a very different perspective. The Conference might indeed represent a triumph of the nation-state in the post-colonial world. It might privilege the very same "new states" that the United States would make the objects of its anti-communist "nation-building" and in that sense serve its regional purposes well. These pluses notwithstanding, Bandung threatened US influence in Southeast Asia at a far more fundamental level, for it challenged the landscape that made US influence in Southeast Asia even remotely feasible in the first place.

It has become a truism to observe that the idea of Southeast Asia as a region dates from the time of World War II, that that idea took shape in large part in the minds of outsiders rather than Southeast Asians, and that it assumed in consequence an unfortunately political significance.[20] The frequent contemporary identification in spheres far beyond the political of "Southeast Asia" with ASEAN, a collection of polities, does much to confirm this latter point. But these wartime considerations prove insufficient as an explanation for Washington's eventual definition of Southeast-Asia-without-China. For, in the immediate post-war period, the United States envisioned a Southeast Asia in which China still figured. Nothing illustrates this vision so much as the role of the Republic of China, agreed on at Potsdam, in accepting Japan's surrender and disarming its forces in Indochina north of the 16th parallel.[21] Ironically, this role prefigured the participation, so unwelcome to the United States, of China—albeit this time as the People's Republic—at the Geneva Conference on Indochina in 1954.

By that latter year, of course, containment had already become the well-established basis of Washington's approach to China, in Southeast Asia as elsewhere.[22] The PRC's role at Geneva represented precisely the sort of Sino-Southeast Asian connection that Washington wanted to block. In the post-1945 period, American policy makers had conceived an extraordinarily brash and in the end failed re-orientation of Asia's modern political economy as it had developed during the past century. Southeast Asia would, they hoped, serve in China's stead as market for and supplier of a newly prosperous and therefore non-communist Japan.[23] If Washington had seen that role as a means of de-linking Japan from China and severing pre-war economic relationships between the two, the policy had another purpose, too. Southeast Asia's assumption of this new role would supplant any reintegration of the region with China.

The irony of the activities of James Lilley and his fellow agents in watching the PRC from Southeast Asia thus becomes clear. By the time of Bandung, and well before Lilley first reached Manila, Washington's Southeast Asia had long since taken shape. It was a transmogrification of the wartime idea of Southeast Asia as a zone distinct from China (and India) to a Southeast Asia quarantined from and unconnected to China. In the abstract, the region as Washington understood it made sense as a region only if walled off from the PRC. Two concrete US efforts in the region underlined this understanding. In Southeast Asian perspective, neither had any room for Bandung.

First, of course, was SEATO, formed in the immediate aftermath of Geneva and with memories of China's role there still fresh. The alliance epitomised in most respects Washington's geopolitical strategy of the time: forging multilateral military-*cum*-security pacts to contain global communism.[24] In regional terms, however, and despite including only two Southeast Asian states—the Philippines and Thailand—among its eight members, SEATO was meant to wall Southeast Asia off from the PRC. In its global dimension, Bandung's emphasis on non-alignment flew in the face of Washington's commitment to pacts. But in the Southeast Asian context, the presence of China at the Conference defied Washington's vision of the region. Equally seriously, and as Amitav Acharya has pointed out, in the minds of at least the British, Bandung scotched prospects for an expanded SEATO, one that included additional Asian states.[25]

Second came what one historian has aptly termed "the basic rationale of the Vietnam War, namely to contain and isolate Communist China."[26] In regional terms, the United States' intervention in the Second Indochina War must be seen as above all an attempt to sustain its post-1949 vision of Southeast Asia. Bandung challenged that vision directly, both in the Sino-Southeast Asian contacts that proved a highlight of the Conference and in its implications for SEATO expansion. SEATO's failure to attract additional members or to apply in any convincing or even legal way to Indochina meant that the United States would pursue war in Vietnam on its own.[27]

The Fragility of Washington's Southeast Asia

In other ways, too, Bandung illustrated the fragility of Washington's Southeast Asia. The run-up to the Conference saw Washington urging Manila and Bangkok, SEATO's two Southeast Asian members, to attend the Conference with the express purpose of checking the PRC as it reached out from behind its post-1949 isolation in search of renewed ties with the region.[28] But, again, to check the PRC meant to engage it, if only indirectly. That engagement, along with China's participation at Bandung and Zhou Enlai's success in presenting such an appealing face for the regime that he represented, was irreconcilable with Washington's vision and definition of the region.

What is more, at the time of Bandung and in the period immediately thereafter, whether to write China out of Southeast Asia remained very much at issue even in Washington's Philippine and Thai client-states. While each of these states had committed troops to the US-led UN forces in Korea earlier in the decade, in neither one was there a clear commitment even among political elites to envisioning a Southeast Asia unconnected to China.

In the former, the year of Bandung saw leading elite nationalist Senator Claro M. Recto break with his party and his party-mate President Ramon Magsaysay over the issue of Philippine willingness to join the United States in defending Taiwan. Recto's position represented his consistent advocacy of an "Asia for the Asians" approach to foreign relations, very much in tune with the Bandung Spirit.[29] But Recto's position had more local origins, too. Economic nationalism, prompted above all by continued US domination of the Philippine economy, impelled Recto to call for opening trade relations with the PRC. Indeed, he saw those relations as a resumption of historical connections between the Philippine archipelago and China.[30]

In Thailand—where SEATO maintained it headquarters—too, elite politics in the mid-1950s produced a series of remarkable, largely forgotten, overtures to the PRC and considerable resultant skittishness in Washington. On Field Marshal Phibun's express instructions, Thai Foreign Minister Wan Waithayakon reached out to Zhou at Bandung. The subsequent period, through mid-1957, saw Phibun speaking to the Thai parliament about China in language scarcely distinguishable from Claro Recto's, back-channel discussions of Sino-Thai diplomatic normalisation, the easing of economic and cultural contacts with the PRC, and the dispatch of a series of official and semi-official delegations to Beijing. At least two of these delegations met with Mao Zedong and Zhou. It is impossible to understand Bangkok's sustained campaign of contacts with and openings to Beijing in these years without placing them in the context of rivalries among the military cliques then dominant in Thailand's politics. The magnitude of US influence in the country gave neutralism a certain domestic political appeal. But the inclusion of figures from Thailand's civilian political left in missions to Beijing also bespoke the broader appeal of renewed Sino-Thai contacts of the sort that the country's American patrons so fervently wanted to block.[31]

Bandung's apparent success in exemplifying and even making attractive a non-aligned alternative to the Dullesian two-bloc view of geopolitics notwithstanding, regional resistance to walling China off had roots in the domestic politics of Southeast Asian states. In this sense, Southeast Asian resistance during the 1950s to hostility towards the PRC presented the mirror image of political pressure for toughness towards the PRC in the United States itself.[32] Across Southeast Asia, such domestic and regional concerns mattered. They would define regional interactions with China, or the lack thereof, far more than would the Bandung Spirit as conventionally understood in terms of non-alignment and peaceful coexistence in the global arena.

If non-alignment had a tortuous, disappointing post-Bandung history,[33] Southeast Asian regionalism fared much better. But the understanding advanced in this chapter, the argument not only for Bandung's regional significance but also for its irreconcilability with the US approach to Southeast Asia at the time, both suggests and in fact demands reinterpretation of that regionalism.

ASEAN and the Triumph of Washington's Vision

ASEAN stands at the centre of narratives of Southeast Asia's successful regionalism. Its record is such that one may understand its success from a number of perspectives. During the past quarter-century, it has played a significant role at both the regional and global or geopolitical levels. At that latter level, and as a collection of just the sort of nation-states whose centrality to the post-colonial order the Bandung Conference affirmed, it has allowed its Southeast Asian member-polities often, if not always, to punch above their individual weights.

ASEAN's geopolitical role dates, in fact, back to its creation in 1967 as a grouping of five non- (or anti-)communist states: Indonesia, Malaysia, the Philippines, Singapore and Thailand. One need not deny ASEAN's subsequent record to consider its origins from the perspective developed here.

Central to ASEAN's early and lasting credibility was its status as a Southeast Asian undertaking, not a creature—like SEATO—of outside powers.[34] In regional perspective, however, two features of this undertaking appear striking. First, for all its Southeast Asian roots, ASEAN initially represented the formalisation of Washington's vision of the region, of a Southeast Asia walled off from China. Bandung long seemed to belong as little to ASEAN's history of the region as to Washington's. Second, and surely not unrelated, ASEAN represented in regional terms not so much a collection of non-communist states as a group of regimes that had bested what we must call—descriptively, and for lack of better terminology—more progressive, alternative forces within their own polities.

The geopolitical focus on ASEAN serves to obscure its connection to the domestic political histories of its members; the group's vaunted non-interference principle has served, likewise and perhaps unintentionally, to deepen this obscurity. Emphasis on ASEAN as a Southeast Asian creation begs the questions of which Southeast Asians created ASEAN and what their vision of the region was. Too rarely have observers of the region paused to consider these questions, let alone their implications.

The cases of the Philippines and Thailand, treated briefly above, prove instructive. In Manila, Ferdinand Marcos remained a constitutionally elected first-term president at the time of ASEAN's creation; he would launch his Martial Law dictatorship only five years later. But Recto, crushed in the 1957 presidential election, had died. The 1961 election had again exposed the narrow appeal for the Philippines' mostly rural poor of the late senator's brand of economic nationalism.[35] Even before Bandung, the Philippine Republic had crushed the progressive forces that appealed to that majority with the illegal suppression of the Democratic Alliance in 1946 and the defeat of the Huks in the early 1950s.[36] In Thailand, a similar situation obtained. The 1947 coup had stripped power from the collection of civilian progressives more or less associated with Pridi Phanomyong. A decade later, Sarit Thanarat's seizure of power ended even the residual influence that they had on the Bangkok government in the period after Bandung. By 1967, Sarit had succumbed to cirrhosis; his former Thai Army protégés Praphat Charusathian and Thanom Kittikhachon perpetuated his dictatorial regime.

The regimes in power in the remaining three of the original ASEAN Five also by 1967 reflected the defeat of the progressive forces in Southeast Asia to which the immediate post-1945 period had offered such promise. Singapore's People's Action Party—its astonishing single-party-dominant, pro-business, developmentalist regime then rapidly abuilding—had been rescued from its own former left wing through the mass arrests of "Operation Coldstore" of 1963.[37] Across the Causeway, in Malaysia, the ruling coalition of Chinese tycoons and Malay aristocrats provided an apparently stable climate for enduring British business interests; the cracks in this order revealed by the ethnic riots of 1969 remained largely unimagined. Mass murder on a scale previously unknown in Southeast Asia had brought the end of Sukarno's Guided Democracy in Jakarta. The ghoulishness of General Suharto's New Order, while already very much apparent, had only just begun by the time that Indonesia joined four of its neighbours in founding ASEAN.

If ASEAN proved a face-saving way to ease the tensions resulting from Konfrontasi, from the perspective adopted here this accomplishment had mainly short-term significance. Of longer-term importance was ASEAN's success in giving institutional form to a grouping of pragmatic or anti-progressive Southeast Asian regimes and to their shared vision of a Southeast Asia quarantined from China. Considerations of space preclude extended, counterfactual discussion of the regional vision that would have informed an ASEAN constituted by regimes that afforded more political space to alternative political forces at home. In any case, what ASEAN's founding leaders could not have guessed was how soon the long-time promoters of their 1967 vision in Washington would themselves abandon it.

Intellectual Buttresses of the Vision: Bandung's Absence from Southeast Asian History

Convergence towards Washington's vision for Southeast Asia had its intellectual dimension, too. In his public remarks to fellow participants at the conference out of which the present volume has emerged,[38] Anthony Reid noted that Bandung had had little or no impact on the historiography of modern Southeast Asia.

How to account for the failure of either the Bandung Conference or the Bandung Spirit to appear as much more than a quaint footnote in thematic and narrative treatments of the region's recent past? Reid stressed the absence from Bandung of such important components of Southeast Asia as then still not independent Malaya and the Straits Settlements, which as Malaysia and Singapore would of course number among ASEAN's co-founders. He emphasised the importance of the Bangkok-Kuala Lumpur-Singapore-Jakarta "corridor" in integrating the region. This answer has much to recommend it. Certainly among Anglophone students of the region, Malaya, Malaysia and their historiography have assumed very probably disproportionate importance in shaping understandings and informing frameworks. Neither could an "ASEAN Three" have ever launched so successful an organisation as did, in 1967, the ASEAN Five.

Nevertheless, an alternative to the explanation offered by Reid also suggests itself. This explanation stresses those present—or at least one of those present, China—at Bandung rather than those absent from the Conference. Rather than view it as an assembly of states from far too far afield to have specific significance for the region, one might emphasise two other factors. First, of course, is engagement between China and Southeast Asia at Bandung, in most ways the highlight of the Conference. Second is the effective writing both of China and of linkages with China out of the historiography of the region in which mainstream Western and Southeast Asian specialists on the region participated between the creation of their field and just the past decade or so.

Reid himself has been among the pioneers in re-integrating China into the history of Southeast Asia.[39]

Repeated assertions that Southeast Asian "area studies" were in their origin a Cold War project long ago became tiresome and unproductive, but we need to understand why the re-integration that Reid has spearheaded proved necessary. For that need was a function of the solid intellectual foundations that scholarship gave Washington's—and early ASEAN's—conception of Southeast-Asia-without-China in the golden age of Southeast Asian studies in US universities. This scholarship included not least the work of many of the more progressive specialists on the region. Confidence in the coherence of Southeast Asia as a region and in its logic as a unit of study resulted as much from an understanding of what Southeast Asia was not as from an emphasis on what it was. Ironically, and in a surely unintended tribute to Bandung as Abraham understands it, that confidence also extended to viewing the nation-states of the region—like those of Europe—as more or less natural and inevitable results of long-term historical development. They were worthy both of national histories reaching far farther back into time than the idea of the nation-state itself and of studies of their Chinese populations as, effectively, "national minorities" rather than reminders of interactions in an era before the triumph of the nation-state.

A different conception of the region, one less in line with Washington's and early ASEAN's determination to draw a line through Sino-Southeast Asian connections, would and almost doubtless will give Bandung the place in the historiography of Southeast Asia whose lack Anthony Reid points out. As that historiography takes shape, it will also doubtless put Washington's effective erasure of that line just a decade and a half after the Conference, to which the following two sections of this chapter turn, in a new, more critical, perspective.

Appreciating Bandung: China and Ending the "Vietnam War"

In the third volume of his memoirs, Henry Kissinger—the man, not least, who sent James Lilley to Beijing in 1973—attributes to Richard Nixon three motivations in joining Mao Zedong to launch a "geopolitical revolution" in 1971–72. These motivations were "to extricate the United States from Vietnam, to create a counterweight to Soviet expansionism, and to draw the sting from the militant peace movement at home."[40] Within a short time, of course, Nixon's domestic troubles would exceed anything that a foreign-policy breakthrough could help. Nevertheless, the first and second of these motivations, one of intense regional importance for Southeast Asia and the other a matter of the global balance-of-power politics of the day, each merit emphasis.[41]

From the vantage point of 2005, serious worry over Soviet "expansionism" in Asia or elsewhere could easily appear ridiculous. Perhaps it always was, even in the early 1970s. The worry may simply have been symptomatic of Washington's late-Cold-War habit of continuing to map its North Atlantic concerns onto the rest of the world. At the same time, Beijing viewed US difficulties in Vietnam in relation to China's own contest with the USSR. To the degree that Vietnam diverted US resources from confronting the Soviets, the PRC had an interest in helping Nixon end the war.[42] The history of the long, failed and perhaps always ill-conceived "Vietnam peace process" lies outside the scope of this chapter. In retrospect, however, it is striking how very seriously Nixon took the possibility of PRC assistance in bringing US involvement in Vietnam to an end.[43] That the PRC numbered, unlike the USSR, among the dozen signatories and guarantors of the Paris peace agreement of 1973 comes in view of that seriousness as little surprise.[44]

Kissinger credits Mao with effecting the PRC's rapprochement with the United States through "a return to classical patterns of Chinese statecraft" and the foreign policy of "the so-called Middle Kingdom."[45] While without specific reference to Southeast Asia, he notes that the commitment between Mao and Nixon to cooperate in Asia embodied in the 1972 Shanghai communiqué "marked a far more significant departure from prevailing US Wilsonianism than from Chinese traditions."[46] Kissinger was himself no Wilsonian; his memoirs make clear his easy readiness from the time of his earliest discussions with Zhou Enlai in Beijing to treat the PRC as a deserving participant in the geopolitics of Asia.[47] Washington's post-1949 vision of a quarantined Southeast Asia evidently meant little or nothing to him.

What purpose, in Southeast Asian perspective, had the United States' long-term military commitment to Vietnam served, if not the enforcement of that quarantine? Among the few scholars to appreciate, in contrast to Kissinger, the degree to which Washington's geopolitical and regional or Southeast Asian interests in reaching out to Beijing therefore represented two rails of the same track rather than two temporarily parallel tracks is Walter LaFeber. The United States had previously used "Vietnam to contain China," he writes.[48] Now, the United States' need to get out of Vietnam and its concern over the flourishing Moscow-Hanoi alliance led Nixon to "use China to contain Vietnam."[49] The new track reincorporated China into the international politics of Southeast Asia as Washington understood them. It represented an unwitting show of appreciation, just over a decade and a half after the Conference, of the regional variant of the Bandung Spirit. This appreciation both resulted and was made evident in a series of ironies and odd or awkward developments, for the United States, for China and for Southeast Asia.

First came the spectacle of Washington's belated acknowledgement of the PRC's legitimate interest in events across its immediate southern border. The United States had long feared that the People's Liberation Army would intervene directly in the Vietnam conflict.[50] So its denial of that interest had been disingenuous from the start. In their early discussions, however, Zhou assured Kissinger, if anything far more disingenuously, of the PRC's lack of concern with or knowledge of not only Vietnam but also the rest of Indochina.[51]

Second, among Southeast Asian states the regional variant of the Bandung Spirit had perhaps less appeal than ever. A half-decade after the formation of ASEAN, the chaos of China's Cultural Revolution and the renewed activity of Chinese-backed communist parties in the region made for little interest in renewed Sino-Southeast Asian ties.[52] Relative to 1955, Washington and many Southeast Asian governments had now changed places.

Third among these ironies was the role played by the paramount foreign-policy "realist" Henry Kissinger in reopening the possibilities of those romantic April 1955 days in West Java. A less likely proponent of any of the ideals of Bandung would be very hard to name. In his own effort during the Carter administration to counter the Soviet Union, Kissinger's long-time academic rival, fellow self-regarding geopolitician, and eventual successor as American national security adviser Zbigniew Brzezinski would reinforce Kissinger's opening to China. By that time, however, US interest in renewed Sino-Southeast Asian connections had begun to grow far more explicit and purposeful.

Embracing Bandung: China, ASEAN, and Solving the Cambodian Problem

Cambodia loomed as an issue in Sino-American relations even before Henry Kissinger's secret trip to Beijing in 1971 gave those relations serious impetus. From China's point of view, Washington's attitude towards the country following General Lon Nol's coup against Prince Sihanouk in March 1970 showed little regard for PRC interests in Indochina. The PRC remained determined that the terms of any rapprochement with the United States include at least tacit acknowledgement of those interests.[53] Following the Kissinger and Nixon trips, as the Sino-American relationship gained momentum, the problem of Hanoi's growing influence over the whole of Indochina numbered among those matters with which Beijing wanted Washington's strategic cooperation.[54]

At a more tactical level, Kissinger actively sought in his discussions with Zhou Enlai and Deng Xiaoping Chinese participation in efforts to end the crisis into which Lon Nol's failure to defeat the Khmer Rouge insurgency had thrown his country.[55] Kissinger pursued these efforts as a follow-on to his apparent success in bringing peace to Vietnam with the Paris Agreement of 1973. They proved that China's doubts of just several years before about US unwillingness to afford China a role in the international politics of Southeast Asia had little foundation.

Well before Vietnam's invasion of Cambodia at the end of 1978 and its toppling of the Khmer Rouge's Democratic Kampuchea regime in early 1979, then, Cambodia offered a demonstration of US sincerity about the Shanghai communiqué. At least in Southeast Asia, its commitment to including Beijing in the international politics of Asia and the Pacific extended beyond the narrow case of China's immediate neighbour Vietnam and Washington's search for an expedient way out of its quagmire there. Nevertheless, it required that invasion and the fear that it provoked across the region before Washington's friends in ASEAN would come to share its spirit of inclusiveness towards China. Further, as with preceding chapters in the curious history of Bandung's legacy for the United States, this development resulted from overlapping global and regional factors.

Chief among the former were shared Chinese and US concerns over Soviet ambitions in Southeast Asia and Vietnam's status as a putative Russian proxy in the region. Zbigniew Brzezinski appeared to discover Southeast Asia for the first time when he leapt to the conclusion that Cambodian-Vietnamese border skirmishes in late 1977 made the region a theatre in a larger Sino-Soviet conflict.[56] Brzezinski's geopolitical priorities determined which side he would take in such a confrontation. Unlike Kissinger, who viewed the Sino-Soviet-American triangle in terms of balance-of-power manoeuvring, Brzezinski had an active interest in besting the Russians. His trick, in the course of the year preceding Vietnam's invasion of Cambodia, was to have the United States take China's side, too. Despite the resistance of Cyrus Vance and the Department of State, Brzezinski transformed the Kissingerian policy of welcoming Chinese participation in Southeast Asian affairs to a policy of clear alliance with the PRC in Indochina.[57]

While the result of geopolitical calculations, the United States' radical new stance had its greatest impact at the regional level. It is important to emphasise that the Nixon administration's opening to China had not led all of Southeast Asia to follow along with equal eagerness.[58] Southeast Asia would accept the restoration of linkages with China only in stages. Antipathy towards long-vanquished communist rivals in domestic politics and continuing unhappiness over China's apparent support for those rivals led some regimes to proceed slowly. Among the ASEAN Five, while Malaysia, the Philippines and Thailand had normalised relations with the PRC by mid-1975, it was not until 1990 that Indonesia and Singapore followed suit.[59] During 1978, too, the arrival of large numbers of Vietnamese "boat people" on their shores led the ASEAN states to focus more on Washington's relations with Hanoi than on its ties with Beijing. They urged normalisation of US relations with Vietnam in the hope that it would end the refugee crisis.[60]

Vietnam's invasion of Cambodia quickly changed ASEAN's focus. So much did it affect regional perceptions that even China's willingness to use force against a Southeast Asian neighbour, as when it launched a massive attack across its border with Vietnam in February 1979, left ASEAN's members unfazed in comparison. Their readiness to welcome Chinese participation in checking what they cast as Vietnamese aggression took numerous forms. On the diplomatic front, as early as the 1979 United Nations General Assembly session China and ASEAN worked together to see that the toppled Democratic Kampuchea regime retained Cambodia's seat in the body. In both that year and in 1980, the United States, which had also begun early behind-the-scenes efforts to organise a coherent alternative to the Vietnamese-backed Heng Samrin government in Phnom Penh, chose expressly to follow the lead of its Chinese and Southeast Asian allies.[61] On the ground, the same period saw similar cooperation. US "humanitarian assistance" and tacit approval backed Chinese and Thai efforts to support the rebuilding of Khmer Rouge forces along the Thai-Cambodian border.[62]

Work in diplomatic circles and along that border would come together in 1982, when China, ASEAN and the United States orchestrated the creation of the Coalition Government of Democratic Kampuchea (CGDK).[63] Bringing together, at least ostensibly, the Khmer Rouge and the followers of Prince Sihanouk and of veteran Khmer politician Son Sann, the CGDK would serve both as the internationally recognised government of Cambodia and a useful fig leaf for principally Khmer Rouge military action against the country's Vietnamese occupiers. Along with Washington's economic boycott of Vietnam and a decade's worth of patient negotiation under ASEAN auspices,[64] joint Chinese, ASEAN and US backing for the CGDK would bring Vietnam's withdrawal from Cambodia in 1989 and the subsequent peace settlement.

Washington's willingness to end its efforts to wall China off from Southeast Asia had initially related to its difficulties in Vietnam. Its need to extricate itself from the conflict there pushed it out ahead of its friends among ASEAN's member-states in envisioning a resumed Chinese role in the region. The Cambodia problem proved what it took to induce those states to follow where the United States had led. It is important to note important disagreements among the Association's member-states over how closely to cooperate with the PRC on Cambodia. By the late 1980s, however, ASEAN achieved consensus and operated effectively despite those disagreements. It was thus that the Association won its reputation as the exemplary regional organisation in Asia.[65]

By the time of the Cambodian settlement, too, China had re-emerged as a recognised participant in Southeast Asian affairs, not just briefly but as permanently as could be foreseen.[66] The political, economic, social and cultural transformations of the region in the three and a half decades after 1955 notwithstanding, the Southeast Asian variant of the original promise of Bandung saw realisation.

Conclusion: China in Washington's Southeast Asia, 2005 and Beyond

This chapter is very much a product of its times. Five decades after the remarkable gathering in Bandung in April 1955, Southeast Asia, as both an idea and a reality, seems today to fare better than non-alignment and perhaps even peaceful coexistence. These are also times in which China's "peaceful rise" has come largely to define the international politics of Asia; among the most intelligent media commentators on that rise, from his perch at the American Enterprise Institute in Washington, is retired Ambassador James Lilley.

The prospect of China's rise and the accelerating significance of Sino-Southeast Asian interactions make it futile to speak of or understand the region without reference to its great neighbour to the north and east. Few in the region might today understand these interactions as a legacy of Bandung. In the United States, the number would be fewer still; after all, the US policy in Asia between the late 1940s and the early 1970s of opposing such interactions was in fact so aberrational as to be only dimly recalled today. From the perspective of 2005, however, Bandung's most important legacy concerns neither Afro-Asian solidarity nor even non-alignment or the rather paranoiac Dullesian fear thereof. Rather, that legacy concerns Southeast Asia and the post-1945 US construction of the region. It also relates to the promptness with which—just a decade and a half after Bandung—American policy makers found Washington's construction of the region obsolete, both conceptually and politically.

That discovery came, of course, in an Asian context much changed in the years since 1955. Like its non-communist neighbours in Southeast Asia, the PRC had in those years shared in the post-colonial triumph of the nation-state noted by Abraham. Despite, or perhaps because of, domestic political turmoil, it was more firmly consolidated as a polity and thus more evidently ready to participate in the arena of state-to-state relations. Washington's hard line towards the PRC and its effective attitude towards Chinese populations in Southeast Asia had in any case long differed considerably. Across the region, local Chinese, such as those on whom Lilley had focused his attention in Manila and Phnom Penh during the 1950s, emerged in time as assets far more than threats to US goals. By the 1970s, the *de facto* policy of rejecting PRC influence but embracing the roles—above all commercial, financial and industrial—of local Chinese had begun to look like a retrospectively ingenious approach to quasi-capitalist "economy-building" in Southeast Asia. The resultant growth did much to make several of the non-communist "new states" of the region viable. For all its effort to draw a line between the PRC and the region, too, the United States welcomed from the 1960s onwards an enhanced role in Southeast Asia for China's East Asian neighbour Japan. Japanese development assistance and investment, not least in partnership with Southeast Asian Chinese, succeeded where Washington's earliest post-war vision for Japan-Southeast Asia ties had proved abortive.[67]

US foreign policy has long had, in all parts of the globe, a much stronger regional aspect than is clear to observers fixated on geopolitics or such global struggles as the Cold War or "democratisation." In its Southeast Asian dimension, Washington's recourse to Beijing for help in addressing the problems of Vietnam and Cambodia was a nod-and-wink undertaking. It brought no specific repudiation of Washington's Southeast Asia as conceived of *circa* 1955. In that sense, too, it reflected a failure to appreciate the principal legacy of Bandung for the United States.

That legacy lay in US failure to see in the gathering either the fleeting possibility for early reincorporation of China into Southeast Asian affairs or the inevitability of eventual reincorporation. If, in US understanding of the histories of Southeast Asia or of Southeast Asian regionalism, Bandung hardly figures, it should. For, like the exclusion of China itself, the exclusion of Bandung from those histories will make progressively less sense.

Notes

[1]   The comments on an earlier draft of this chapter by Patrick Jory, Walter LaFeber, Shawn McHale and Barry Wain inform many specific points and general arguments made herein; the chapter has also benefited from the research assistance of Jay Cheong Hanwen and the criticisms of several anonymous readers. The ideas of Shiraishi Takashi have, over many years, greatly influenced the author's understanding of the place of Southeast Asia in post-1945 Asia.

[2]   See James Lilley, with Jeffrey Lilley, *China Hands: Nine Decades of Adventure, Espionage, and Diplomacy in Asia* (New York: Public Affairs, 2004).

3   Ibid., pp. 90ff., 98ff.

4   Jamie Mackie, *Bandung 1955: Non-Alignment and Afro-Asian Solidarity* (Singapore: Editions Didier Millet, 2005), pp. 54–5.

5   Ibid., p. 30, offers a list of participating states at Bandung.

6   Ibid., p. 66.

7   Evelyn Colbert, *Southeast Asia in International Politics, 1941–1956* (Ithaca: Cornell University Press, 1977), p. 322.

8   Mackie, *Bandung 1955*, pp. 58, 78–83.

9   Howard Palfrey Jones, *Indonesia: The Possible Dream* (New York: Harcourt Brace Jovanovich, 1971), p. 415; Mackie, *Bandung 1955*, pp. 115ff.; and J.D. Legge, *Sukarno: A Political Biography* (3rd Edition, Singapore: Archipelago Press, 2003), pp. 380ff., offer discussions of Sukarno's political and ideological vision.

10   Mackie, *Bandung 1955*, pp. 78–83.

11   Ibid., pp. 108ff.

12   Mackie, *Bandung 1955*, p. 48; Colbert, *Southeast Asia in International Politics*, pp. 321–2. This dimension of Bandung's legacy has proved especially important in China, of course. The astonishing film *Zhou Enlai in Bandung* (directed by Wei Lian; produced by the Beijing Film Studio of the China Film Group, The Movie Channel, and Century Hero Films Investment Ltd., 2003) represents just one of the more recent manifestations of this legacy. The makers of the film devoted evident, lavish attention to the recreation of the Southeast Asian settings of a half-century ago, as if—one might surmise—to make concrete the Sino-Southeast Asian relationships and connections that the Cold War served temporarily to sever.

13   Mackie, *Bandung 1955*, pp. 62–3.

14   Martin Stuart-Fox, *A Short History of China and Southeast Asia: Tribute, Trade, and Influence* (Crows Nest, N.S.W.: Allen & Unwin, 2003), pp. 168–9.

15   Mackie, *Bandung 1955*, pp. 83–7.

16   Stuart-Fox, *A Short History of China and Southeast Asia*, pp. 171–2; Michael Yahuda, *The International Politics of the Asia-Pacific, 1945–1995* (London: Routledge, 1996), p. 196; Mackie, *Bandung 1955*, p. 85.

17   Stuart-Fox, *A Short History of China and Southeast Asia*, pp. 173ff.

18   Chen Jian, chap. 6 in this volume; see also Yahuda, *The International Politics of the Asia-Pacific*, p. 196, and Colbert, *Southeast Asia in International Politics*, p. 321.

19   Itty Abraham, chap. 3 in this volume.

20   See Donald K. Emmerson, "Southeast Asia: What's in a Name?" *Journal of Southeast Asian Studies* 15, no. 1 (1984): 1–21, see pp. 7ff.

21   Colbert, *Southeast Asia in International Politics*, pp. 53, 60.

22   C.M. Turnbull, "Regionalism and Nationalism," in Nicholas Tarling (ed.), *The Cambridge History of Southeast Asia, Volume II: The Nineteenth and Twentieth Centuries* (Cambridge: Cambridge University Press, 1992), pp. 585–646, see p. 598; Mackie, *Bandung 1955*, p. 49; Michael Oksenberg, "U.S. Politics and Asia Policy," in Ezra F. Vogel, Yuan Ming and Tanaka Akihiko (eds.), *The Golden Age of the*

U.S.-China-Japan Triangle (Cambridge: Harvard University Asia Center, Harvard University Press, 2002), pp. 17–37, see p. 23.

23   William S. Borden, *The Pacific Alliance: United States Foreign Economic Policy and Japanese Trade Recovery, 1947–1955* (Madison: University of Wisconsin Press, 1984), chaps. 2 and 3 (pp. 61–142). John Foster Dulles spoke very explicitly to this point at a private dinner meeting of an Asia study group of the Council on Foreign Relations in October 1950; Walter LaFeber, *America, Russia, and the Cold War, 1945–1980* (4th Edition, New York: John Wiley and Sons, 1980), pp. 110–1. See also Bruce Cumings, "The Origins and Development of the Northeast Asian Political Economy: Industrial Sectors, Product Cycles, and Political Consequences," in Frederic Deyo (ed.), *The Political Economy of the New Asian Industrialism* (Ithaca: Cornell University Press, 1987), pp. 44–83.

24   See Leszek Buszynski, *SEATO: The Failure of an Alliance Strategy* (Singapore: Singapore University Press, 1983), pp. 1–43, for background.

25   Amitav Acharya, "'Why Is There No NATO in Asia?': The Normative Origins of Asian Multilateralism," paper presented at the Weatherhead Center for International Affairs, Harvard University, 22 November 2004, pp. 22–4.

26   Zhai Qiang, *China and the Vietnam Wars, 1950–1975* (Chapel Hill: University of North Carolina Press, 2000), p. 201.

27   Yahuda, *The International Politics of the Asia-Pacific*, p. 51.

28   Mackie, *Bandung 1955*, pp. 65–6.

29   Armando Doronila, *The State, Economic Transformation, and Political Change in the Philippines, 1946–1973* (Singapore: Oxford University Press, 1992), pp. 101–2.

30   Emerencia Yuvienco Arcellana, *The Life and Times of Claro M. Recto* (Pasay City: Claro M. Recto Memorial Foundation, 1990), pp. 242ff., 294–9.

31   Colbert, *Southeast Asia in International Politics*, pp. 328–31; Daniel Fineman, *A Special Relationship: The United States and Military Government in Thailand, 1947–1958* (Honolulu: University of Hawaii Press, 1997), pp. 205–42. See also David A. Wilson, "China, Thailand and the Spirit of Bandung," *The China Quarterly*, no. 30 (June 1967): 149–69, and no. 31 (September 1967): 96–127, for an exceptionally broad early survey of Thai-Chinese relations and the significance of Bandung for those relations.

32   Mackie, *Bandung 1955*, pp. 51, 124–5.

33   See Mackie, *Bandung 1955*, p. 108ff.

34   Turnbull, "Regionalism and Nationalism," pp. 604–5, 615ff.

35   Doronila, *The State, Economic Transformation, and Political Change*, pp. 108–13.

36   See Benedict J. Kerkvliet, *The Huk Rebellion: A Study of Peasant Revolt in the Philippines* (Berkeley: University of California Press, 1977), pp. 149ff., 233ff.

37   T.N. Harper, "Lim Chin Siong and the 'Singapore Story'," in Tan Jin Quee and K.S. Jomo (eds.), *Comet in Our Sky: Lim Chin Siong in History* (Kuala Lumpur: INSAN, 2001), pp. 3–55, see pp. 34–46.

38   "Bandung Revisited: A Critical Appraisal of a Conference's Legacy," organised by

the Institute of Defence and Strategic Studies, Nanyang Technological University, Singapore, 15 April 2005.

39   To cite one example among very many, see Anthony Reid, "A New Phase of Commercial Expansion in Southeast Asia, 1760–1840," in Anthony Reid (ed.), *The Last Stand of Asian Autonomies: Responses to Modernity in the Diverse States of Southeast Asia and Korea, 1750–1900* (London: Macmillan Press, 1997), pp. 57–82.

40   Henry Kissinger, *Years of Renewal* (London: Weidenfeld and Nicolson, 1999), p. 139.

41   Ezra F. Vogel, *Introduction*, in Vogel *et al.* (eds.), *The Golden Age of the U.S.-China-Japan Triangle*, pp. 1–14, see p. 6.

42   Zhai, *China and the Vietnam Wars*, p. 197.

43   Ibid., pp. 196, 199; Zhang Baijia, "Chinese Politics and Asia-Pacific Policy," in Vogel *et al.* (eds.), *The Golden Age of the U.S.-China-Japan Triangle*, pp. 38–51, see p. 39; Soeya Yoshihide, "Japan's Relations with China," in Vogel *et al.*, pp. 210–26, see p. 212.

44   See Kissinger, *Years of Renewal*, p. 485, for a list of the 12.

45   Ibid., p. 139.

46   Ibid., p. 140.

47   Ibid., p. 157.

48   Walter LaFeber, *The American Age: United States Foreign Policy at Home and Abroad since 1750* (New York: W.W. Norton, 1989), p. 613.

49   Ibid.

50   Kissinger, *Years of Renewal*, p. 147.

51   Ibid., pp. 156–7.

52   Stuart-Fox, *A Short History of China and Southeast Asia*, pp. 184–5.

53   Zhai, *China and the Vietnam Wars*, p. 182.

54   Kissinger, *Years of Renewal*, p. 868.

55   Ibid., pp. 507, 511, 874.

56   Elizabeth Becker, *When the War Was Over: Cambodia's Revolution and the Voices of Its People* (New York: Simon & Schuster, 1986), p. 394.

57   Ibid., pp. 395–402.

58   Oksenberg, "U.S. Politics and Asian Policy," p. 23.

59   Stuart-Fox, *A Short History of China and Southeast Asia*, pp. 196–7, 212.

60   Becker, *When the War Was Over*, pp. 399–400.

61   Kenton Clymer, *The United States and Cambodia, 1969–2000: A Troubled Relationship* (London and New York: RoutledgeCurzon, 2004), pp. 132–5.

62   Ibid., pp. 135–7.

63   Ibid., pp. 139ff.

64   See Kishore Mahbubani, "The Kampuchean Problem: A Southeast Asian Perspective," *Foreign Affairs* LXII, no. 2 (Winter 1983/84): 407–25, for a prescient, quasi-official statement of ASEAN's approach. Mahbubani served at the time of its publication as Singapore's deputy chief of mission in Washington.

[65] It is not the purpose of this chapter to narrate the long process, spearheaded by ASEAN, resulting in the Cambodian peace settlement of 1991; for a thorough, accessible narrative of the process, see Jin Song, "The Political Dynamics of the Peacemaking Process in Cambodia," in Michael W. Doyle, Ian Johnstone and Robert C. Orr, *Keeping the Peace: Multidimensional UN Operations in Cambodia and El Salvador* (Cambridge: Cambridge University Press, 1997), pp. 53–81.

[66] Stuart-Fox, *A Short History of China and Southeast Asia*, p. 209.

[67] A general discussion of this transitional role for Japan is available in Sudo Sueo, *The Fukuda Doctrine and ASEAN* (Singapore: Institute of Southeast Asian Studies, 1992), especially chap. 3, pp. 53–67; see also note 23 above. The author thanks Shawn McHale and an anonymous reviewer for NUS Press for urging him to consider the perspectives offered in this paragraph; he nevertheless accepts full responsibility for the conclusions drawn.

INDEX